Little Stories of Life and Death @NHSWhistleblowr

Little Stories of Life and Death @NHSWhistleblowr

Dr David Drew

Matador
9 Priory Business Park,
Wistow Road, Kibworth Beauchamp,
Leicestershire. LE8 0RX
Tel: (+44) 116 279 2299
Fax: (+44) 116 279 2277
Email: books@troubador.co.uk
Web: www.troubador.co.uk/matador

ISBN 978 1783065 233

British Library Cataloguing in Publication Data.
A catalogue record for this book is available from the British Library.

Cover design by Nathan Bennett

Typeset in 11pt Aldine401 BT Roman by Troubador Publishing Ltd, Leicester, UK

Matador is an imprint of Troubador Publishing Ltd

Printed and bound in Great Britain by TJ International Ltd.

Dedicated to the memory of

Kyle Keen

(20th February 2005 to 30th June 2006)

Unlawfully killed following catastrophic failures in basic
safeguarding at Walsall Manor Hospital

Contents

Foreword

Read It and Speak

The NHS will always need whistleblowers. Healthcare is complex, rapidly changing and dangerous; staff are fallible, variably trained and widely spaced; and demands are huge and resources limited. No matter how much is spent on regulation and risk management, harm will always happen – mistakes, incompetence, inhumane treatment and corruption.

But the same harm doesn't need to keep on happening. If it's picked up and acted on, many lives and much money can be saved. Whistleblowers should be the heroes of our time, praised and rewarded for speaking up and putting patients before corporate, political and personal interests. Yet too often they are vilified for doing the right thing. They become professionally isolated, rumours are circulated about their mental health and counter accusations are made (and often invented) against them.

Unsurprisingly, whistleblowing is very bad for your health. Stress-related illnesses, relationship breakdown and financial hardship are common. Even if you win it can feel like a defeat. More often it is the whistleblower who has to leave their job and finds it near impossible to get another in the NHS. Usually they are poorly represented by their unions and professional bodies, savaged by NHS lawyers paid out of the public purse and end up heavily in debt. Which begs the question, why would anyone blow the whistle in the NHS?

The beauty of this book is that it gives us the hinterland behind David Drew, a well known, loved and respected NHS paediatrician and whistleblower. Whistleblowers tend to be known to the public from the point that they go public – already harrowed, unhealthy and under enormous pressure – and we rarely get an insight into what sort of person they are, their values, beliefs, happier times and back-story. This book traces David Drew back to his roots, and we see that raising concerns and speaking up for patients come entirely naturally to someone grounded in public service values. This is a book the NHS has been waiting for, written with extraordinary honesty, openness and insight.

When I was a junior doctor, the 'must read' book was the darkly satirical *House of God* by Samuel Shem, a pseudonymous American psychiatrist. *Little Stories of Life and Death* deserves the same status, not just for the craft of the writing and the history of the NHS and medical training, but the fact that Drew has unashamedly 'gone public' about both himself and his journey of speaking the truth to power. There are no pseudonyms here, just glaring honesty backed up by thousands of pages of supporting documents and other evidence. Given the fate that befalls most NHS whistleblowers, it is brave almost beyond belief. Drew is the doctor who wouldn't be silenced. And he deserves to be listened to. The truth and reconciliation the NHS so badly needs starts here. Read it and speak.

Phil Hammond, doctor, journalist, broadcaster, medical correspondent for *Private Eye* and Patron of Patients First

Preface

The NHS is a wonderful institution. It largely provides what its founders intended: good medical care for all from cradle to grave, free at the point of use and funded by general taxation. It is, to use a bit of religious language, a great blessing to us. Nevertheless, it is not perfect. In recent years its flaws have been exposed to detailed scrutiny. Scandals at the Bristol Children's Heart Unit in the 1990s and, more recently, at Stafford General Hospital, Furness General Hospital and Heart of England Foundation Trust, amongst others, have shaken public confidence. Abysmal care and, worse, the cover-up of patient harm and avoidable death, have come to light.

There has been a growing concern over healthcare professionals who witness this and, contrary to their ethical codes, fail to raise concerns. The oppressive culture prevalent in some NHS hospitals and other institutions actively discourages this kind of feedback. Doctors and nurses are reluctant to speak up for patients, partly because they have low expectations that anyone will listen but also because they fear retaliation, especially from senior managers. These fears are well founded, as the experiences of many show. Three truths are now generally accepted: professionals have a duty to blow the whistle on patient harm, patients' lives and limbs depend on this, and, yet paradoxically, blowing the whistle can be a career-ending act.

It is against this background that I offer my own story. I was one of those doctors who spoke up for patients and suffered the consequences – the end of a long, productive and enjoyable career as a children's doctor. My whistleblowing occupied the years from 2008 to 2010, but I have set this period in the context of my wider and much less troubled professional and family life. No one knows better than I do what immense suffering whistleblowers can bring upon their own families.

I tell my story for one purpose only: to hasten the advent of an NHS culture in which frontline staff are treated with the respect they deserve, enabling them to concentrate on excellent patient care. This culture already prevails in the best of our hospitals, but in others disrespect, bullying and dishonesty are still the all too common day-to-day experience of many.

A huge number of people have supported me through these difficult years. I am grateful to them all: I would not have survived without them. My wife, Janet, my grown children and their families have all suffered with me and remain fiercely loyal. They helped save me from despair. Ian McKivett at the BMA was not just an adviser but a wise friend. My medical and nursing colleagues have been solidly behind me, both in legal proceedings and at a personal level. My lawyers fought the good fight and lost. I asked everything of them and they gave it. What more is there?

This book arose from the ashes of my professional life. It had to be written. But without the skills of my eldest son, Simon, it would not have been. Simon is a palaeo-ecologist. His expertise is unravelling and reconstructing the past. How well we have succeeded together in reconstructing my own history only time will tell. I am grateful to my editor Sue King. From our first contact I recognized Sue's intuitive grasp of my story. Its telling would have been poorer without her insightful criticism.

Finally I have included three appendices, a timeline, a list of dramatis personae and a list of acronyms. These may be helpful particularly to readers not familiar with workings of the NHS.

David Drew
March 2014

1

The End of All Things

This hearing is not about the loss of a job. It is about the end of a career.
> Martin Brewer, Walsall Hospital's Solicitor at my Internal
> Disciplinary Hearing

…and never being able to practise medicine again
> Sue Hartley, Nurse Director and Disciplinary Panel Chair

On the 21st of December 2010 I woke and made tea at 5am. First light showed we were in for a deep white Christmas. Ian McKivett, my British Medical Association representative, and I had an appointment at the Hospital Learning Centre in Walsall. We were going to hear the panel's decision following my recent two-day disciplinary hearing. I was calm but tired, as I'd had a long and tedious drive from Kent the previous night. Five hours on the M25 had given me plenty of time to think about this meeting. Ian had already told me he thought the outcome predetermined and that I would be dismissed.

He drove. I opened and re-read the letter from Irene Lemm, the Human Resources secretary, to check the date and time. "I confirm the venue for the reconvened hearing, which will take place at 10am…" We parked and walked to the main entrance. It had stopped snowing and the new hospital looked quite beautiful in the morning sunshine. The Private Finance Initiative building had enabled the Chief Executive to embellish her portfolio ("I delivered the PFI at Walsall Hospitals NHS Trust", "My gift to Walsall patients" etc.) but it had also helped sow the seeds of my undoing.

We went up the escalator through the atrium. This was arguably the most impressive building in Walsall but to me it reeked of venture-capital-funded extravagance. Like that ancient ziggurat of Babel it was as much about human ego as anything else. Most clinicians, and probably managers if they were honest, knew it would be a millstone around the Trust's neck for years to come. I was greeted by the Learning Centre receptionist as if it were a normal working day. It was for her. We were shown into Study Room 2.

The room smelt new. It was unimaginatively minimalist. There was no window. There was no air. I'd been a lifelong sufferer from claustrophobia after being locked in a cupboard for several hours as a child. Even at 63 I was still vulnerable in a restricted space. The panel sat on the far side of a long table: Sue Hartley, newly appointed Director of Nursing, who had chaired my disciplinary hearing, and on either side of her Nigel Summer, the Trust Vice Chairman and Colin Holden, an external HR consultant.

They made no eye contact. It was hard to know whether they were ashamed, embarrassed or just dismissive. Sue Hartley spoke: "Sit down." We sat. "This meeting will not be recorded. I am going to read the letter agreed by the panel and you will receive a copy of it in the next few days by post." She began to intone. It was a dreary monologue and I soon lost the thread. Towards its end the essence came into sharp focus: "The unanimous decision of the disciplining panel is that you should be dismissed with three months' pay in lieu of notice. This will be paid into your bank account at the end of January 2011. Your P45 will be sent to your home address. You should return your ID badge and any equipment to the Trust."

She stumbled to the end: "There's nothing more to say. Now, go home and this letter will follow." I looked for eye contact but still got none. Ian began to stand but saw I wasn't moving. "I'm sorry but I do have something to say." Nervously, one by one, the panel members raised their eyes to meet mine. "I'd like to say thank you for hearing my case. And I'd also like to wish you all a very Happy Christmas." We stood and left. Outside, Ian roared with laughter.

At that moment two angels rose into view as they reached the top of the steep escalator from the ground floor. Ann and Irene, retired volunteers in angelic dress, were on their way to the hospital wards bearing Christmas tidings of comfort and joy.

"Ladies, the Lord still sends his angels to those in trouble, I see."

"But you're not in trouble, Dr Drew."

I gave them a brief account of what had happened to me.

"That's disgraceful, Dr Drew. Everyone who knows you knows that's wrong. Do you want us to write to the paper?"

"I thought angels might have a bit more influence than that."

"Sorry, Dr Drew, we're only tinsel angels."

They left to carry out their sacred duties. Ian and I drank a Costa coffee, exchanging a few pleasantries. After ten minutes we walked out into the worst English winter for 42 years. Ian drove me home. On the way we saw many unfortunates with cars stuck in the snow. We stopped to give an old lady a push. "Bless you," she laughed when we got her going. I walked the last half-mile home as our road was snowed in. "Thanks, Ian", I said. "Have a Happy Christmas." He laughed and drove off.

My wife, Janet, was in the kitchen when I let myself in.

"That's it," I said, "I've been sacked."

"Thank God" she answered.

Neither of us needed to say any more. We'd rehearsed this moment more than once. My work as a children's doctor had been a huge part of my life, and it had been taken away at a stroke. On the other hand, everything else that was important to me, including my family and my conscience, was intact.

"Glass of sherry, Dr Drew?"

"Just a small one."

It was small-ish – one of Dick Swiveller's modest quenchers.

After lunch we packed our bags and drove to Newcastle upon Tyne for a family Christmas. The next day I was reading Maurice Sendak's *Where the Wild Things Are* to my grandchildren: "Let the Wild Rumpus begin!"

Six months later Phil Hammond's article about my case in *Private Eye* began, "Whistleblowing paediatrician Dr David Drew had an unblemished career for 37 years, the last 18 in Walsall, until he was sacked in December 2010 for 'gross misconduct and insubordination'." My story is about the dark side of the NHS. It is about what happened to one particular doctor in one particular Trust but it's a story that will resonate with many other NHS healthcare professionals. It didn't happen to them for all kinds of reasons. But many will know the possibility was never far from them.

In 2010, in the preface to his consultation paper *The NHS Constitution and Whistleblowing*, Secretary of State for Health Andrew Lansley referred to NHS Trusts that promulgate a culture of "secrecy and fear". He named Stafford General Hospital as an example and following the Francis Inquiries that name has become a byword. In these Trusts, doctors, nurses, managers and others are actively discouraged from exercising their professional responsibility to their patients: when they report poor care, patient harm, wrongdoing and even fraud they are often ignored. If they persist, senior managers are likely to perceive a threat to the organization's reputation and their own position. The whistleblower is then pursued with bullying and threats, exclusion, allegations of mental instability, disciplinary investigations and hearings, vexatious referral to the GMC and, ultimately, as in my own case, dismissal.

At some point in this process, the offender is likely to be offered a generous severance payment. This may come with the promise of a good reference to enable continued employment at another Trust. To ensure that this provides closure for all, the employee will be expected to sign a gagging order. That will normally be the end of the matter. Any dirt, including patient harm or wrongdoing will be swept unsafely under the carpet for good. In my case this involved the death of a patient following catastrophic mistakes at the hospital and the subsequent concealment of those mistakes from the family.

The alternative to caving in and accepting the offer is facing loss of reputation, unemployment, financial ruin and often ill health. Everything then becomes subject to the vagaries of employment law. The Trust will have excellent legal advice. Trust lawyers will have been on the case for many months. Once a case is taken to law there is virtually no limit to the legal costs the Trust may incur, all at public expense. This has, in some cases, amounted to millions of pounds – money that should have been spent on patient care. The employee will depend on his or her union, the British Medical Association or the Royal College of Nursing, for legal representation. These bodies tend to be wary of the potentially high legal costs and usually prefer settlement with a gag. It makes sense to accept what is on offer. The problem is that this is usually in breach of the professional's own ethical code.

The need for professionals to blow the whistle on poor care and the way they are treated when they do are both markers of the dysfunctional organizations Andrew Lansley referred to. Organizational culture is largely determined by its leadership. This story is about my own struggles in such an organization and with such leaders. Everything that happened to me is well documented. I will not tediously repeat this assertion for each event I describe. I cannot prove everything that I report from private conversations with colleagues but I believe my own account will bear the ring of truth.

This is a true story. It is the story of an NHS Hospital Trust whose leaders were, I believe, more concerned about their own reputations than the care of the sick children they were ultimately responsible for. As clinicians we worked skin to skin with patients but senior managers kept their distance and were unable to see what was happening on the ground. I have used real names for everyone in the story. There is no reason to do otherwise. All are easily identifiable. Many have been named in the media already. If any of them wish to contest the facts they will have every opportunity to do so. And I will be well prepared for that.

This is the story of a rumpus. So, let the rumpus begin.

2

In the Beginning

*People ask me why I didn't go to university. In my family you didn't
have expectations. You didn't plan to go to university. You lived in a
fog, one day at a time.*

after Colin Wilson: *The Outsider*

I was born in Belper, an old mill town on the River Derwent on the
southern edge of the Peak District. I had been conceived in the Great
Winter of 1947, when the temperature was permanently sub zero
and, as our dad once loved to tell us, the snow was up to the rooftops
for weeks on end. My mother often told me how as a 19-year-old
she had held me for the first time on a windy October day at
Babington Hospital. A few months later and I would have been
delivered in the world's first universal healthcare system,
Beveridge's NHS. My father was a coal miner and my mother
worked in a draper's shop. I was the oldest of five brothers; only
three of us survived young adulthood, but that's another story.

My whole childhood was spent in a warm, loving, working-class
home. We lived a semi-rural existence, outside as much as possible.
We knew the countryside and its seasons intimately. There were few
books in our house. We didn't discuss ideas. We took the *Daily Mirror*
but I never got beyond Andy Cap and Garth. I had no expectation
of life that I can remember.

My dad once promised me, "When you're 14 I'll take you down
the mine. Then you can make your own mind up what you want to
do." I was six or seven at the time. He never kept his promise and I
never got to go down the mine with him, which I regret. My life

7

took a different direction a few years later, when I was required to sit the 11-plus test for grammar school entry. We were told one day to go to another classroom because we were going to be tested. I was unhappy with this. My experience of being tested was unpleasant. I was a failure at arithmetic and spelling tests. I found it hard to understand how the severe canings I received as a result would help me improve.

I had no idea why I was there or what this test was for. It was a test unlike any I'd done before and I still remember enjoying it. Weeks later, a teacher gave me a letter addressed to my parents. I took it home and gave it to Mum. She opened it and told me I'd passed my 11-plus. I had no idea what it all meant but she seemed quite pleased. There was only one other child on my estate who went to grammar school that year

My dad went out and bought me a new bike, a Palm Beach Tourer. It was red and gold with 3-speed Sturmey-Archer gears. That was what you got in those days for "passing". If you were lucky. If you had a good dad. I loved that bike but was embarrassed that I was the only kid to get one. It sort of cut me off from the others. My first distaste of privilege.

In the autumn of 1959 I started my new life at the Herbert Strutt Grammar School. I spent much of that time in a daydream. I was always, always in trouble. Homework didn't get done. I lost my school cap, my pen, my protractor, everything. I turned up to PE with no kit. My marks were poor. But, when given a copy of *Tom Sawyer* on a Friday and told to read the first chapter by next lesson, I turned up having finished it and able to tell my teacher that I was halfway through *Huckleberry Finn*. I longed for the freedom of living on a raft. And that was where my appetite lay, with stories. The headmaster reported at term's end "David spends half his life in another world." (My parents were distressed by this.) "He will see me in my office at the beginning of next term." More therapy was coming my way, compounding my generally angst-ridden existence.

But then, unaccountably, the wind changed. I got good marks, passed nine O levels and found myself doing four Science A levels.

Mr "Buster" Beecroft taught my A level Biology class. An oversize teacher originating from South Africa, he was totally serious. He brought in old scholars to teach us on recent developments in the embryonic sciences of genetics and molecular biology and I found that not only could I remember what he taught I could understand it as well. I admired Mr Beecroft and for the first time in my life understood "Don't mess." I developed a passion for Biology.

In those days there came a point when you were expected to decide what you would do with your life. At 17 it had never crossed my mind, but it was Mr Beecroft who told us that that point had arrived. "It's time for you lot to think what you're going to do with your lives," he announced at the beginning of a Friday afternoon double period. There were only twelve in the class and we were seated in a horseshoe arrangement. I was on the extremity of one limb and luckily for me he started at the other end. I was amazed how, when named, each of my classmates, with an easy confidence, could state their ambition and even explain why they held it. "Doctor!" "Dentist!" "Vet!" "Teacher!"

I grew quite anxious as the question approached me. Nick Dawes sat on my right. "I want to be a doctor, a surgeon in fact. Yes, it's the knife for me." He went on to speak of things I'd never heard of. He spoke as if a he was a doctor already. "And what about you, Drew? What are you going to do with yourself?" All I knew was that I wasn't going to be a coal miner. "I want to be a doctor as well." I heard myself say. I was hard pressed to say why. "It's a good job, sir. You can help people and you get well paid." I was deeply conscious at my shallowness. But the die was cast: from then on I was going to be a doctor.

I knew of three or four doctors in our town. They were all GPs and lived in the posh houses overlooking the Derwent Valley. My only contact with them was as a patient: I was quite often ill. I only saw them from a distance in their smart suits and gold-rimmed spectacles. They were the social and intellectual alphas of our town. They lived a world away from me and my community, a different species almost. And now I had signed up to be one of them. It didn't strike me how unlikely that was. That was not my way of thinking at all.

When school finished that day I went home and over dinner (it was called tea in our house) I made my announcement.

"Mum, I'm going to be a doctor."

I still remember her response.

"I doubt it."

The subject was not discussed again until several months later, when I had to fill in my application form for medical school. There was a brief struggle, a more concerted effort to dissuade me. It was over in days. I had no idea why there should be any resistance and it wasn't something we discussed. Eight years later, when I was working as a paediatric registrar in Birmingham, my younger brother Stephen was drowned in a boating accident on the River Derwent. In the aftermath of his death we talked more than we ever had. One night it all came tumbling out of Mum.

"We want to say sorry for trying to put you off becoming a doctor. We didn't want you to get hurt. We didn't think it was possible for you to do it. Not from the working classes. We were wrong about that. I don't know what we were thinking. Anyway, you've done it. And we're proud of you."

I had a small crisis about my origins following that. I began to understand my own history, the lack of ambition, and the low expectations. I was reading Colin Wilson's *The Outsider*. Life itself is an exile. The way home is not the way back. Therefore a man must leave his father and his mother. My brother's death and the openness it produced became a defining moment for me. It reconciled me to my parents, whom I loved dearly but who had signposted me to a different future. That revelation, however, was years away; in the meantime I struggled with an ambition that seemed contrary to my parents' wishes.

In 1967 I received an invitation for an interview at Bristol University Medical School. It was a lonely train journey but when I arrived I was intoxicated by the bustle of Temple Meads Station. I was ill-equipped for an interview: in those days, in my world at least, coaching was unheard of; Buster had told me to be myself and I would be fine. That was all.

The interview went badly from the start. The usual questions about why I wanted to be a doctor. I wasn't sure. Questions about my life experience, which was very narrow. I was struggling. Then, one kindly professor asked me, "Do you know *Stand up, Nigel Barton?*" I did. "I do. Dennis Potter." I'd seen the play and been mesmerized by it and its sequel *Vote, Vote, Vote for Nigel Barton.* "Well, Mr Drew, as you'll remember, Nigel was starting his political career and was interviewed on TV. He's talking about where he's come from and where he's going. He comes to a moment of realization. 'I don't feel at home in either place. I don't belong. It's a tightrope between two different worlds, and I'm walking it.' That's you, isn't it? That's the position you're in."

It was a rare moment. I knew the answer as it struggled to form itself. I didn't know what I was going to say until I heard the words coming out of my mouth. "My uncle's a tightrope walker in the circus. He says the secret is not to look down. Or back. Just look ahead. He says that's where your future's waiting, on the other side." It was the only decent answer I'd given in the whole interview and only God knew where it had come from. And I hoped they weren't going to ask any questions about my uncle. I always loved stories.

"That's a good answer. Thank you."

The sages on the interview committee looked at each other and nodded. I left feeling exhilarated but knowing that the interview was the end of me. A few weeks later I received a conditional offer of a place at medical school. I got the required grades and spent the summer working as a labourer on a building site. But in October I would be going up to Bristol. Up to Bristol. La di da, Doctor Drew.

3

University

doctrina vim promovet insitam [knowledge promotes innate power]
Horace – motto of Bristol University

The local paper announced my departure for medical school with the headline "Local lad to train as doctor." and gave a fair account of my achievement. "But what does it mean?" asked a neighbour. "It means nothing," I replied, "But it might mean something one day." The neighbour died while I was at University and it never meant anything to him. Nor to most of the people I knew apart from my family. My past life slipped away unnoticed into a mythical country where not a great deal had happened.

I went to Bristol University in 1967, at the back end of the Summer of Love. October found me once again in the bustle of Temple Meads station but this time with a small bag and an old metal trunk. As with so much of my life up to this point the transition was marked not by excited anticipation or great expectations, more a puzzled acceptance. I was met at the station by older students and accompanied to Badock Hall, my home for the next year.

I quickly came to love Bristol. Badock was up on the Downs, two beautiful stretches of limestone heathland on the edge of the city. I could walk out onto them from my room within minutes. They echoed the semi-rural environment I had been raised in and helped me settle quickly. A brisk walk over the Downs of 20 minutes or so took me to the Avon Gorge and the spectacular Clifton Suspension Bridge. I discovered it for myself in the early morning within days of arrival. I stood, breathless, saying to myself over and again, "How marvellous are your works, O Man." Later I discovered the man's name, Isambard Kingdom Brunel. I wished someone had been a bit more imaginative with my own name. But I doubted I could live up to one like that. I was a country boy; cities were not to my taste but this one was beautiful. Lack of cash limited my ability to enjoy it but I made the most of everything that was free.

I arrived at the start of freshers' week. Everyone was rushing round signing up to Dramsoc, the Folk Club and a hundred other activities. They seemed to be having the time of their lives. I tried a couple of clubs but felt little enthusiasm. Students quickly settled into cliques based on common interests. I remember spending a lot of time on my own. Many of the students I met in the first weeks were from a different social class. They'd been to public school or came from professional families and it showed. Most were, it seemed to me, quite well to do. Some drove cars, others motorbikes. One delightful Greek student pitched up every day in a red Jaguar. I was ill at ease when I found myself amongst them.

The first two years, the pre-clinical course, were filled with lectures and practicals. An endless stream of anatomy, physiology, biochemistry, histology and, innovatively at that time, behavioural science washed over me. In the first week we were ushered into the anatomy dissection room. It felt like a warehouse, cavernous and impersonal. Thirty stainless steel tables, each draped with a white plastic sheet, concealed the thing that I dreaded. I had never seen a dead body before. Three or four students were allocated to each table according to a list at the entrance. I was relieved. It automatically made me part of a group that I didn't have to break into. We stood by our table as the demonstrator gave a short talk. Then he told us to remove the sheet. One of our group lifted the corner of the sheet. He looked up in mock horror: "Oh no! It's not... human!"

It was indeed a pale imitation of its original owner, all traces of humanity washed away by months of immersion in preservative. But I saw the person. It could have been my grandfather, who had died recently. I carried a photograph of him in uniform at Ypres in the Great War. "Cover him over with violets of pride, purple from Severn side." The pathos of Ivor Gurney filled that moment out for me. "Your journey's over, friend, but mine has scarce begun." On the next table another student had lifted the drape off his cadaver's thigh and was absent-mindedly playing noughts and crosses, scalpel on skin. I dare say we all had our own ways of dealing with this initiation. The whole of the first term was spent dissecting the upper limb. I found working in three dimensions difficult. I was poorly motivated and slipping behind.

But, I was pretty average in everything else. Biochemistry was tough. Our lecturer was German and delivered mainly in his mother tongue. I didn't speak German and was puzzled that others seemed to have little difficulty understanding him. I was lonely a lot of the time and didn't make friends easily but I wasn't the only one having difficulties. A dozen or so students simply disappeared, never to be seen again. One told me. "I'm off tomorrow, Drew. I won't be back." "What's up," I asked? "I'm only here because my parents want me to be. From what I've seen so far doctoring's not for me." I didn't want to be there either but unlike him I had no idea how to get out. So I stuck at it.

One experience in the first term was to prove decisive for the rest of my life. I was reading late on Saturday night when my next-door neighbour came in. "Where've you been?" I asked. "Christian Union." I laughed and made a rude comment. We had a brief conversation and then he gave me a book called *Basic Christianity* by John Stott. I went to my room but couldn't sleep so I read the book. I finished it at about 4am. At the end there is a short prayer in which you commit to follow Christ. I read it and then prayed it. It made perfect sense to me and without a single trumpet being sounded I entered the kingdom. Stott suggested that if you had prayed the prayer you should go and tell someone. So I went outside looking but everyone was abed.

At about 8 o'clock I went down to the refectory for breakfast, aware that something had happened to me. There were only three other students there. I sat at a table on my own eating Weetabix. An unshaven, heavy-eyed lad came and sat across from me.

"Is it OK if I tell you something?"

"What's that?"

"I became a Christian last night."

He looked at me with weary irritation. "Oh for fuck's sake, mate, not at this time in the morning. Please!" He picked up his breakfast and moved to another table. I was amused by that and not in the least put off. I laughed out loud. And he laughed back. At a distance. The next person to sit down was a young woman a bit older than me. I got a completely different reaction, intense interest. She told me she was a Christian herself. We had a brief conversation and I never saw her again.

Over the rest of the term I tried to shake off my new-found faith. I was away from home for the first time in a threatening environment. Religion was a crutch. But this didn't feel like religion and it wouldn't go away. One evening in November I came in late and sat down exhausted. Five books on the shelf caught my eye. They sat there accusing me. I'd borrowed them from the school Biology departmental library earlier in the year and had not returned them when I left. The next day I parcelled them up in brown paper and sent them to my old Biology teacher with a covering letter:

Dear Mr Beecroft

University is difficult but I'm doing my best. I became a Christian recently and I'm trying to tidy my life up a bit. I borrowed these books from the library months ago. I never got round to bringing them back. I suppose that's theft technically. But it's 90% idleness. As an act of penitence I am returning them with a cheque for £15 towards new books for the department.

My parents had instilled honesty into me but something else was at work now. I wanted to realize that honesty in my personal relationships. I somehow felt that I'd wronged Buster personally after all the good he'd done me. In those days £15 plus postage was a heavy price to pay even for peace of mind. The importance of honesty has been a dominant theme in my life from that point. I have not always been as honest as I should have. But I have suffered when I have not. I had a brief exchange of letters with Buster and then he wrote to say he was going to live in New Zealand.

My first term ended badly. I was bottom of the class in the exams with 26%. I went home for Christmas and my mum expressed alarm that I was talking so posh. I didn't want to go back for the next term but I didn't have the nerve to say so. I re-read *Animal Farm* and resolved to follow Boxer's example and work harder. I was always looking for clues like that. I read Joshua's exploits in the Old Testament with a commentary and was encouraged by his experiences. Even at that stage I found myself sceptical of some of the narrative detail. In January I went back to Bristol. I worked harder if not very hard and with a mark of 49% was halfway up the field by term's end. By year's end I was among the top students.

The following year I met, in a sense for the first time, a girl who I'd shared the same street with since we were small. Her name was Janet. She lived at number 36. I lived round the corner at number 64. I proposed in Hyde Park, like the farm-boy I was, by telling her that we were going to make a great team. We were engaged in 1968 and married in 1971. She was a trainee teacher in Manchester and we had a difficult long-distance relationship for several years before we married.

After two years of pre-clinical studies I started work in the hospital. I was immediately at home with the patients, many of whom had a background close to my own. When I began my paediatric posting at Bristol Sick Children's Hospital I experienced for the first time a burst of wild enthusiasm. John Apley, my consultant teacher, told me I was going to be a paediatrician. It was, he said, my manifest destiny. So many things were lost on me in those days.

In 1972 I won the Richard Clarke Prize in Paediatrics after written and clinical examinations. The prize was £27. I took my new wife out and we blew the lot on a beautiful summer dress for her. We were broke most of the time but, as has often happened in my life, the impulsive heart overruled the rational head.

My mum and dad came for my graduation in 1972, along with my five-year-old brother. It was a proud day for them and they said so. The university years had flown. I was a qualified doctor and I was going to be a paediatrician. We were newly married and frighteningly happy. I had learned a lot at university, though not as much as I might have. I knew that Socrates, having been declared the wisest man in Athens by the Oracle at Delphi, had claimed to know nothing. Long painful years of learning that deep truth lay ahead of me. I had developed a mildly arrogant streak. A common ailment among the medical profession.

John Apley on his teaching rounds would give a small notebook to one of the students, usually Chris Lee. Every so often he would come out with a pithy maxim. "Write it down, Lee, write it down." They became known as Apley's aphorisms. "The child is not a mini adult." "Most abdominal pain is non-organic." "A father attending with a child suggests family pathology." Times change and some of his pronouncements are now redundant but they always added depth to our technical medical education. My personal favourite was "The retrospectoscope is a remarkable instrument". Looking back I can agree with him. It is.

4

Training in Bristol

Tell me and I forget. Teach me and I remember. Involve me and I learn.

Benjamin Franklin

As my undergraduate years drew to a close in the summer of 1972, I faced the prospect of my first real job. It was standard to do six months in surgery and six months in adult medicine. Successful completion of these posts was required for registration with the General Medical Council. Etiquette required an approach to the senior clinician on the team you were applying to join, seeking his permission to apply. (It was always a he in those days.) The first senior surgeon I spoke to looked me up and down. I had spent six weeks as a student on his team but he could not remember me. He asked two questions. Which school had I gone to? What did my father do? I don't suppose that would be allowed today. I crossed him off my list.

My postings were approved before we set off for a brief summer holiday in Derbyshire. In August I would start work in Gloucester with John Kilby, a delightful surgeon I had met but not worked for. In February I would return to the Bristol Royal Infirmary to do diabetes and cardiology. Meanwhile, we were completely broke. At that time getting an overdraft was unheard of. So, when I saw an advert for a medical locum at a nearby hospital, I rang immediately.

On the evening of my first day as a locum, with no previous experience, I found myself alone while the registrar left the hospital to attend to some personal business. I will not forget the first patient to arrive, a lady in her seventies. She was brought into the ward with severe asthma. By rights she should have been in the A&E department. She was *in extremis*. The nursing staff were frantic. She was given oxygen but did not improve. I rang the registrar. He was on his way but would be 15 minutes. He told me to give her a dose of an asthma drug called aminophylline by slow intravenous injection. I put in a cannula while the nursing staff drew up the drug. I gave it very slowly as instructed. She began to improve. I relaxed and so did the nurses. Then the patient quite suddenly died. She stopped breathing and I could hear no heartbeat. We did our best to resuscitate her but without success. We had just given up when the registrar arrived. I gave him a slightly hysterical account of what had happened.

"It's the aminophylline," he said bluntly. "Respiratory arrest, abnormal heart rhythm, it happens. Can you talk to the relatives?" It wasn't a question; he turned and walked off the ward. I delivered the bad news to the relatives and they left. The next day I would write out the death certificate and cremation form and that would be the last I would ever hear of it. The past is a foreign country; they did things differently there. Bad things happened. Questions were rarely asked. Tomorrow was a new start.

Janet had stayed up in Derbyshire with her parents and I was living alone in hospital accommodation. At midnight I went back to my room to lie down. I walked in and threw up on the carpet. — *Dear Diary, This is for your ears only. I think I killed a patient tonight.* But after a few hours' sleep, a shower and a piece of toast I was ready to present the newly admitted patients to the consultant. I survived the fortnight and moved on to Gloucester with enough money to get us through until the next payday.

At Gloucester Royal Hospital I was part of a three-man surgical team. I enjoyed it from day one. John Kilby was the role model every junior needs: talented, confident, cheerful, helpful and genuinely compassionate. The registrar was an Iranian doctor, Mohammed, with a wicked sense of humour. They both made me feel like an indispensable member of the team, which is what I was soon to be. After several weeks Mohammed had to return to Iran for three months and no replacement could be found. John Kilby took me aside. "We're on our own from Monday, David. You're a quick learner and I'm a good teacher. We'll be fine." His confidence was infectious.

We were on call on Monday. I admitted a young man with appendicitis. "Right, David, you can do this one," he told me as we scrubbed up in theatre. I had already seen and assisted with a few appendicectomies, so we were moving on to stage two of "see one, do one, teach one", a common teaching strategy at that time. He talked me through it. As he had predicted, I was fine. The patient recovered quickly and never learned that he had been operated on by a neophyte. The next time I rang the boss out of hours to tell him I had an appendix he simply told me to do it. "And, David, it's a patient with appendicitis. Not an appendix," he chided. The theatre sister would assist, he told me. It was, I found, a massively inflamed appendix but I got it out and once again the patient recovered quickly. — *Dear Diary, This will never last. My luck will run out.*

But it didn't. Everything I turned my hand to went well. I had my own weekly minor operations list. I learned how to do above-knee amputations. The patients were mostly diabetics or heavy smokers. "Make sure you talk to them, David. Find out how they feel. It's a big thing," counselled the boss. I was never happier than when I was assisting him in more complicated operations. A senior registrar came up from London for an interview and "Mr Kilby" brought him around the ward. He introduced me as his pre-registration house officer.

"How many appendicectomies have you done, Jim?" he asked him.

"Seven."

"How many have you done, David," he asked me, mischievously. "About fifty, but I'm not counting now." I answered. "This is the place for you, Jim. Experience m'boy, that's what you need." The boss winked at me.

In February 1973 I laid down my scalpel and we moved back to Bristol to live in a flat at the Infirmary. I was brimming with self-confidence and although I'd loved surgery I was a physician at heart. My two new consultant bosses were men of gravitas. They were not unkind but a rigid hierarchy put them beyond reach. I was at the bottom of the hierarchy with my house officer colleague. Directly above us was the ward clerk, who took an instant dislike to me. A clerk had the power to ruin you in those days. After six months of working alternate nights and alternate weekends as a surgical house officer I was frazzled. To make things worse, I had determined to take the exam for membership of the Royal College of Physicians at the earliest opportunity. This necessitated long hours of study outside work. I made the serious mistake of mentioning the arduous rota to one of the consultants. "When I was a house officer I only left the hospital once in six months. That was to get a haircut. And I still managed to get a bollocking off my consultant," he told me without a trace of humour.

By March, only a month after starting in Bristol, I was ill with a cold and sore throat. It quickly turned to pneumonia and I was off work for two weeks. This caused immense pressure on the remaining house officer. Janet took calls most days asking when I was coming back. The day I could stand I returned to work. But I had extensive cold sores covering half my face. The consultant caught me in the corridor. "Where are you going, Dr Drew?" I stuttered something. "You can't come back looking like that; you'll scare the patients to death. Go home till it clears up."

When I did go back I worked harder than ever. But I had blotted my copybook and everyone let me know it, especially the ward clerk. I arrived early and stayed late. I volunteered for extra tasks; but it was no use, I could not redeem myself. In the midst of these miserable circumstances Janet announced good news. She was pregnant and expected to give birth in October. It was time to look for my next job. I applied for a senior house officer job in paediatrics at Bristol Children's Hospital. I no longer felt so confident of my manifest destiny and John Apley was not on the interview committee. I was passed over for my peers, who I believed had shown nothing like the promise I had with children. One of the interviewers briefed me in a single sentence. "There's a question mark over you, David. The reference from your last job was awful."

I was at a clinical meeting weeks later with no idea what I was going to do. An Indian GP told me he'd just failed his MRCP for the 8th time. He joked about a friend of his practising back home with a sign above his surgery 'MRCP (Failed)'. He planned to stop work for six months to swot and have one last attempt. I told him my own situation and he asked me to look after his practice while he was away. "Come up and do a surgery with me and meet my partner." I drove to Filton the next day, arriving as Concorde was taking off on a test flight. I liked the partner, an amiable Irishman, and agreed to do the locum. Ten pounds a day was all they could afford to pay me. Nothing in writing. It was more than I was currently earning so I accepted. That's the only time I have ever been paid a day wage as a doctor.

At first I struggled with the volume of patients and what seemed to me the enormous complexity of their complaints. I encountered situations that medical school had not prepared me for: historical sexual abuse, patients with terminal illness, childhood behaviour problems, psychosomatic symptoms, teenage girls asking me to check their breasts. And a host of physical conditions I had read about but not seen before. The patients told the receptionist they liked "the new kid". Recognizing the importance of professional credibility I tried to put on a few years by growing a beard.

In late October I went to the practice dropping Janet at the maternity hospital on the way. She rang mid-morning to say her waters had broken and I went to see her as soon as I'd finished the last patient. Little happened over the afternoon and we agreed that I should go and do the evening surgery. As the first patient came through the door I heard the receptionist bawl across the waiting room, "Hey, Charlie! Don't you keep the doctor now; his wife's having a baby. You've only got a boil on your bum!"

Afterwards, I raced to the hospital and was present at the birth of our firstborn, a son, Simon Drew. We laughed and cried with joy and I stayed until I was thrown out. We were renting a cottage at the time on the road out to Weston-super-Mare. I yelled out loud on the way back home, "I've got a son. I've got a son." I was stopped for speeding but quickly forgiven when I explained my excitement. I did not sleep a wink.

Before Christmas I heard that the posts at the Children's Hospital were being advertised for the following February. I rang and made an appointment to see the professor. I told him I was applying and wanted to be a paediatrician.

"What are you doing at the moment, David?"

"General practice."

"Are you enjoying it?"

"It's not what I expected. I love it. I could do it for the rest of my life."

His face lit up.

"Every paediatrician should do some general practice but I'm damned if I can get anyone to believe me. I did three years as a GP before I started. OK, apply. Success is more or less guaranteed, I should say." I was appointed and in February I became engaged to the love of my professional life, clinical paediatrics.

Those six months confirmed John Apley's prophecy. I was made for this. Sub-specialization was in its early stages and every consultant was a good generalist. I simply could not believe my luck. Every day I was engaged head and heart in the best job in the world.

The paediatricians didn't have their own college so I sat the first written examination for membership of the Royal College of Physicians and passed.

To my surprise, as well as having a medical role, I found I was house officer to the professor of surgery. In those days there were no paediatric surgeons in Bristol. His senior registrar asked me to assist him in theatre with a child with appendicitis. I asked if I could do it. He was incredulous but when I told him I'd done more than 60 on John Kilby's team he agreed. I got it wrong from the start. My incision was in the wrong place and too large. My dissection into the peritoneum was untidy. My purse string would allow leakage. He allowed me to finish but by then I knew I was useless. No doubt he meant it well. *— Dear Diary, What happened? I used to be able to do that with my eyes closed. In another universe.*

The surgical senior registrar rang me at 6am one Sunday.

"Have you heard?"

"What?"

"Prof's dead. Heart attack we think, in the night."

"Oh no, that's terrible."

"Why, was he your reference as well?"

I had a much more basic human sentiment in mind. But I had learned from personal experience that references could be a matter of professional life and death.

In general the consultants and registrars were good clinicians, worthy role models and enthusiastic teachers. I was now fully committed to paediatrics. When a rotation was advertised in Birmingham I applied.

Janet was not happy. For three years we had regularly driven from Bristol to see our families in Derbyshire. En route we would pass the smog-bound conurbation that was Birmingham. "Promise me we'll never live here," she often joked. But I got the job and had to break my promise. In fact Birmingham did not look half as bad from the inside as it had from the outside.

5

Training in Birmingham

Life is so short, the craft so long to learn.
Hippocrates

In August 1974, two days before our third wedding anniversary, I started work in the Special Care Baby Unit at Sorrento Maternity Hospital in Birmingham. This was an astonishing time to be setting out as a young paediatrician. Sorrento was the first SCBU in the country, having been established by Dr Vickie Cross some years earlier. I had the privilege, as an undergraduate in Bristol, to be taught neonates by Professor Peter Dunn. He told us that there had been little medical interest in babies in the first half century – possibly because their numbers were surplus to requirement! Paediatricians became more involved when exchange blood transfusion was introduced to prevent Rhesus babies getting brain damage. This technique had been invented in the 1920s but had taken many years to catch on. At Sorrento Vickie Cross had been ahead of the game, designing her own cots, doing her own blood tests and post mortems and setting up the country's first human milk bank. She had reluctantly retired, and died soon after, in the previous year. When I arrived the unit was run by Dr Brian Wharton, a neonatologist with an interest in nutrition.

The British Paediatric Association (later to become the Royal College of Paediatrics) and the Department of Health started to take more of an interest in neonatal care in the early 70s, recommending the establishment of specialist consultant posts. Mechanical ventilation of babies with respiratory disease had started and greater attention was given to investigating baby illnesses. There were few books. The bible was the Hammersmith manual, *Medical Care of Newborn Babies*. I quickly learned every word in it, every diagram and every algorithm. The unit at Sorrento ran like clockwork, with one consultant, one non-resident registrar, three house officers and a band of dedicated neonatal nurses. It was a continuation of frequent nights and weekends but that had little impact on us. We were running on enthusiasm.

At 5pm on my first day the other doctors went home and left me on call overnight. I could call a registrar in, but with babies things happen too quickly for that to make any difference. At 6pm I had my first crash call to a newborn who wasn't breathing. I tried stimulation and oxygen but without benefit. In those days the next step was to put a tube into the lungs to inflate them. I did this for the first time in my life. Ten minutes later I was handing the baby to his mother, pink and healthy. There were two similar cases that night, which again I managed on my own. It was a great way to learn and grow in confidence, so long as all went well. Over the coming years better methods of resuscitation would evolve but in those days being a slick intubator badged you with credibility. It's called the halo-effect. St David.

I've met some non-paediatric doctors who seem to think babies suffer from a quite narrow range of illnesses. An orthopaedic surgeon asked me in my early career, "What do you lot do? I didn't think babies got ill." He was wrong about that and we encountered an endless variety of medical and surgical conditions at Sorrento. The consultant came round one day and put his hands on a newborn baby's abdomen. "What's this?" he said. I put my hand where his hand had been and felt a hard lump that turned out to be a rare kidney tumour. I had examined the baby only an hour earlier and missed it. — *Dear Diary: A near miss. Everything counts. Everything.*

One Friday afternoon I saw a six-week-old baby in the follow-up clinic and couldn't contact either of my seniors. There were signs that reminded me of a description I had read of congenital syphilis when doing my membership. The baby was well enough to be sent home with an appointment to return to see the consultant after the weekend. Later that afternoon the consultant dropped in to his office. I told him of this possible diagnosis. "That's an overactive imagination, David. I haven't seen congenital syphilis since I was in Africa." On Monday morning I had a call from a doctor at another Birmingham hospital.

"Did you see this kid on Friday?" he asked. In those days I had a near photographic memory for names.

"Yes, I think he's got congenital syphilis."

"Why do you say that?" I told him what my findings had been.

"It looks like you're right. He pitched up here on Sunday. Oh, we're keeping him. Our first case in ten years."

Subsequent tests confirmed the diagnosis. I told the consultant about this but was wise enough not to make much of it. I've seen a number of diagnoses suggested by juniors pooh-poohed by consultants.

I enjoyed every minute of my first neonatal job but after six months I knew baby medicine was not for me. I needed patients who talked back.

In March 1975 I moved on to the Heart Unit at Birmingham Children's Hospital. Paediatric cardiology was also in its infancy. Echocardiograms were only just coming in. Most children were investigated before surgery by cardiac catheterization. The catheter, inserted through a vein or artery, measured pressures and oxygen levels in different heart chambers and vessels. Dye could also be injected to produce beautiful images. Every week we had a conference with cardiologists, surgeons and x-ray doctors present. It was my job to present the case history, and show diagrams of the catheter data. After the conference we would do the rounds and see patients we had discussed.

One Wednesday we went down to the ward to see a child whose

family I had got to know well. Casual chatting with the children and their families was my favourite pastime. The cardiologist gave the parents a dazzling account of the child's problem, including the catheter data and what the surgeon intended to do. The father looked puzzled. "Well, thank you, Dr Silove, but I think my wife and I would like to hear what Dr Drew has to say about that." I blushed. My quick-witted consultant looked from the father to me and back again. "Er, that *was* Dr Drew's opinion, wasn't it, David?" I nodded. That was not the only time my junior opinion was given more weight than it deserved simply because I was willing to spend time building a relationship. But my consultant never let me forget this one. "Can we have Dr Drew's opinion on how we manage this complex case?" he'd joke. Yawn.

I did my final examinations for membership of the Royal College of Physicians at Great Ormond Street Hospital. By then there was a separate examination for paediatricians. I breezed through data interpretation. My viva was conducted by two senior female professors. The questions came like machine gun fire. I was on top form. The bell rang and I left with a polite thank you. Outside the senior registrar who was supervising looked nonplussed.

"Ooops, I dropped the bell. You've only had five of your 15 minutes."

"I thought that was quick. Shall I go back in?"

"How were you doing?"

"Great."

"Better leave it then."

In the afternoon I was examined on a child with a very rare condition called Gaucher's disease. The previous week I had coincidentally admitted a child with the same condition in Birmingham. I had also just attended a lecture by Philip Evans, an expert on that group of conditions. And there to examine me on my case when I went in was Dr Evans himself. A Royal Flush.

"You seem pretty knowledgeable about this?" he said after I'd finished.

"I heard your lecture at the Institute last week."

"What did you think?"

"Brilliant."

I passed and was admitted as a member of the Royal College. To celebrate, Janet and I took Simon for a beach holiday to Menorca. When we came back I applied for the paediatric registrar rotation in Birmingham. I was appointed and committed to spending the next three or four years working in gastroenterology, neurology, endocrinology, neonatology and a load of other ologies. Janet was pregnant again and due in August. The future was assured.

On a Saturday afternoon in June 1975 I was seeing a child in A&E. Switchboard rang with an outside call. It was my dad. My 21-year-old brother, Stephen, had been drowned in a boating accident on the River Derwent. I was six when Stephen was born and he was the delight of our lives. Our world was turned upside down in one dreadful instant that has remained with me. After a week off I returned to work on the psychiatric ward. I was met in almost every corner of the hospital by profound expressions of sympathy; strangely though, I found in the psychiatric unit, where I was working at the time, only coldness and silence. Hospitals usually have an overarching culture whose tone is set by their leaders. The full picture is much more complex. Even in a great hospital little subcultures of negativity can exist in the last place you might expect to find them.

Meanwhile, I had to give urgent consideration to the needs of my family because when I was appointed registrar we were given notice to quit our hospital accommodation – and our second child was due in only a few weeks' time. Through an over-zealous understanding of certain Bible verses we had decided never to buy a house, but now, finding it cheaper to buy than rent, we allowed common sense to prevail and went house hunting. As usual, however, we had no spare money and so could not afford a deposit. I saw a junior admin officer sitting on his own one lunchtime and struck up a conversation. He was also thinking about buying a house. I explained my dilemma. "Under the terms of your contract you're entitled to an interest-free loan to be repaid over five years", he replied. "That'll cover your deposit. And you get removal expenses." I thanked him and rushed off to tell Janet. Shortly afterwards we brought a small house with a garden ten miles north of the city and Ben, our lovely second son, arrived safely in August. Our cup, surely, was running over with good things.

It was a huge pleasure to come home and find Janet and the children in the garden on a sunny day, but still I was weighed down by a deep sadness about Stephen. Around that time I met a mother who had recently given birth to twins. One, tragically, had died. "What am I supposed to do?" she asked. "Do I laugh for joy or cry at my loss? It's so hard to be happy and sad at the same time." I didn't usually give advice in such situations. Now I found myself telling her she would need to find a way to do both. As for me, I resolved that I would put the living first. My sons had a right to lives not blighted by my grief. I did what I could for my grieving parents, which was very little, and kept my grief for Stephen to myself.

My years at Birmingham Children's Hospital flew. In 1977, in the last six months of the rotation, I started to think seriously about the future. One of the consultants suggested I apply for a senior registrar job at a certain London teaching hospital. The four years were split equally between London and Brighton. I'd always wanted to live by the sea so I went to Brighton to have a look around the day before the interview, which was in London. The interview was going well when I was asked a question I had not expected. Nor did I have a decent answer. Where did I expect this senior registrar job to lead? I gave a poorly thought-out account of my intention to practise in Africa for some years. Not the answer they wanted. This post, I was informed, would lead to an NHS consultant appointment in the next three to four years. I obviously lacked clarity and commitment to the job. I was not appointed. A signpost to somewhere else.

The professor of paediatrics in Birmingham was a tough individual, as I recollect. She called me to her office one afternoon shortly after this. "I've got three years of Medical Research Council funding for a research project on coeliac antibodies. It's a real opportunity. Do you want to do it?" I didn't. I could feel an upset coming on. I'd not thought my future through but I knew it did not involve lab research. I was not the type. I explained my intentions. "Well then, off you go to Africa. Go and get it out of your system. Or into it." It was my own fault. I kept putting myself in these embarrassing situations. I was coasting in a job that I was now on top of. The future needed addressing.

It had long been our intention to take the skills I had learned to what in those days we called The Third World. This was motivated by our Christian faith but I never saw myself doing conventional medical missionary work. I had been reading extensively in my spare time to explore the possibilities. The most impressive read by far was David Morley's *Paediatric Priorities in the Developing World*. He was now Professor of Tropical Child Health at Great Ormond Street Hospital. I rang him and went to spend a couple of days there to meet him and pick up some ideas.

I was as impressed by the man as by his message. He was later nominated for a Nobel Prize. No mere theorist, he had revolutionized child health in the area of Nigeria he had worked in, with a massive reduction in under-five mortality, achieved cheaply and without using any complex technology. Prior to his arrival in Ife, an ancient Yoruba city in Western Nigeria, measles killed five per cent of all children. He used vaccination to eliminate the disease from this community, the first time this had been accomplished anywhere in the world. When I left his department I was brimming with ideas and enthusiasm. I couldn't wait to get out there and do some good.

I later heard that the new University of Ilorin, where David Morley had also worked, was recruiting doctors, and sent in an application. I was interviewed in London and appointed as lecturer in paediatrics. I asked about the start date and travel arrangements. No one on the committee seemed to have thought about this. Janet had given birth to our beautiful daughter, Rachel, in May and my family was my main concern. I left having been told I would hear something soon.

Months went by and I heard nothing. I wrote but got no response. In September I was reading through the Acts of the Apostles. I have always found this an intriguing piece of writing by Luke, who had himself been a doctor. In Chapter 16 I read, "During the night Paul had a vision of a man of Macedonia standing and begging him, 'Come over to Macedonia and help us.'" A few days later I was browsing the overseas section of the *British Medical Journal*'s job adverts. A large boxed advert for "Two Refugee Camp Doctors in Thailand" immediately caught my eye.

After a brief job description a short plea was appended: "Please come and help these needy people." The words so resonated with Paul's Macedonian call that I went home and told Janet about it. She was as excited at the prospect as I was. I put in my notice at the hospital the following day, certain this was for us. I contacted World Vision, the Christian organization running the camps, and had a telephone interview with the in-country medical director. As a result, we rented out our house, sold our car and said a long series of goodbyes. In six weeks we were packing our few belongings and preparing our three small children for a journey into the unknown. Irresponsible madness, of course. As some told us.

6

Thailand

Choose a job that you love and you'll never have to work a day in your life.

Confucius

I knew little about Thailand but the day before we flew I read in the press that Bangkok, the capital, was under curfew. The student massacre at Thammasat University in 1976 had brought an end to three short years of democracy with a military coup. As we were booking our flights in October 1977 a second coup resulted in even more instability. But we were young and foolish then – and full of faith. It never occurred to us to revise our plans.

We were met by a friendly World Vision Thai national at Don Muang airport in Bangkok. Our meagre collection of luggage was thrown in the taxi's boot. The welcomer barked, "*Saladang, soi song*" at the driver. Instantly we were on the road to Bangkok Christian Guesthouse. If ever we were lost in Bangkok all we had to do was give that address to any taxi driver and for a few *bhat* we would be taken home. In Thai even a bark has a beautifully melodious ring to it. We drove through the polluted streets, competing with *tuk-tuks* and *sam-lors*, the ubiquitous motorized and pedal-powered three-wheelers, alongside the fetid *klongs* and past the floating markets. The two Thai men chatted enthusiastically in rising and falling tones. But we were soon falling asleep, unable to take in this magical place.

We spent ten days in Bangkok. The guesthouse was a little American haven, with all types passing through, missionaries, medics, refugees, investigators searching for soldiers missing in action following the war, hush-hush groups. Our older son was amused when we found ourselves sitting at the dinner table with Mr Wee and Mr Poo. Our smiles faded when, after the meal, they showed us the barely healed gunshot wounds they both sustained in their escape across the border with Laos.

It was monsoon season, and on our first trip out to an ice-cream shop on the notorious Patpong Road (aka Brothel Row) we were stranded by flooding following a monsoon downpour. Adventures by their nature are full of inconveniences and we grew used to their regular occurrence. I went daily to the World Vision headquarters for extensive briefings. They were miles ahead of the NHS at that time, it seemed to me. The accountant, a large Texan called Al Stetz, told me I would be running my own budget for two large refugee camps. "Only one rule, doc," he drawled, "One 'n' one is two. An' it aint anythin' else. Balance your books every month." I never managed that. There were much more important things to do.

And then our little family, with only a dozen words of Thai between us, was on its way to the wild North. For the first month we lived in a rented house in Chieng Kham. Our Chinese landlord lived in an ecologically sustainable project at the bottom of the garden. His house abutted a fish farm he'd hand dug. "We shit into the pond and with some waste scraps the fish grow fat. We eat the fish and any scraps go to these pigs. He showed us his four pigs with pride. Pig shit goes on the vegetable patch over here." Small wonder Thailand was a parasitologist's paradise.

My job was to run medical services in two camps about 80 kilometres apart. The Chieng Kham camp was nearby. It was the smaller but in the first month I visited the larger camp at Chiang Khong only three times weekly. The first thing I did was to hire a translator. Mr Lo Chiem Pibul-Sack Srisombat was sent by the Lord. He spoke four languages, including beautiful English. He became a personal friend. The camps were populated by about twelve different language groups, which created some difficulties and made his services indispensable.

In November we moved to Ban Mai Tung Mot, "the village at the end of the plain", only two kilometres from the larger camp. The house was built of hardwood on stilts, eight feet above the ground. In case the annual monsoon flooding breached that level there was a small boat tied up in the garden. A few hundred yards across the paddy fields was the Mekong and beyond its muddy waters the steaming jungle-draped hills of Laos.

This was a beautiful but troubled place. The refugees were mostly from the hill tribes. The majority group was Hmong, who I grew to love and respect. They had been recruited by the CIA to prosecute a secret war against Pathet Lao, the Laotian communist army. The Americans bombed Laos on average every eight minutes, twenty-four hours a day, for nine years. In 1975 the CIA Headquarters in Long Tieng fell, and huge numbers of refugees began to flee the country over the Mekong into Thailand. Although this had settled down by the time we arrived in late 1977, we heard gunfire most nights and refugees still arrived regularly at the old ferry point. We were surrounded by living oral history. These people had suffered and come through, often leaving loved ones behind. Books were redundant.

We soon settled into a routine. Janet looked after the children with the help of a Thai woman and ran the most northerly sanctuary in the country for any passing expatriate. Life with a small butane-run fridge and no electricity required endless ingenuity. As I left for work in the morning there was always something wonderful happening. A herd of elephants came ambling down the road, the leader reaching into our garden to uproot a banana tree. "Dad, come and look, it's elephants in our garden." A huge water buffalo lumbered by, bullied to its work by a small boy perched on its back. Our Thai remained vestigial but the children picked it up effortlessly. "Dad, it's his buffalo. He's the only one in the whole

world can ride it." The kids might be fishing for catfish in the
flooded ditches. Buddhist monks were passing by, stopping to help
our *tambun*. Basically this involved us giving them stuff so that we
accumulated merit for our next reincarnation. And snakes
insinuated themselves everywhere. I remember shuddering
occasionally when we had close contact, but we never lived in fear.

I worked at the nearby larger camp every day and visited Chieng
Kham twice a week. The lab services were run by Maurice Bauhaun,
an ex-Vietnam US Army lab technician. He provided, in the
circumstances, an excellent service, including blood transfusion. He
registered and typed a volunteer group at Chieng Khong. We both
had a longstanding interest in intermediate technology but he put it
into practice. The camps were surrounded by a twelve-foot-high
barbed wire fence.

"What do they need that for, Maurice? Frightened they'll
escape?" I asked.

"No, it's to stop the locals getting in. Conditions are better in
there when it comes to free food supplies and medical care than
outside," he answered.

We were sure we were doing a good thing but soon understood
there were other ways of looking at this. We developed a deep
friendship with a Welsh missionary, Dorothy Jones, who'd been
living and working with the Hmong in the hills for forty years.

"David," she told me one day with a sigh, "You're probably
doing as much harm as you're doing good. The Hmong are the
toughest, proudest, most independent people in the world. Last
week I had a Hmong man visit me asking for a handout. I never
thought I would see that happen. You're creating a dependency
culture." It's unusual to find someone so kind but so outspoken.

We trained up a large group of paramedical workers and nurses.
I knew enough about getting the community on side to ask the camp
committee to be involved in the selection process for paramedic
training. I explained the role and the kind of people we were looking

for and suggested we had interviews and appoint for a probationary period. The local chief of police was also on the committee and felt he had a better idea: "You choose half and I'll choose half." I knew I had lost the argument against this idea before I opened my mouth. I spoke to power with every argument I could muster. And lost. Afterwards we had a beer and a good laugh together.

We employed a 13-year-old girl who could speak eight languages to do translation. One day she asked if she could try inserting a cannula. I found that with practically no training she could get a drip into almost any vein. Once, after seeing me do a cut-down when we could not get a cannula into a collapsed child she asked if I would teach her. I did and I never needed to do a cut-down again. Our medical workers were lovely, polite and enthusiastic – apart from a few rogues, that is. I used my budget to have a simple hospital uniform made, the same for all staff, including cleaners. When I arrived at the hospital wearing it myself they were delighted: one of my early attempts at flattening hierarchies in the interest of patient care. It would be another 30 years before the NHS got to thinking about that.

The paramedics soon managed the bulk of the simpler cases. I observed them at work regularly. They didn't think outside the box but were brilliant with algorithms. They had to deal with quite a lot of worried well and we produced red and green placebo by the gallon. I'm sure quite a lot of animistic belief came into consultations but in general I didn't interfere with that. These things take time.

As well as the routine complaints there were a lot of exotic conditions. Parasitic disease abounded: roundworm and hookworm were universal but also rarer conditions like Paragonimus (a lung fluke). Maurice managed to find a supply of bithionol, which at the time was the only treatment for this infestation. An expatriate friend and his wife both developed a severe form of cystercercosis after eating poorly cooked pork. It was complicated by epilepsy, a reminder of the everyday dangers we faced. Opisthorchis, a liver fluke, was common and the cause of liver cancer in longstanding infestation. Rabid dogs occasionally appeared and we had one clinical case of human rabies. His family knew the score and took him off to die.

Thalassaemia abounded in the Thai population. We had a huge measles epidemic, which the paramedics struggled to cope with. There had been no vaccination programme. We had to do outreach at a moment's notice when called on. One night, very late, 300 refugees, including many children, crossed the river. They were in bad shape, malnourished and malarial from months in the jungle. Some had gunshot wounds. We took a team out to the ferry point, long fallen into disuse, to help. Within twenty-four hours many had disappeared into the bush to find relatives who'd arrived earlier.

Once we were known, local people arrived at the house at all hours. A tribal family came at midnight with a sick four-month-old baby. I drove them to the camp with Maurice. A lumbar puncture showed pneumococcal meningitis. At that time even in the UK 50 per cent of babies with pneumococcal meningitis died and 50 per cent of the survivors were severely handicapped. After ten days of antibiotics (cannula courtesy of a 13-year-old refugee girl) the baby was well. Many months later the family visited us to show us the "miracle child". The child's father repaid us by taking us on a hair-raising fishing trip up the Mekong.

One Sunday a man in the village brought his eleven-year-old daughter to the house. She'd been ill for a week and I diagnosed appendicitis. The girl was very sick and I was worried about operating myself. I drove her with her parents to the provincial hospital in Chieng Rai about 200 kilometres away. It was a large hospital but we were told there was no surgeon available that afternoon. We drove back to the camp, where I removed a huge gangrenous appendix under ketamine anaesthesia. The operation didn't go entirely without incident. An untrained "assistant" came in as I was about to start and quick as a cat picked up a sterile pair of Spencer–Wells forceps off the instrument tray, calmly walked over to the wall and used them to crush a cockroach crawling up it. He knew no better. The next briefing ensured that was the last time such a thing happened. The patient survived and I gave her the appendix in a jar preserved in Mekong whisky. Days later, I received an instruction from a World Vision manager to stop treating non-camp personnel and to stop doing operations. I went to Bangkok with our medical director, a very supportive New Zealander.

"What am I supposed to do in these situations?" I asked.

"Behave in a way that does not jeopardize our whole programme," replied the manager.

"How will my helping sick people jeopardize the programme? That's what I'm here for."

"It is strictly against policy."

"I have sworn an oath." I said.

My medical director supported me and I went back north, following my conscience all the way. There was one unforeseen consequence to this meeting. Later that year I applied to have my contract extended. I was turned down. World Vision had already contracted a doctor from India to replace me.

Leaving was one of the saddest days of our life. We all cried. The Hmong gave me two crossbows that would kill a man at 100 metres. "This is the boy's crossbow," the chief told me when he handed it over. "I know you cannot draw the man's." If you saw the man's crossbow you would know there was no shame in that.

I was encouraged before we left to receive a letter from the Liverpool School of Tropical Medicine. I had applied for a place on the Tropical Diseases course to start the following January. The letter informed me that every year one applicant was chosen on the basis of their CV to work as a clinical fellow in tropical diseases with the Reader, Dr Dion Bell. The post was for six months and paid at Whitley Council rates. Attendance at the three-month course was included and the costs waived. I would just have to do a few hours' work each evening. "The Lord is with you, Dr Drew," said Janet when I read this out. "And with you, Mrs Drew."

We boarded the plane at Don Muang airport in Bangkok late in the afternoon, sad to be leaving but suddenly homesick for our families and friends.

7

Back to Blighty

This blessed plot, this earth, this realm, this England
                                    Shakespeare: *Richard II*

We were home before Christmas. That was the time when we really missed our families in Thailand. Christmas may be a Victorian invention more lately hijacked by commerce but we relished it. In our own land, with our own people. I was due to start the tropical medicine course at Liverpool in January so there was a short time for rest and relaxation. We spent Christmas Day with our parents, who lived close to each other in Belper. There had been a communication failure and both sets had cooked Christmas dinner for us. We were due at one house at 1pm and the other at 4pm. We explained to the children what was expected of them and they did us proud, cleaning up two lots of plates in four hours. They were all rather underweight so it did them no harm. But I found it hard to eat. I felt as if I was developing flu. We had a lot of fun but our children's insistence on eating everything with their fingers caused some grandparental concern. It was no use trying to explain that this was their cultural norm.

The next day it snowed and I was sent out to buy plastic sledges. I felt like staying in bed. I found it difficult to pull even our youngest along. I was weak, nauseated and out of breath. I had a sense of foreboding. It grew cold and we went in for tea and bath-time. I ate nothing. I was ill.

I crawled out of bed the next morning from a sense of duty. Janet had already given the children breakfast. "Go and have a look at yourself in the mirror, will you." I didn't recognize the yellow-eyed zombie that stared back at me. "I'm jaundiced." Doctors make awful patients. I wanted to go back to bed and sleep it off but Janet was already on the phone to Barry Kenyon, our GP and a personal friend. Half an hour later he came into the bedroom, took one look at me and said, "I don't know what it is but it looks tropical." By lunchtime I was in bed in the nearest tropical diseases unit.

The clinical examination and tests quickly confirmed that I had a liver inflammation, and over the next couple of days this was shown to be hepatitis B. Had I been given any injections or blood transfusions (that being the usual mode of transmission)? As it happened I had. Two months earlier I had developed severe renal colic late one evening in Ban Mai. I'd had several kidney stones that hospitalized me in my training years and this was an inconvenient recurrence. The communist insurgency in our province meant we could not travel safely at night. In wave after wave of agony I paced around under the house until first light and then drove to Chieng Rai with the whole family. I was demented with pain and given 10mg of intravenous heroin on arrival. I had three further doses, which I did not object to at all and was discharged after three days. That was the most likely explanation for my hepatitis: a dirty needle.

There was no treatment for it and after a few days I asked to go home. I was told I was too ill. The tropical diseases professor came around in the afternoon. I told him I wanted to discharge myself. I explained that I was due to start in Liverpool in less than a week. "If I miss this boat there won't be another one." I told him. "The Ferryman will take you over the Styx any day of the week, Dr Drew," he cautioned. I looked and felt like death but I'd made my mind up. He let me go.

The next few days were busy. I'd met a young Burmese nurse, Mala, in the Golden Triangle, six months earlier. She was also starting a course at the Liverpool School. We'd asked her to stay with us for a few days so that I could take her up with me. I rested as much as I could, aware of the pressure on Janet. At the weekend I drove Mala to Liverpool and dropped her off at her digs. Then I went to find my room at Sefton General Hospital, where I was staying and supposedly working. This was the one thing I was anxious about. The deal was that I would fit registrar duties in with the tropical diseases course. I was too weak to work.

I picked up my room keys and a kindly old porter showed me the way. He explained that the ancillary workers had been on strike for weeks and the ward I was to be working on was closed. The course lasted more than three months and in that time the strike held. I only had to see half a dozen patients in the time I was there. — *Dear Diary: I'm wondering if that Scouser was some sort of angel. "Don't be afraid, I bring you good news," says he.*

I started the course, which was intense. Ironically no one noticed that I was jaundiced. My boss at Sefton was the Reader in Tropical Diseases, the late, magnificent, Dr Dion Bell. I met him after a few days, a warm and charming man. He asked about my personal arrangements and explained about the strike at Sefton. Finally he asked, "Do you know you're jaundiced?" I told him I had hepatitis B and that he was the first person to notice. "David," he replied, "powers of observation are not what they used to be."

The course ground on, and for me it was a hard grind. There was a cinema next to the school and most afternoons as soon as classes finished I would buy a ticket and a coke and collapse on the back row. After seeing *The Heroes of the Telemark* for the third or fourth time I'd struggle back to the hospital and go to bed. In the three months I lost two-and-a-half stones. I was thin before I became ill. Doing any amount of clinical work would have been out of the question. Some weekends I didn't have the energy to go home to Janet but lay in bed doing nothing.

I rang home when I could. At the end of January Janet seemed unusually upbeat. "I've got some good news for you." We were short of money. "Tax rebate?" I suggested hopefully. "I'm pregnant." The last ounce of strength drained from me. "Fourth and last, eh?" I groaned. "Definitely." We were under pressure but in truth we were both delighted. We were never, thank God, the worrying kind.

The few patients I did see were ex-FEPOWs (Far East Prisoners of War). I spent many fascinating hours listening to them and learning that my own experience of the Orient was tame. The course was drawing to a close. Soon I would get my diploma and be on my way. Time to think about our next move. I had seen an advertisement for a paediatric clinical lecturer post in Nigeria in the *British Medical Journal*. It appealed to me and Janet also thought it would be a good move. But I was too tired to do anything about it and mislaid the ad. One afternoon, at the end of his lecture the Professor of Community Medicine asked if I would come to his office at 5pm. I went, intrigued. He pushed a paper across the desk at me. "This came in the post today asking if there was anyone I could recommend. Your name came to mind." I didn't think he even knew who I was. "Senior Lecturer post in Paediatrics at the University of Jos, Nigeria," it read. The post I had intended to pursue.

After the course finished I went home and started to regain weight. I did a few registrar locums and realized that the hiatus in my career had made me if anything a better and more confident doctor. Joseph, our fourth and last child, was born in September. His name means "God will increase" but we made a policy decision that we had increased enough. He was a bonny baby and, along with our other three children, the principle source of our happiness. I was allowed to bring the other children in to see mother and new baby brother in the afternoon. That would have been unthinkable a few years earlier. Two weeks later we had a letter confirming my appointment as Lecturer in Paediatrics at Jos University Teaching Hospital (JUTH), Plateau State, Nigeria.

The following month was hectic, saying goodbyes, selling our car and renting our house out again. We were invited for a week of induction into African life at Farnham Castle in Kent. All manner of people, indigenes and expats, were there to help us understand what we were letting ourselves in for. We heard a lot of great live music and tasted a variety of African food. We heard tales of the ordinary and the extraordinary, horror stories and magical adventures.

But our dominant impression was of the larger than life Nigerians themselves. One expansive Nigerian speaker I got talking to was candid: "We Nigerians love, we love the ostentatious display of wealth. Even if we don't have it." He began his talk by proclaiming in a booming voice, "There is nothing good enough I can say about Nigeria. And there is nothing bad enough either." A Ghanaian sitting next to me whispered, "Nigeria, land of the big talk talk, eh?" We went home full of eager anticipation. And in the twinkling of an eye we found ourselves landing at Kano Airport in arid sub-Saharan Northern Nigeria. We disembarked into Bedlam: a scene so noisy, so chaotic, that we felt afraid. Janet looked at me as we headed for the baggage lounge. "Nothing bad enough either." I said.

8

Nigeria

Nigeria is what it is because its leaders are not what they should be.

Chinua Achebe

We were the last to clear customs. Casually dressed, in a sea of suits and traditional costumes, we struggled with our four children, the youngest, Joseph, only six weeks old. We must have looked like refugees to the custom officials. But that didn't stop them trying to fleece us. We had our first taste of the *dash* culture. Money, even a small amount, talks. I didn't pay a *kobo*, hence our slow passage. When we got through into arrivals the promised welcome failed to materialize. We were on our own. A taxi driver told us of a hotel in Kano where University people stayed. He took us there at a fare that would have been generous in London. After a hasty meal of cow-heel stew and pounded yam, which the children demolished, we fell exhausted into bed without washing. So far so good.

At 6am I went down to the lobby to ask about transport to Jos. The receptionist was asleep. I woke him to be told, "A vehicle will come before noon." How did he know, I asked. Too late, his head was down on the desk again. I picked up a week-old national newspaper. "Woman Gives Birth to a Goat," its front-page headline announced. Paediatric practice was obviously going to be quite different here.

After breakfast we walked in the hotel grounds, taking in the new and strange sights and sounds and smells. The early sunshine restored our spirits and our children shrieked with delight at the lizards lazing on the walls — "If men were as much men as lizards are lizards/ they'd be worth looking at." About noon a driver arrived in a long-wheelbase UNIJOS Toyota Landcruiser to take us to Jos. We sped across the plain at 100 kph, having to slow to a crawl every so often to negotiate deeply eroded sections of road. I'd read that road-accident mortality in Nigeria, expressed as deaths per hundred thousand miles, was a hundred times greater than the European average. The two serious accidents we saw within ten miles of each other supported this.

The scrublands were dotted with pools where naked children splashed and butterflies teemed. It grew hotter until we started the slow ascent to Jos. At 5,000 feet above sea level Jos sits atop a massive volcanic intrusion at the heart of Plateau State. Before we reached the cooler air of that altitude the Landcruiser ground to a halt. "Broken fan belt," the driver told us helplessly, "No spare." Janet opened a bag, pulled out a pair of maternity tights and showed him how to fit them on the pulleys. He looked doubtful but we held a steady 60 kph after that and two hours later rolled into the car park at the Plateau Hotel, where we would stay until a house was allocated to us.

We lived at the Plateau Hotel for six weeks. It would be hard to overstate the difficulties of that time for all of us but it was also a great adventure. On one occasion the Nigerian President, Al-haji Shehu Shagari came to town and commandeered the whole hotel. We had to move out for two days to make way for the great man. After a few days I went to see the Dean of Medicine, Professor Ikeme. I also met many of the pre-clinical teaching staff, a friendly, cosmopolitan bunch. My office at the hospital was in a new single-storey block. We were possibly the only clinicians in the world whose offices were guarded overnight by one old man with a bow and arrow. In the first week I heard a dreadful commotion outside. A thief had been caught in the market. He was knocked unconscious with a club, doused with petrol and thrown onto a pile of tyres. He was ablaze when I arrived. "Leave this, white man," someone shouted at me and I went back inside.

Eventually we were allocated a large bungalow in the Student Village. Our neighbours were a thousand mostly delightful university students, whose only serious fault was their love for playing loud music into the early hours. "We love to share our music, sir," they told us. Home life settled down to a routine such as we had never known before. No running water for the first two years, frequent power cuts, haggling in the markets. Simon and Ben spent the first year in a Nigerian school. At night their main game was taking it in turns to be "teacher" and chase the other with a stick shouting, "I'll beat you. I'll beat you. I'll beat you."

Water was a daily problem. Each house had a raised water tank and, twice a week, a university truck came to fill it, but this was contingent on paying the driver a small bribe. In my commitment to honesty as a Christian (please remember I recognize that you atheists can be just as committed) I refused to pay. Consequently we went without and I had to hand-carry what we needed. One day we watched the truck pull up next to our tank. The driver jumped out, connected the hose and filled it. As he was getting back into his cab I ran out to thank him, "*Sannu de aiki!*" We exchanged a lengthy Hausa responsive greeting. Then I pulled out a five-*naira* note and asked him to take it for his troubles. "No, thank you, sir. I'm a Christian, I don't take bribes." And off he went.

Wild life was everywhere and natural history became our main interest. Under every stone were toads and mice, scorpions and snakes, sometimes sitting in apparent harmony. We accumulated a menagerie of pets and creatures from the bush: love birds, a goat, chickens, chameleons, guinea pigs ("but they is for *chop* [eating]," said Mary, our house help) and lizards. Lizards laid eggs all over the house, even in the keyholes. One Sunday we returned from church and Simon noticed one egg quivering. We sat and watched three of five eggs hatch, and the most tiny, perfect, baby lizards slip off to their new lives. We spent hours watching sand lions catching ants in their conical sand holes. And ruling the roost there was Eric.

"Looney Eric." He was a ginger tom born of a bush cat we had adopted. He would often climb 15 feet up our water tower and jump off just for the hell of it, thus earning his sobriquet. Eventually he developed a paralysing disease and I had to put him out of his misery. 30 years later we still talk about him as though he had been a family member.

My medical work began in earnest. Jos University Teaching Hospital, JUTH, was the revamped Murtalla Mohammed Hospital, which once served as the district general hospital for Plateau State. The paediatric ward was old, cramped and completely inadequate, but it was replaced some time after my arrival by a new facility. 400 children arrived each day in general outpatients. They were triaged in a way I never fathomed and never made any impact on. The worst cases were sent to our outpatients department or the ward. Many children were malnourished; diarrhoea, pneumonia and measles were rampant. But there was, alongside this, the whole complex gamut of conditions that I had seen in the UK. The workload was unmanageable and I had to learn to go home at night with much undone.

The maternity block was in a backwater. 12,000 deliveries a year meant 30 to 40 births a day. Many women delivered and then, if the baby was OK, they picked it up and went home. The first baby I saw in the nursery had gross hydrocephalus and was inappropriately on three antibiotics. Other babies died of umbilical cord sepsis because the parents could not afford one antibiotic. Vince Knight, an English doctor working in the physiology department, came to visit occasionally. I gave him a detailed tour and described our working day. "It's not a medical facility, David; it's an ecological disaster zone," he told me.

We had no telephones. If I was wanted in the night a hospital car was sent to my house. On one such night I went into the ward at 3am to find pandemonium. Two children lay dead on a table. Another cradled by his mother was *in extremis* with an obstructed airway. The one nurse on duty was asleep. I woke her and asked where the doctor was. He'd gone for food. The obstructed child vomited blood and died. I asked the driver to take me home. I'd been in Jos more than a year but I was still shocked by what I saw. At home I got into my own car and drove to the Dean's house. I roused him with a long blast on his doorbell. "Professor Ikeme, please come to the hospital with me." He didn't ask why, just went in, got dressed and climbed into my car. I gave him an account of what I had seen an hour earlier.

The ward was quieter when we arrived; the sleeping nurse was on her feet and a doctor and another nurse had appeared. Two of the dead children had been taken away and the other covered over. If the Dean thought I had been exaggerating he did not say so. He took it seriously. We walked around, spoke to the staff and some parents, and then I took him home. We sat in the car outside his house. I was about to tell him I was going back to England when he said, "I've got no answers. I do know that it's better that you are here than that you are not here. There's more chance things will improve if you stay than if you go. You came because you thought you could do some good. So, do it." I went home for breakfast. I'd been a doctor for ten years and that was the first time I consciously decided that I had to put my patients before my own interests and probably, as it seemed, my family's interests.

We started teaching clinical paediatrics formally in my second year, and other faculty members, mostly Polish and Indian, joined us. The paediatric professor was a formidable Polish lady from Warsaw. She appeared at meetings with an enormous folder emblazoned with the word "DIDAKTIKA." We disagreed about the course content, teaching methods and lots of other things. I'd read a lot of David Morley, the father of tropical child health, Oscar Gish on developing health systems and some of the early medical educational literature. She hadn't heard of any of them. Our students had been educated in an authoritarian system and although didactic teaching was needed they had to learn that things were true for other reasons than that your teacher said so. I took to carrying an equally huge folder with "SOKRATIKA" stencilled on its front. A subtitle declared "I know nothing." I tried to explain what this meant but failed. I found myself on one side of a mini cold war. But it didn't last. The wall came down. We found a way of living together.

Corruption was everywhere. Before our new wards were opened I asked a clerk about equipping them. "Contracts are already signed, sir," he told me. He showed me the inventory, which included 200 bedpans and other useless stuff. I went off to the Dean again. Whoever signs the contract takes a ten per cent cut from the provider: that was the norm in those parts I was told. At least on this occasion something happened and money appeared that could be used honestly by people who knew what they were doing. But I made enemies in the process.

The ordinary Nigerians were more victims of this culture than we were. But they were cheerful, philosophical and an antidote to self-pity. I cultivated the habit of getting to know everyone, drivers, messengers, secretaries, cleaners, any old nobody. That was where the local intelligence was, where you found out what was really going on.

We graduated our first students after working frantically hard to get them up to scratch. For six months I held three one-hour seminars between 2 and 5pm every Monday, Wednesday and Friday to ensure they got experience of learning in small groups. I sometimes felt I never wanted to teach again.

The clinical finals examinations in 1983 were memorable. John Dodge, a paediatrician from Cardiff, came as external examiner in paediatrics. We were walking up to the hospital canteen one lunch time and I noticed the obstetric and gynaecology examiners team walking behind us. That evening I met one of our gynaecology consultants, Isaac Wright, socially. The O&G external examiner was

Bill Whitehouse, an eminent doctor from London. He told stories of his obstetric practice at London Zoo and showed us a deep scar where a pregnant orang-utan had bitten him.

"David, Mr Whitehouse said something about you today when we were walking up to the canteen," Isaac said, smiling.

"Oh yes, what was that?"

"Well, he pointed to you and said, 'There goes a man with no future.'"

I recognized the truth in that immediately. I had been away from British practice for seven years and I would find it difficult to get back on the ladder at home. But needs must. I had achieved most of what I could at JUTH. Things were still chaotic but less so. By 1984 we could not afford to send any more of our children to Hillcrest Academy in the autumn. I was chronically tired. We decided that it was time for us to go home. I saw Janet and the children off on a KLM flight in late summer and stayed behind alone to tidy up the many loose ends.

Getting out of Nigeria was a complex bureaucratic exercise. One large form had to be completed and each section stamped and countersigned. That completed form was a requirement for getting through customs. All library books had to be returned and the university librarian's signature and official stamp obtained to guarantee none were outstanding. I had no library books but this was hard to prove. It took three visits. Next was NEPA, the Nigerian Electric Power Authority or "No Electric Power Always", as it was then known by our Nigerian friends. All electricity bills had to be settled and the form signed and stamped. On my fifth visit, (required because the man with the stamp was never "on seat"), I became agitated. That was always counterproductive. I pushed the bill and the exact sum over the desk at him.

"I'm not taking money today."

"Why not?"

"I need some help first."

"I've brought the exact change."

"Come back tomorrow."

"I'm here now. I'm paying now."

"Tomorrow." I went and sat down.

"Tomorrow."

"I'll wait here until tomorrow."

I waited until closing time. I kept my nerve. I knew he would not lock up and go with me sitting there. He took my money and stamped my card without making eye contact.

"German dog! You bloody German dog!" he shouted after me as I left. That was the only time I ever experienced any unpleasantness from a Nigerian. The ordinary people, unaffected by wealth or status, are among the most companionable people I have met.

I ploughed a lonely furrow for the last month, collecting my stamps and finishing my work at the hospital. A Polish pathologist asked me to visit him and have a few drinks one Friday evening. I stayed overnight and at 5am he woke me and said we should climb the mountain at the back of the staff quarters. The view from the top overlooked the local polo ground, a colonial relic where we had had a lot of good fun as it was also used for horse racing. But now, on a Saturday morning, it was to be used for a non-recreational purpose. The increase in armed robbery had resulted in the reintroduction of death by firing squad for that crime. Far below three men were brought out, tied to posts and shot. "I'll be seeing those three gentlemen on Monday morning I expect," my friend said in a matter-of-fact way. But I found myself thinking that each one of them had a mum and dad somewhere and that in a different world... And I longed for my English home and my own children.

9

The Locum Years

"What makes the desert beautiful," said the little prince, "is that somewhere it hides a well."

Antoine de Saint-Exupéry: *The Little Prince*

October 1984: I landed at Heathrow on a grey afternoon, to be cheerfully ferried north by my brother Chris. Any depression I might have felt was dissipated when I saw our children, all anxious to tell me of their adventures since arriving home. Janet had moved the family back into our little house in Sutton Coldfield and they had been overwhelmed: "Is this our house? Our own house? Are these our spoons?" All four had already settled into the same local primary school. I insisted on fish and chips for my first meal back home and after we had eaten and tucked the children up in bed we sat and talked for hours. We'd been away in Nigeria for more than five years. It felt like a dream. I went to bed intoxicated and wide awake — "Is this our bed? Our own bed?"

The alarm at 7am signalled the beginning of a military-style operation to get four excited children ready for school. We walked them there together, greeting people I had not seen for years. The kids didn't hang around at the school gate but ran off with their new friends. One shouted, "My dad's home." Life is an exile. Home is the way back. We walked for an hour in Sutton Park, reminiscing, laughing our heads off most of the time, attracting a few very English stares. Culture re-entry shock. We avoided talk of the future.

For the next few weeks we were busy with the mundane. Our house had become dilapidated and the garden neglected. The outside had to be painted and I had to fit a new window. The gardening skills of our tenants were revealed when our next-door neighbour reported finding them encouraging bindweed to grow up a trellis intended for honeysuckle. We spent whole days outside at our favourite time of year. Season of mists. We visited family and friends and re-established ourselves in the church. It was strangely difficult to communicate what had happened to us over the last eight years. Simon, Ben, Rachel and Joe adapted much more quickly than we did. And Janet much more quickly than me.

At some point I had to face the future that I didn't have. A friend came to me with an offer of a partnership in general practice – subject to my doing a bit more hospital training: "Good money, good life." But even though I had taken a massive diversion in my career I knew paediatrics was the only girl for me. So, one November morning, I took the train to the medical school library in Birmingham. I picked up the four most recent copies of the *British Medical Journal* and found a quiet corner. I was looking for job opportunities but, according to my longstanding habit when reading that journal, I turned first to the obituaries section. There on page 1390 in the 17 November 1984 edition was a familiar face staring out of the page at me: Mr "Bill" Whitehouse. He had died two weeks earlier, at the age of 57, on my birthday. The worst side of me was tempted to make a smug comment but the truth was I had found him a decent person with the rare gift of plain speaking. It would have been better if he had spoken plainly to me. There goes a man with no future.

But I was going to prove him wrong. When I first told Janet about Bill Whitehouse's prophecy she pulled out a Bible and read to me from Psalm 37: "There is a future for the man of peace." One of the journals carried an advert for a senior registrar post at Birmingham Children's Hospital. I visited a couple of my old consultants to ask for advice and a reference. "God, David, we thought you'd died in Africa," one told me. They were both intensely interested in what I had been doing. I was promised good references and went away feeling optimistic. I was called for interview but didn't get the job. Dick White, the nephrology professor, gave me a detailed and helpful debrief. I'd worked for him in 1975 and he had written to me a number of times about my clinical work in Nigeria. "It's always down to who's the best candidate for the job, David. But the committee was unanimous that someone of your experience and maturity should go and find a consultant post now." He told me that a nearby hospital was looking for a locum consultant. A week later I was working as a consultant in the NHS at Sandwell District General Hospital only ten miles from home.

I experienced a huge culture shock. The volume of extremely sick children and high mortality I'd become used to had desensitized me. It wasn't that I didn't care. I had four children of my own and knew how it felt when they were threatened by illness. My difficulty was that in comparison with the last eight years many problems seemed trivial. There were other challenges as well. I had seen virtually no non-accidental injury in Nigeria but now I was asked to do examinations every time I was on call. I had to completely re-orientate myself in the care of the newborn. We were regularly ventilating small premature babies and encountering babies with rare complex diseases who we would have left to die in Jos. Pharmacy rang me one day; I had prescribed a drug that had been withdrawn two years earlier because of dangerous side effects. Getting back on the ladder was only a small part of my problem. I raised the issue with a number of senior colleagues of how a doctor removed from paediatric practice for so long could just walk back in to the NHS. No one seemed remotely interested in this idea. And it wasn't in my interest to make too much of it.

I was saved from failure by three factors: a continual, almost visceral, delight in the challenge of clinical practice; the frequency of direct patient contact with only two consultants and no registrars;

and freedom, as a locum, from most of the department's administrative work. After a year a permanent post was advertised. I applied and did not get it. I was disappointed. I was so confident of being appointed that I put a bottle of champagne in the fridge before going to the interview and told my children they could have some when we celebrated later! We drank the champagne anyway. My children to this day insist I was crying but of course they were under the influence of Veuve Clicquot and would not remember.

Once again I was on the scrap heap. We'd made a conscious decision that our children's education would come first. We could not unsettle them again. So, I would wait for a consultant job to come up within the statutory ten miles travelling distance from home. That put quite a number of hospitals in range. Meantime I was happy with locum work. The head of the regional neonatal intensive care unit rang and offered me a six-month locum while his colleague went on maternity leave. It suited my development needs precisely. I had been registrar there ten years earlier. I realized on my first day that the whole discipline had been reinvented in that time. I soaked up the change and emerged more up to date and possibly more competent than most general paediatricians I knew.

But I was back at the same point with no permanent post that I could put a mark on, no security for my family. I would not have chosen that way of living but through the retrospectoscope it appears to me now a blessed country. For the next six years I worked as a locum, mostly in the West Midlands and Yorkshire. That was a strange and rather vulnerable position to be in. It provided an opportunity to see at quite a senior level how the departments I worked in functioned. In some the medics got on with each other, in others not. Some were full of enthusiasm and innovation but others felt world-weary. I encountered all kinds of inconsistency and individual practice. Clinical governance with practice guidelines and audit were not even on the horizon. I made the mistake of saying at one clinical meeting that the barefoot doctors I had trained in the refugee camps were more consistent in their management of diarrhoea and dehydration than our primary and secondary care doctors. I was asked to keep that kind of opinion to myself in future.

No one ever took any interest in or responsibility for my professional development. As a locum I got paid for the days I worked. There was no study leave and no refund for meeting or course fees. It was all down to me. My learning was needs driven. I took every opportunity I could to understand the patients that I was seeing. I learned quite a lot from making diagnoses that other consultants had missed – and likewise from diagnoses that I got wrong. I rarely met an individual consultant who minded being challenged on clinical practice. Any who did were likely to be insecure personalities. Sometimes with good reason. These were, in my experience, the really dangerous ones.

I arrived at one hospital fresh from my six months at the regional neonatal unit. The locum post came up because a consultant had fallen ill. One premature baby was being ventilated in the unit. It was normal by then to use a morphine infusion to keep babies pain-free and comfortable until they could breathe for themselves. I wrote the morphine prescription and made up the right dilution myself. When I came back in the late afternoon I noticed that the drug had been crossed off the treatment chart and the infusion stopped. I asked the baby's nurse who had done this. The unit sister, concerned about this novel practice, had rung the sick consultant at home. He had then driven in, crossed the morphine off and left a message for me: "Please tell Dr Drew we do not practise euthanasia in this department." I rang him at home but he was too ill to speak to me. Before I left it was normal practice on that unit to give babies pain relief when required.

I saw all manner of clinical incidents over those years, some resulting in death. There was no reporting mechanism and no formal way of dealing with patient harm. Babies and small children would be ventilated on adult intensive care units and, in several hospitals I worked in, on the general ward. Patients received overdoses of drugs and underwent inappropriate procedures. Parents were told in full, in part, or not at all, what had gone wrong. There was a general attitude that accidents happen. Some doctors put their hands up, some did not. I never encountered parents who, having been told the truth and given an honest apology, took it any further.

I was sometimes asked about the practice of colleagues. Especially as a locum that was possibly the most difficult situation I faced. The "Three Wise Men" came to visit me at one hospital. This was a trio of very senior consultants who at one time helped "self-police" (some said protect) the consultant body, though the custom fell into disuse long ago. Had I noticed anything unusual about a certain colleague's behaviour? Were there problems with his practice? Did he turn up for appointments? Did he ever smell of alcohol? In truth I knew there was a problem but it had no serious effect on his practice. I ducked the issue and said that as far as I knew there was no problem. I then dropped some hints to the consultant to let him know he was under scrutiny. For the rest of my time in that hospital I lived with the anxiety of knowing something could go wrong. A few years later I heard that things had got worse and he subsequently died of an alcohol-related disease. Knowing how to deal with fellow consultants was never easy.

And so it continued, year by year. Life was punctuated by pleasure and pain. In the summer after our return Janet's eldest brother, William, was drowned while punting on the Cherwell at an Oxford reunion. He couldn't swim. His best friend dived in to save him but also drowned. I was working away. Once again I received the telephone call we hope we'll never get. Someone is getting it every day. Janet was heartbroken but busy with four lively children. "Happiness or sadness, which shall we have today?" she asked. "Both, love." —*Dear Diary: this is the real world. No turning back.*

I saw an old friend, a paediatrician who was a few years my

senior. "What's happened to you, David? What are you doing with your life? You were a contender." I was only occasionally troubled by self-doubt. I served my seven years as a locum drinking deeply from the well of the experience they provided. Both my personal and my professional life were enriched. In that time only a couple of suitable consultant posts had come up within travelling distance of home. In 1991 I was 44 years old and my eldest son had left for university. Then, four posts were advertised within weeks of each other. One of them was at Walsall. I had worked there for a year in 1987 when a consultant was on sick leave. Janet reminded me that some of my happiest memories were of that time. I sent in my application and was shortlisted.

The Walsall interview was informal but demanding. The professional adviser on the interview committee was Paul Rayner, a consultant I'd worked for years earlier. I'd seen a lot and picked up a lot of good ideas in my wanderings and had developed quite strong opinions of my own. The advantage of my year in Walsall as locum consultant enabled me to give a good account of what I thought the department needed. I was told that if I waited the committee would make an immediate decision. Ten minutes later I was called back in: "We would like to offer you the job." I was pleased but had agreed to attend another interview the following week. Paul Rayner laughed, "What's a matter, David? Don't you think Walsall needs a missionary doctor?" I asked to be given a week to decide. The CEO, John Rostill, was in the chair. He agreed to give me two weeks.

The other interview, at a hospital within walking distance of my home, went badly. I couldn't resist pointing out a couple of ambiguities in one of the panellist's questions. "Have you had any personal experience of physical abuse?" "No, my parents were really decent people." That foolish act of pedantry was not received well and provoked a barrage of difficult and hostile questions that I could not answer. "Don't mess with us, Dr Drew." I was not appointed. I rang Walsall the same day: "I'm coming."

10

Walsall

*Ya know what? You're a goddam swordboat captain! Doing what
you were made to do. Is there anything better in the world?*
Captain Billy Tyne in *The Perfect Storm*

On the 4th of January 1992 I drove into Walsall Manor Hospital as a
substantive full-time consultant. I'd worked there for a year as a
locum four years earlier. I was replacing a consultant I'd worked
with over that time. He'd taken early retirement and gone to open
a bar in Spain. A few years later we heard he'd had a heart attack and
died. I would be working with two consultants whose duties I'd
covered as a locum during their lengthy illnesses. It was a threadbare
department even by the standards of the time. The three of us shared
a secretary and we had no office. The wards were located in a
Victorian workhouse, and the maternity and neonatal unit in a
draughty, old prefabricated building.

The situation had been transformed beyond recognition by the
time of my dismissal in 2010.

My two new consultant colleagues, Dr Rashid Gatrad and Dr
Pat Howse, were warm and generous people. I'd known and
worked with both of them before, at Walsall and Birmingham
Children's Hospital. I don't believe I ever had a cross word with
Rashid: he got on with his work and left me to get on with mine. I
had an enjoyably sparky relationship with Pat, and we quite often
failed to see eye to eye. If she was losing an argument she would
typically say, "David, you used to be my registrar and that's how I
still think of you." It was all very good-humoured, though, and we
often laughed about our spats. Within weeks I knew I was in the

right place. Once more Janet had proved that she knew me better than I knew myself.

Walsall is an area of high socioeconomic deprivation and its paediatric unit was accordingly very busy. Besides the normal nine-to-five weekdays, we worked one in three nights and weekends and covered each other when we were on leave. We were called in most nights, sometimes simply because a junior doctor couldn't put a drip up on a baby but usually for much more serious things. My long years as a locum stood me in good stead. Shortly after my arrival I went to a GP meeting where the Director of Public Health presented his annual report. Scanning his cosmopolitan medical audience he opined, "Many of you were born in the third world and you will feel perfectly at home in Walsall: Walsall is a third-world country." That would have caused an upset locally, I imagine, if it had been made public. But some of the statistics he produced supported his statement.

Junior staffing levels had not improved since 1987. There were three house officers and only one middle grade, Dr Barathan. He'd been lured to Walsall by promises of further training and a consultant post, but by the time of my arrival this seemed unlikely. He lived in the hospital and made himself available for emergencies at any time of day or night. He was intelligent, hard-working and totally dedicated. In other circumstances he would have made a good consultant. The managers who treated him so shoddily at the end of his working life neither knew nor cared about his history of long and loyal service to the hospital. The poor staffing meant that we largely ran a consultant-delivered service. The nursing establishment was the best I had met in my travels and every trainee went away praising the nurses for helping provide an excellent learning experience. Departmental managers at that time were ex-clinicians themselves, so we tended to have a better rapport with them than with the "Sainsbury" types who arrived later.

My consultant colleagues decided that I should run the neonatal unit, and as I was enthusiastic and still relatively young I eagerly agreed. Care of the newborn here was primitive compared to what it was in the regional unit but the basics were in place and we set about creating clinical guidelines, training the staff in resuscitation and upgrading equipment. Clinical governance had recently been introduced nationally but had not yet reached Walsall. I did the first paediatric clinical audit on ventilated babies. On every practice audited there was considerable room for improvement but we started to produce some results for subsequent re-auditing. Unlike some other neonatal units I had worked in, Walsall's was open and very friendly. Care of the babies came before every other consideration, including personal rivalries.

We had no up-to-date books in the department. One day a grateful dad whose baby had died approached me in the corridor and said he'd raised £270 for the unit. That was a small fortune in those days. I was delighted but afraid that the crushing hospital bureaucracy would delay our using his gift. I was in a hurry so I asked him to give it me in cash. He did, the next day, and I went straight to the university bookshop and bought or ordered a small library for the unit. I sent the receipt to the dad. No one would get away with that level of initiative now. It was always difficult to get funds for non-essentials – as books were once described to me by a non-clinical manager. When we needed more books my request was denied. I found a story in the medical press of a doctor who had given the wrong treatment to a patient on the basis of an outdated textbook. I resubmitted my request for funds with a copy of the article and the hospital's potential liability underlined: "Can we take the risk of using out-of-date information?" £500 was made available for the purchase of books. Those were kinder times and I never had a single cross word with that manager, although I had to resort to unconventional methods to get my way.

Before long I realized that the workload was unsustainable and we applied for funding for a new consultant post. This was rejected. The adult physicians and surgeons had a louder voice than ours and in those days it was certainly true that children were an unrecognized priority. In my first outpatient clinic there were 57 patients on the list and no junior doctor to help. When I walked into clinic at 1:35 the nurse, Debbie, a delightful Black-Country woman, chided me, "Doctor, you'm late. It's a big clinic." Each patient was new to me and took a considerable time. We finished at 8 pm. Debbie told me that my predecessor would have "polished that lot off before 5 o'clock". The problem was that many patients had been badly mismanaged. I began to find, for example, children with heart disease who had had abnormal chest x-rays and ECGs for years and who had not been seen by a cardiologist. Months later, a mum told me that her daughter had recently had heart surgery. When she had compared notes with the mums of the three other children admitted for operations she found that they had all been referred by me. This was a backlog of neglect. We were so busy and there were so many problems that I did not tell parents about this. I didn't have the time.

One morning I woke with a temperature. That comes with the job. I told Janet that I'd got flu and wasn't going in. "The babies need you," she said. She dispensed a hot cup of tea and two paracetamol. This worked wonders and I arrived at the clinic on time to find a list of 45 patients, again with no help. A clerk came in to tell me that Debbie had been transferred to the ear, nose and throat clinic by the outpatient manager. I called the manager and told her that if Debbie wasn't in my clinic in five minutes I was going home to bed. I was ill and could not do such a large clinic with an inexperienced nurse. But the manager was in charge. The manager knew better. And I was genuinely ill. No sign of Debbie after ten minutes, so I did as I said I would.

I went to my car and drove home via my GP's surgery. "You're ill but you're also exhausted," he told me and wrote out a sick note for two weeks. An hour later I was in bed with a hot toddy and more paracetamol when the phone rang. It was the Medical Director. "David, I'm sorry about this morning. Can you come and do your clinic. Debbie's there, waiting." But I had succumbed to flu and it was all over for me. Sorry. I slept until late afternoon. The phone rang again. This time it was Dr Gatrad. He'd been called by the Chief Executive Officer, John Rostill, in the wake of the morning's events and John had agreed to appoint a locum consultant immediately for six months. This would give us time to write a job description for a substantive appointment to follow. When I went back to work we were four consultants.

In my second winter I noticed a recurring pattern of babies and small children on the ward having respiratory or cardio-respiratory arrests. This was happening with frightening regularity and on one particularly bad day the resuscitation trolley had not been restocked after use by the time another baby arrested. This was a largely preventable problem and was solved by training all doctors and nurses in Paediatric Advanced Life Support (PALS). I taught on these courses from the beginning and Walsall became one of the largest provider centres in the UK. Phil Jeavons, the Trust Resuscitation Officer, was the organizing power behind this. We were good friends and had similar unconventional ways of getting things done. Some of these were hilarious but since Phil is still working it would not be fair to give any details. He fell foul of management, who picked up on this and began to rein in his enthusiasm. As far as I could see, his training programmes started to decline from that time. We considered writing a book together: "The Art of Stifling Innovation".

Instead we wrote a successful book on practical newborn resuscitation, which sold in 18 countries and made us a significant amount of money. Without his entrepreneurial drive it would not have been written. I had no taste for writing. I wanted to be like

Jesus. He went around doing good and left the writing to others. I found writing more stressful than running the courses and after we published I vowed never again. The improved outcomes for acutely unwell children and babies from this work were self-evident. It became extremely rare to see a child collapse on the ward. It was also reflected in children being transferred to outside intensive care units in better shape, with improvements in survival rates as a result. There was a minor revolution in the delivery suite, with midwives and neonatal nurses taking over the bulk of resuscitation.

Eventually Pat Howse retired and a Muslim consultant was appointed to replace her. Heavily bearded, softly spoken and traditionally dressed, he was an unknown quantity. A senior manager railed at me after his appointment: "Walsall people will never accept someone dressed like that." Some months after his appointment Debbie came to tell me that I had been displaced as the most popular doctor in clinic: Dr Muhammad had won his patients' hearts by his quiet, cheerful compassion. Walsall people tend to be kind and generous in their opinions, which is why so many of us enjoyed serving them.

The years passed and I settled into one of the most stable and enjoyable periods of my professional life. We continued to be an understaffed and under-resourced unit. We were remote from the West Midlands deanery. We were judged fit to provide training for our three house officers but not the higher-level training required for registrars. The range of medical and surgical conditions that we saw at Walsall was greater than anywhere I could remember. Children came with their illnesses neglected and sometimes beyond repair. This was an excellent training ground for young doctors but we were outside the mainstream.

I was a good doctor in a good team. Not everyone was happy with me of course. I got things wrong. I looked after a set of twins with an identical handicapping condition. The parents were slow to hear what I was telling them about the future. I picked up on this and did my best to adjust my pace to theirs. I was unaware of the strength of their feelings towards me until one night they brought both babies in to the paediatric assessment unit in the middle of the night. They rang the doorbell.

"Hello, who is it?" asked the nurse on the desk.

"Mr and Mrs Whatsit with the twins."

"OK, I'm opening the door, come on in."

"Thanks but we're only coming in on one condition."

"What's that?"

"We're only coming in if Dr Drew's nowhere within two miles of the building."

I was fast asleep in bed ten miles away. The next day I arranged for the twins' care to be transferred to another consultant.

In Walsall a practice of domiciliary or home visits had grown up at that time. Ostensibly these were done when the patient was unable to attend hospital or there was no bed available. Management decided at some point that these were unnecessary and funding was withdrawn. But at that time, when community paediatrics was underdeveloped, they provided us with an opportunity to get out into homes and see life in the raw. And often it was raw. One of my first visits was to see the baby of a single mother. They lived alone on the 12th floor of a tower block. The lift was broken. The stairwell was filthy. In the living room was a cot with the baby, a chair and a small Christmas tree with flashing lights. It was February. I dealt with the baby's problems and asked mum how she found life in the flat. She was cheerful and told me she was happy and could stay with her mum any time she wanted. "I like it here," she said, "Look at that view." I gazed with her at the panoramic view of Walsall spread out below us — "The city now doth like a garment wear the beauty of the morning."

I was privileged to spend most of my time in clinical practice and teaching. It was admittedly my own slightly idiosyncratic idea of teaching. I had no other ambitions. I carried my share of administrative work and was always ready to join in politicking for the good of the department. I enjoyed nine hard but carefree years. On the rare occasions I thought to look ahead I saw only more of the same and then a happy retirement with Janet — *Dear Diary: The boundary lines have fallen for me in pleasant places; surely I have a delightful inheritance.*

11

Walsall 2

Shades of the prison-house begin to close upon the growing boy.
William Wordsworth: *Intimations of Immortality*

In 2001 my life took a distinct turn for the worse. Dr Gatrad had been Clinical Director of paediatrics for five years and he'd had enough of it. The Trust approached me to take over from him. I didn't want to do this but when I was told there was no one else who could do it I gave in gracefully. The formalities had to be observed: the job was advertised internally; I wrote a short letter of application; I received an invitation for an interview with the Medical Director and Director of Operations, both of whom I knew well.

Before the interview I rang the Medical Director's secretary and asked if there was a job description. "Never been asked before. I'll have a look and get back." There was one and I went to collect it. When I read the four pages of tight script describing what was expected of the Clinical Director I took fright. To me it had the look of a death sentence. I showed it to Rashid and he told me he'd never seen it. "What do you actually do then?" I asked. "Most of it's meetings," he said. "Take something to do. Ninety per cent of it's a total waste of time."

I went for the interview and was told at the outset that my application had been successful. Did I have any questions? I asked how much time I would be given to run the department. "You'll be paid four extra hours of work a week. That's it. It's yours. Make what you want of it." There was no question of cutting my clinical

70

workload. We still had only four consultants. I took on the role and suffered for it for the next seven years.

No formal managerial training was required for this position. Just as well: I had none. As I got to know other clinical directors I discovered that at that time they were all in the same position. I attended a couple of courses but found them unhelpful. I bought books but they were poorly written and dull. For the first six months I went to meetings and did little but ask questions. It was rare to get a straight answer. There was a lot of talk, mostly aspirational. There was little action. My clinical responsibilities were the same as other consultants' but were continually interrupted with administrative matters. After a few months I felt hopelessly dejected.

In August tragedy struck us for a third time. I arrived at work and Janet rang to tell me that my youngest brother, Robin, had been killed. He had fallen from a high building in London the night before. A late blessing in my parents' life – in our family life – Robin was born only months before I left for medical school and so I had missed much of his childhood, but we were good friends. He was a software designer and had gone to London to pursue his career. My parents were bereft. I had four days off work to help them with practicalities and another for the funeral. The church seated 300 and was full to bursting. It was the saddest occasion I can remember. Over the next weeks I met the black dog for the first and only time in my life. He kept me from sleep at night and woke me at 4am sharp. I was so preoccupied with thoughts of Robin and my parents that I had no interest in food or any other pleasure. I would find myself in polite company involuntarily blurting out, "This is a fucking nightmare." Every moment at work was tedious. I found I could not listen to people telling me about their problems without thinking, "That's nothing. What about Robin? What about my mum and dad? What about me?"

And then, one morning I woke and it was gone. I did not cry again for our three brothers for another five years. I remember visiting the crematorium with my parents on Stephen's anniversary. The book of remembrance recorded one stark fact: "He was 21 years old." I found that unbearable and burst into tears.

My life was dominated by more and more meetings. Rashid had been right: much of the time was spent with managers engaged in discourse that made no practical difference to patient care. But every so often something important cropped up. There was the annual equipment bid that we used successfully to refit the neonatal unit with monitors and ventilators. That had to be fought tooth and claw and I could shroud-wave as good as the rest. I tried to get the Trust to recognize how understaffed we were and doggedly pursued funding for a new paediatric consultant. When it came down to it, the bigger and more powerful blocs were given priority. We were turned down again and again.

We were short of consultants compared to other similar size units. We were running a largely consultant-delivered service. The only new post in the last 20 years had been established when I abandoned my over-size clinic through illness. It was time for me to take action again.

In October 2002 Janet and I spent three weeks in Ethiopia with missionary friends. I spent a week trekking in the Simian Mountains and then did some medical work. Janet was up to all kinds of good. She came home with a missionary from a local school for deaf children having promised to raise money to provide all the children with shoes and uniforms. The next day I visited the school myself and saw children with exactly the same range of medical problems as are common in Britain. I could see how these beautiful children had won Janet's heart. Within a week of returning she had, with the help of our church, raised the money she had promised and we later received a school photo of the children in their new uniforms.

The problem of consultant staffing was never far from my thoughts. The first week back from Ethiopia I went for a curry with the paediatric doctors and nurses. On my way home in the dark a local GP driving his Mercedes in the opposite direction came over into my lane and hit me head on. By the grace of God (the policeman said), no one was seriously injured. My car was written off. I had to use Janet's car until I could replace it. The following week Janet needed her car and I set off to work on my bike. I usually cycled the 20-mile round trip to work in the summer months but always quit with the end of British Summer Time. My only anxiety setting off that day was that I would be cycling home after dark.

I have never recovered the memory of what happened after I left home that morning. I understand I got to Walsall without incident but as I was cycling down Ablewell Street into town a red Clio came out of a side street at speed and broadsided me. I was taken on a blue light to the hospital I had been heading for. My first recollection was of the A&E consultant saying, "Call the anaesthetist. They're ready in CT. We need him intubated. Now! Can somebody wipe this blood up?" "Naj, I don't need intubating. I'll lie still. I promise," I croaked.

Hours later I was stable and ready to leave the resuscitation room. As we were going through the swing doors a nurse I knew well and who had helped save my life called out, "Hey, Dr Drew, don't come up here telling us what to do in future: we've seen your bum!" When I eventually returned to work I told this story to a senior nurse manager. "I want that nurse's name," she retorted tartly. "That is totally unprofessional. It's a disciplinary offence." Not in my book it wasn't. It was the only thing that had made me laugh all day. Later that day Nick Turner, an ENT surgeon with some plastic surgery experience, took me to theatre to sew my left ear back on. I refused a general anaesthetic. Later, after it had healed, I thanked Nick with a verse:

"I have an ear that through your care

Will not attract a single stare…"

The next day visitors started arriving. More than a hundred members of staff had pitched up in the morning and been turned away. Sister asked me if I would agree to see one visitor. It was the driver who had knocked me off my bike, a psychiatric nurse at the hospital next door. She was beside herself with remorse. I felt really sorry for her. She was in a much worse emotional state than I was. Nevertheless I was glad to hear, months later, that she had been required to take a driving improvement course. Learning is always more important than punishment.

The next day the Medical Director visited. My accident had given him cause to review the consultant staffing arrangements in the paediatric department, he told me. A decision had been made to appoint another consultant. I was grateful but in a lot of pain. That possibly explained my irritability. "I hope I'm not going to have to pull a stunt like this every time we need new staff." Weeks later he changed his mind about the new consultant post and came up with funding for two.

It was a revelation being an inpatient in my own hospital. The sheer kindness and compassion of the nursing staff astonished me. They were clearly understaffed but nothing was too much trouble. And everyone got the same, nothing special for the doctor. I was special though. At 11 o'clock one night the ward sister came to ask apologetically if I could write my drug sheet up as she was unable to find a junior doctor to do it. A few days later a nurse came to put up a fresh bag of intravenous fluid. I told her I'd been drinking normally for 24 hours and had no need of intravenous fluids. "I took the cannula out in the night," I told her. "Well done," she said, "saved me the trouble."

When I went home I lay in bed for two weeks, too dizzy and nauseated to get up. No TV or radio. No newspaper or books. And no boredom. I spent two glorious weeks reflecting on the strange life we had lived. At various points I'd decided it was time to write about our experiences but I never found time.

After about five weeks I returned to do some managerial work. I looked a mess and could barely walk. I started full-time clinical work as soon as the occupational physician cleared me, which was about five months later. I have never fully recovered in that I still have neurological symptoms in both hands from my neck injury. But to set myself a goal I booked a sponsored place to run the London Marathon in April, shortly after I went back to work full time. A week before the run Janet told me she was not happy with me doing it: "You've not done a marathon before and you've done no training." I put my kit on and went down to the track. I ran 20 miles in three hours. It was too little too late. My first marathon at 55 turned into my most unpleasant running experience of all time. I was fine for the first 20 miles. I only finished through the encouragement of a young woman dressed as superwoman. She looked as if she'd been exposed to Kryptonite but had enough life in her to keep me going.

The accident was for me a painful and disastrous episode but as a direct result two new consultant posts were created and I had the privilege of writing the job descriptions. In 2003 we appointed two excellent new consultants. Dr "Nil" Bagchi arrived to lead the neonatal service and Dr Satish Bangalore came as a general paediatrician with an interest in respiratory problems. Bingo.

The department settled down to a time of peace and productivity. Nil proved a brilliant medical lead for the newborn service and Satish took over most of the respiratory work. Since I ran the asthma clinic and had patients with other chronic chest problems this was a great help to me. I started to enjoy some of the administrative work as a result. Chairing the clinical governance committee was one of my most enjoyable and satisfying roles. Unlike the management group, where we were often preoccupied with finance, this was an opportunity to reflect on the quality of the service we were providing and, in perhaps a slightly amateurish way, improve it.

It was usual to serve a three-year term as clinical director but with no heir apparent I carried on. By 2005 the department was running smoothly and, apart from wasting a lot of time on service reconfiguration plans that everyone knew were a waste of time, I was usefully and happily employed. All this was about to change.

12

An Ill Wind

Time and Chance happen to all men.
Ecclesiastes 9:11

2005. Nil came into my office one Friday evening in the New Year with his overcoat on. "OK, boss," he mocked, "See you in three weeks." I'd forgotten he was going home to India on leave. I took the opportunity to ask him how the work was going. His grin said everything. "Have a good break then." He left and I never saw him again.

Two weeks later my diary entries read:

Saturday 22nd January 2005
Dear Diary:
10 easy road miles in 1hr 26. Steaming.
Off to Birmingham for Rwanda support meeting.
Then to Electric Cinema. Motorcycle Diaries. A doctor with
    a difference. Ché.
Home by 9 pm. 7 voice messages from work on landline.
Voices laced with fear. "Ring me. Ring me. Ring me."
Rang Rashid. "Get ready for a shock David. Nil Bagchi is
    dead. And his wife."
And his children; are they orphans? My first thought. I loved
    and admired him.
Irreplaceable, with his hilarious expletive-riddled humour.

Sunday 23rd January
Dear Diary:

I wake from the nightmare. But it's true. Nil is dead. Unthinkable. Dear God.

Monday 24th January
The dark side of midnight.

Work: Anguish on every side.

Gyan [Dr Sinha, a consultant colleague] is like a broken twig, hanging on to anyone nearby for support.

Met Sue James (Chief Executive). She agreed to hold a memorial service. Did she know Nil?

Does she know any of us? Do we know her?

Nil had been killed in a road traffic accident. He was as good a colleague as you could have wished for: intelligent, hard-working, amenable and very funny. He was the first consultant who had ever come to ask if he could wear shorts to work when on call on summer weekends. "Depends on the shorts," I said, "and the legs." Both were OK-ish and he did his rounds in baggy shorts to the amusement of some of his young patients.

The nursing staff in particular, but all of us, experienced a wave of grief. A memorial service was held in the education centre and was packed out with Nil's friends and colleagues from all over the West Midlands. As head of department, I paid tribute to his many excellent qualities and I did not have to exaggerate. "Has anyone here seen our friend Nil? Can you tell us where he's gone? He was loved by a lot of people; we just looked around and he was gone." It sounds corny now but it was genuine and heartfelt. Tears were shed openly. I finished with "We'll not see his like again." I was right. He was a one-off. A garden of remembrance was planted for him in the neonatal unit courtyard. It was and still is lovingly tended by the neonatal nurses. I spent many quiet moments there trying to calm down at the end of a stressful day. The immediate problem was to replace Nil. It took a year. In that time we had some unsatisfactory locums but most of the out-of-hours cover was done by our own consultants. Although this was well paid some did not want to do it and no one was happy doing it. Everybody was struggling with work–life balance. I asked at the deanery if there were any local trainees nearing completion who might replace Nil. There was no one suitable. We advertised in the national medical press. Only two applicants were even vaguely eligible for shortlisting. "That's a thin field," Mike Brown, the Medical Director, told us. As an obstetrician he'd seen a glut of trainees looking for consultant posts in his own specialty but there was a shortfall in the paediatric workforce. There was an irony in planning for babies to be kept safe up to birth but then hoping for the best afterwards. Whose idea was that mismatch?

I was anxious to appoint a replacement, as were all the other consultants. The neonatal unit had been neglected since Nil's death. We needed to reduce our own workload. At the interview one candidate was unanimously deemed unsuitable. The other was appointed. He was an experienced doctor and had held a consultant post in another hospital for six years. Dr Walia, on the first occasion we met him, told us that he had decided on a career change from intensive care to general paediatrics. This was unheard of in our experience. It proved impossible to get any explanation for the intended change. He had been through an assessment in relation to clinical performance by the National Clinical Assessment Service in his last post. His Trust had then arranged some further training and finally, we heard, funded a year's salary for him to work in another hospital. This, it seemed, was the motivation for his move.

I had not encountered anything like this before. I asked the Medical Director if he could make the documentation available but this was dismissed as impossible, allegedly on grounds of confidentiality. I have no idea if Mike Brown himself – or anyone at the Trust – ever saw the NCAS documentation. "His references will be enough if he's had any real trouble, David", the Medical Director told me. Even I could see how naïve that was. The committee was deeply reluctant to make an appointment, as I remember, but we were all swayed by the risks of the post remaining vacant for a long period. Afterwards I checked the individual interviewer comments sheets. They were quite negative. The Chief Executive, Sue James, wrote, "damaged goods" on hers, which meant she was either very astute or had seen the NCAS report. This was my first experience of information being kept secret – against the interests of the service – ostensibly on the grounds of confidentiality. Dr Walia specified on his CV that he needed to catch up on his child protection training. The significance of that only became clear later.

This was many years ago now. My account of what came next is historical and painful for me to relate. I have no intention of harming Dr Walia. It may well be that management at Walsall has taken him in hand and helped him to improve his performance since that time. There was no sign of this happening before my own dismissal. This is a crucial part of my tale. Raising concerns about a colleague's competence is vitally important to patient care and safety. It is perhaps the most difficult and sensitive concern of all to raise. There is now increasing recognition that a poorly performing consultant reflects a system failure at least as much as an individual failure. My complaints as they evolved were much more about the system, or the individuals with responsibility for the system, than Dr Walia himself. My own thinking at that time resonates with all the recent thinking on learning and remediation being more important than punishment. The concerns I expressed about him led eventually, step by step, to my own dismissal. The Chief Executive later claimed that my concerns were unfounded and that I created a toxic environment in the department by raising them. The evidence is completely against that.

Dr Walia started work in January 2006. He was an apparently

amiable person with an unusual communication style. I am a natural optimist. I believed that in the largely supportive atmosphere we enjoyed in the department all would be well. It was not, and within days of his arrival trouble began. Every time I went into the neonatal unit the nursing staff took me to task over the new lead. I was responsible in their eyes as I had agreed to his appointment. "He is a total disappointment," complained the more vocal nurses. "And we're disappointed with you for bringing him here." I asked them to give him a bit of space but I knew they were good judges and likely to be right.

In June a child who was subsequently identified as Child K by Walsall Safeguarding Children Board in its Serious Case Review of his management was admitted under Dr Walia's care. He was treated for a presumed infection and discharged. Suspicious unexplained bruising at sites commonly associated with non-accidental injury was noted during the admission. This was not investigated and Social Services were not informed as they normally would be. A week later Child K was readmitted and died of a non-accidental head injury. This raised further concerns over Dr Walia's practice.

The situation did not improve over 2007. Consultant colleagues made their dissatisfaction known to me. One consultant told me he was unhappy leaving his sick patients overnight in Dr Walia's care. I asked him to come to the Medical Director with me to voice his concerns. He was so certain that this would achieve nothing that he refused. Another consultant, the day he was going away on holiday, wrote in the notes of one baby on the neonatal unit with a particularly complex medical condition that he was happy for any consultant to look after this baby while he was away "other than Dr Walia". I showed this note to the Medical Director not to complain about the consultant who had written it but to illustrate the dilemma we were in. The Medical Director's response was to offer to write to the hospital's consultants telling them that they were not to make disparaging comments about colleagues in the case files as it was unprofessional. I received more than one such letter from him as a consultant myself. It missed the whole point. It was indeed wrong to write such comments. It was unprofessional. But was this unprofessional action justified in view of the reason for it? Did the comment point to a more serious cause for concern? Those were the questions that should have registered. The Medical Director was always mysteriously unworried by such possibilities.

In early 2008 I wrote a long letter to the Medical Director giving an account of Dr Walia's difficulties and with a degree of foresight deposited it with my own lawyer. I stated some of my concerns as follows:

Three or four consultant colleagues have expressed serious reservations about Dr Walia more or less from the time of his arrival. Concerns have been expressed about his clinical practice, child protection work (you are very aware of this, especially his fatally flawed management of Child K), poor communication skills and poor teaching skills. One consultant actually asked me to check that he had a basic medical qualification.

In the job plan for the post Dr Walia took up there was a provision for him to work two half days a week at the tertiary neonatal unit in Wolverhampton. He asked me to initiate this soon after his arrival. The head of the neonatal unit at Wolverhampton refused under any circumstances to have him work there. You refused to get involved in this and it was still unresolved at the time he ceased to be lead. Alyson Skinner [the tertiary level consultant] is a proper neonatologist and I advised you to discuss Dr Walia's practice with her. I do not know if you did. For a long time I tried to meet him with Alyson. She was always willing. He is very insecure in her presence. She is so much more knowledgeable and capable than he is and he almost always wriggled out of it. The Neonatal Network lead, Andy Spencer, has also made negative remarks about Dr Walia, to both me and the divisional director, Gareth Robinson. For more than a year now the consultants have urged me to replace him as neonatal lead with Dr Satish. I have had more than one conversation with you about the difficulties of doing that. You did eventually realize that there was no other choice. It took a longer than it should have."

It is nigh impossible to manage a consultant whose competence is in question by his colleagues without the support of the Medical Director. In this case every consultant at one time or another expressed concerns about Dr Walia. The Divisional Director, who was non-medical and new to managing a clinical department, was extremely supportive and intuitively understood how serious a problem this was. Eventually the Medical Director agreed to discuss the situation over a curry one evening. This proved far too difficult for him. On arriving at the restaurant he ordered two bottles of Pinot Grigio and the purpose of the evening was lost.

The following day the Divisional Director summed up: "You can't get rid of a consultant, David, unless he has actually killed someone. We are going to have to do this through his appraisal." Appraisal was the annual hoop-jumping exercise that all consultants were put through. There was little faith at that time that appraisal as it was practised in Walsall was anything more than a paper exercise. One main driver was that private hospitals required up-to-date evidence of appraisal. So private practice depended on it. It was unlikely, as long as the Medical Director remained wilfully blind to the real problem, that an appraisal would help in any way. The Trust's attitude to Dr Walia, which puzzled me enormously at the time, is nowhere better seen than in the case of Child K.

13

The Avoidable Death of Kyle Keen

We owe our children, the most vulnerable citizens in our society, a life free of violence and fear.

Nelson Mandela

In a paediatric career spanning almost forty years I have seen hundreds of children die. On my worst day ever, in Nigeria, during a measles epidemic, eight children died on the ward. In Walsall for many years I kept a yellow exercise book recording all my patients who had died and my home bereavement visits. I still have it. I have no memory of the children behind some of the names but others still conjure up the most difficult situations I ever had to deal with. Helping families through the death of a child was to me a sacred responsibility.

It is always a tragedy when a child dies. But in Kyle Keen's (Child K's) case it was a compound tragedy. His death at such a young age was entirely preventable. And the circumstances that led up to it in June 2006 were concealed from his family for many years. My own attempts to speak about it resulted in my fall from grace with senior Trust management.

I was on call on 29th June 2006. Kyle was brought to the accident and emergency department unconscious; his mother reported that he had had a fit. The doctor who saw him first was experienced but contacted me to talk through his findings.

When I arrived in A&E several family members were waiting. Kyle, I was told, had been admitted a week earlier with an unconfirmed possibility of infection. Suspicious unexplained bruising had been noticed. He had been discharged by his consultant, Dr Walia, with a letter to his health visitor but he had not been referred to social services. When I examined Kyle he was deeply unconscious and on a ventilator. There was no sign of injury and none of the many tests explained his condition. A brain scan was reported normal. I spoke to his mother about what had happened but she was withdrawn and I got no further than the story of the fit. I met Kyle's father and his paternal grandmother. They looked like ghosts and did not say a word.

I spoke to the paediatric intensive care consultant at Stoke and we agreed Kyle should be transferred. When I spoke to him the next morning he told me that the brain scan on expert review showed evidence of bleeding. The provisional diagnosis was non-accidental trauma. There had still been no admission of injury by his mother. Kyle was not expected to survive and his ventilator was turned off later that day.

About a hundred children die each year of non-accidental injury in the UK. An average-sized hospital like Walsall can expect one such case every two years or so. In a department with ten consultants any one of them will at most see a couple of such fatalities in a working lifetime. This was not an everyday event.

Dr John Porter was the senior registrar working with Dr Walia when Kyle was discharged home. He gave me a vivid account of what had happened. I advised him to write his statement immediately. I had a copy made and have kept it since. After the weekend I heard that a number of staff besides Dr Porter had pointed out the suspicious nature of the bruises and asked Dr Walia to refer to social services. He had refused.

In his statement, Dr Porter gave an account of his involvement in Kyle's care and Dr Walia's actions. Kyle's mother was asked about the bruising by Dr Walia but could give no explanation. Dr Walia himself suggested the mechanism behind the bruising to have been "handling". Referring a child with unexplained suspicious bruising to social services for investigation is mandatory, not an option. The last thing any experienced doctor does in that situation is to suggest a possible explanation for injury and send the child home into an environment about which nothing is known.

According to John Porter's statement, Dr Walia intended sending Kyle home without an appointment until he challenged this. John suggested a social service referral as had other staff but Dr Walia refused. The statement then records, "Dr Walia said he felt this wasn't necessary and that the child would be under his and the health visitors' follow-up. He suggested that the mother would be aware that she was being watched and this would deter anything further." This struck me at the time as the most fundamental error of reasoning I had encountered in my years doing child protection. The day after Kyle's discharge Dr Porter made another attempt to convince Dr Walia that a referral should be made. At that point it was still not too late. John Porter concludes his statement with "I left the matter in his [Dr Walia's] hands and did not separately make a child protection referral, which again retrospectively was a mistake." It was a mistake that cost Kyle his life and one Dr Porter was honest enough to put his hand up to – unlike Dr Walia, who never at that time or subsequently admitted any failure on his part.

The person eventually convicted of killing Kyle was present on the ward much of the time during his admission. Kyle's father was personally acquainted with him. The family knew he had anger problems. They also had photographic evidence that Kyle had sustained injuries including facial bruising pre-dating his first admission. Dr Walia failed to obtain any of this information. Had a social services referral been made, as medical and nursing staff requested and policy and standard practice required, it is near certain the dangerous situation Kyle was returning to would have been identified and the tragedy averted. The hospital admitted this in internal documents.

After the weekend I arranged to meet Dr Walia with the

Divisional Director, Gareth Robinson, to get a first-hand account of what had happened at the earlier admission. By this time we were all aware that something was seriously wrong. At the meeting Dr Walia resisted any questions about his management of Kyle's injuries. After ten minutes he walked out, informing us that he was going to see his lawyer. Gareth and I agreed that he should be suspended from child protection work until the incident had been investigated. I agreed to cover his duties on the rota to ensure confidentiality. Because of the other concerns about his competence I believed that he should be suspended from clinical duties. Only the Medical Director was in a position to make that decision. And this would require NCAS advice.

Later, Mike Brown, the Medical Director, called me to his office. He was not in the least interested in hearing what had actually happened. A murder inquiry was under way, he told me. This was a sensitive case for the Trust. Dr Walia had been to see his lawyer. He, Mike Brown, would be dealing with the case personally from then on "at the board's instruction". "A child has died. And it's our responsibility," I protested. I later put this into writing in the strongest terms but I was overruled.

The internal investigation, a root cause analysis (RCA), was conducted in due course. There were many witnesses. I never saw their statements. The RCA meeting was electric. Dr Walia denied everything. He told the meeting that if I had looked after Kyle properly on his last night there would be no need for an RCA as he'd still be alive. After the meeting Pat Kennerley, the chair, said that it was clear Dr Walia was a doctor with little or no insight into himself. "This is a highly sensitive matter for the Trust and you must leave it to the Medical Director," she told me. This was now, I understood, the Trust's official policy on Kyle's death. It was none of my business.

The recommendations that came out of the RCA concentrated on documentation and the behaviour of nursing staff. The medical and nursing staff were to be "reminded of the importance of discriminating between bruising caused by injury and that caused by disease." Everyone involved with Kyle seemed to have recognized the potential significance of his bruising apart from Dr Walia. Nowhere was there any reference to his failings. No recommendation was made with regard to his practice. To add insult to injury, I was told to implement the recommendations. I told Mike Brown very clearly that the main recommendation should have been an investigation of Dr Walia's clinical competence

A year passed, and in August 2007 Walsall Safeguarding Children Board initiated a serious case review (SCR) into the circumstances leading up to Kyle's death. It took six months to complete. By December 2007 the criminal trials of Kyle's mother and her partner had been held. Or rather, after plea bargaining both had entered guilty pleas. Tyrone Matthews pleaded guilty to manslaughter and was sentenced to six-and-a-half years in prison. Kyle's mother, Kerry McIntosh, had been found guilty of cruelty by neglect and was given a six months suspended prison sentence.

A West Midlands Police Child Abuse Investigation Unit officer was quoted in the local press: "Kerry turned a blind eye to the bruising. It is a responsibility to look after young children, which should be taken very seriously." But Dr Walia, with his professional training and experience in child protection, had also turned a blind eye to the bruising and failed in his responsibility to protect. And hospital management had helped save him and themselves from the embarrassment of this becoming generally known. Of course there was only one person who had killed Kyle. But, at the same time, if even the most basic safeguarding procedures had been followed Kyle would have still been alive and his killer would have received professional help and avoided jail. As commentators usually say when SCRs are published, "Only one person killed Baby X." That always seems a bit of a cop-out when the SCR is describing the failings of those whose professional responsibility it is to keep children safe.

But Kyle's SCR remained a mystery. We never set eyes on it at the hospital. In 2010 Tim Loughton, the then Children's Minister, wrote to the chairs of all Safeguarding Children Boards in the realm. He instructed them to publish all subsequent serious case reviews in full, with only family names "redacted" [that is, omitted]. He recognized the importance of this in the light of earlier cases. The reviews were a matter of legitimate public interest, and full transparency through publication was necessary to restore declining public confidence in the process. He also understood the primary importance of reviews as opportunities for learning. This usually amounted to learning from mistakes. And still does.

We had little opportunity to learn, as we never saw Kyle's serious case review. In 2012 the hospital, in response to an FOI, acknowledged that it had never received a copy. Given that the main objective of the review was for the safeguarding agencies to learn from mistakes, that is highly irregular. The same FOI elicited an even stranger story. The Safeguarding Children Board had held a briefing meeting on the review shortly after completion. The Trust had delegated a non-clinical manager, with no paediatric or safeguarding training or experience, to represent it. He saw, but was not allowed to retain, a copy of the review's report. There were plenty of very experienced clinicians who should have been at that meeting, but we did not even know it was taking place. This meant that no experienced clinician at any time saw the SCR or was in a position to interrogate it. Seven years after Kyle's death that was still true.

The only conclusion I can reach is that this was done to control the flow of information about the Trust's failure to protect Kyle. As a result it was never made available for learning exercises in our department. The culture of secrecy surrounding professional failure was a principle reason for the minister's instruction to publish the reviews. The conduct of Kyle's review was a perfect example of why this was necessary.

Prior to 2010 it was the practice of the safeguarding boards to publish an executive summary of serious case reviews on their websites. Supposedly, this would be timely and include the main findings and recommendations. Kyle's executive summary was not published until almost three years after his death. No explanation is available as to why it took so long. I cannot do justice to the failings of the executive summary of the Child K SCR. One finding was that "The extended family had regular contact with the family (mother and children) and had no concerns about Mother's partner." This was specifically untrue. The review panel had not taken any evidence from Kyle's father or grandmother, who *did* have serious concerns. The executive summary shows no interest in the vital question of why no referral was made to social services. The recommendations concentrate on policy, procedure and paperwork.

The Medical Director and Chief Executive released a press statement on 23rd April 2009 following publication of the executive summary. Both must have known it was misleading, to say the least:

> We also conducted an internal investigation into the case and, based on the facts gathered at the time, there seemed to be no direct evidence of abuse. However in the light of the subsequent events it is clear that an opportunity to detect abuse had been missed. The investigation that we conducted led us to believe that no individual member of staff warranted disciplinary action.

It was clear from the time of Kyle's death that abuse had been suspected early in the first admission. It is recorded in the RCA. I also made this crystal-clear in my first meeting with Dr Walia and to the Medical Director. I asked him to consider Dr Walia's suspension and to conduct a full investigation of his actions. He refused. At no point did any investigation consider disciplining any member of staff. I was head of department at the time and would have known about this.

I also, at a later date, using FOI, obtained all the board minutes referring to Kyle Keen. There was no reference in them to the true course of events. Dr Walia was airbrushed from the narrative. The board would have learned more from reading accounts in the local press than it learned from its own executive officers. At least the papers found it noteworthy that Dr Walia was still working at the hospital. The Medical Director had the responsibility for informing the board about the investigation of Kyle's care. There was no evidence in the minutes that any board member had shown any serious interest in this tragedy.

By the time the executive summary was published in April 2009 a host of other problems had arisen with patient care and child protection and steps were being taken to silence me for good.

As a postscript to this account I should say that I met Rob Keen in Walsall through a third party in 2012. I learned from him that he had never been told anything about the hospital's failings prior to Kyle's death. As a result, I offered to help him get an explanation from Walsall Manor Hospital and Walsall Safeguarding Children's Board (WSCB). Both organizations continued to resist giving any honest account of what happened. I have seen all the responses. WSCB refused to provide Rob Keen with any documents relating to the SCR or to answer any questions on the grounds of data protection. It is difficult to see how, when all SCRs are now published, a father could be obstructed from finding out why his son was sent home to his death using the Data Protection Act as an excuse.

Similarly, I helped Rob Keen make a formal complaint about Kyle's care to the CEO at Walsall Manor Hospital. This produced a response that could only have made him more angry. The CEO was sorry Rob had not been told what had happened at the hospital. It was all a long time ago and things were not done so well in those days. Lessons had been learned. Some of the most searching questions were ignored all together. Repeated requests to see Kyle's notes were ignored. There seemed to be no genuine interest in letting Kyle's family know what happened. That would have been tantamount to admitting the hospital's negligence.

Later, the CEO, who had no personal knowledge of Kyle's case, recognized the hospital's responsibility and agreed to commission an independent review of the investigation into his death. My dad drilled it into me from an early age. "Do it right the first time, lad. Or you'll only end up having to do it again."

14

An Unpleasant Surprise

The world, that understandable and lawful world, was slipping away.

William Golding: *Lord of the Flies*

In October 2007 I was sixty. My family organized a weekend of celebrations including 'This is your Life' on Saturday evening. A mirror was held up to my outrageous style as a father. Versification was in: here's Simon in an extract from "I Kiss His Ass." ... Well, perhaps not. I am generally averse to censorship but this bit of performance poetry has been judged unfit for public consumption.

I enjoyed seeing myself through the gently mocking eyes of my family and friends, and especially our children. Our youngest, Joe, had a vivid unfading and less controversial image of his dad.

I love your beard.

I know you have been told before by other people,
But Dad, this is for the record!
This is in writing!
This is in stone!
Dad, I love your beard!
I still love it now
But I loved it even more then
When it was bushy and wild
When it used to smell of smoke after your catastrophic bonfires.
It was so big it looked like it had never been trimmed,

There was only one other dad at school who could match it –
Tom Lee.
But that didn't matter because he didn't turn up at school very
    much,
There was no competition.
Remember when you turned up at school dad, in assembly.
I was still safe,
Not many people knew you were my dad.
But you soon sorted that out when you got me on stage with
    you,
To help explain what sperm was to the entire school.
I was no longer safe.
I still loved your beard though…

It was a saga and it finished thus:

Retirement is round the corner,
Time for David the grey to become David the white?
It doesn't matter to me though dad, because you will always be
WILD, BUSHY and RED.

And at the end of an evening of poetry, prose, ridicule and laughter
the whole family turned serious. "We want you to retire, Dad. You
and Mum need to enjoy a bit of life. That job is killing you." I agreed
to hand my notice in as Clinical Director. I knew it was affecting
my health. They accepted that compromise. In December I gave
three months' notice in writing. The Medical Director and
Divisional Director refused to accept it. They insisted there was no
other consultant in the department able to take on the role. They
asked me to continue for another year to give them time to appoint
a consultant with management experience. I reluctantly agreed.

The first few months of 2008 were marked by further problems
with Dr Walia. One of the ways performance was measured at this

time was known as 360-Degree Appraisal. It had recently been renamed Multi-Source Feedback. It involved sending out a short standard questionnaire on each consultant to twelve colleagues. The respondent was asked in each section to grade the doctor's performance as acceptable or not. There was a free field for comments. It was administered by a medical secretary, who sent out the questionnaires to departmental staff, including doctors, nurses, secretaries and administrative staff.

It went out on all consultants in the department. There was an excellent return of practically 100 per cent. The performance of every consultant at every point was good or acceptable – apart from Dr Walia. There was a consensus that his performance was poor. More instructive were the comments on these forms. Most doctors attracted brief comments such as, "he is kind" or "very helpful" or often nothing at all. Colleagues responding on Dr Walia's forms were much more expansive – and consistently so. Here is a selection of comments as I listed them in correspondence with the Medical Director a few weeks later:

- Cannot be trusted.
- Very unprofessional.
- Criticizes colleagues, ignoring his own deficiencies.
- Blames middle grades/secretaries for his errors.
- Not constructive in comments made to juniors.
- Not supportive of staff working in the same environment.
- Rather than tackling problems head on with the person involved he will complain to others.
- Appears to shirk duties.
- He is extremely difficult to get a clear answer from.
- He has got no insight.
- He is unsupportive.
- He lacks professionalism.
- Makes mockery of own colleagues and demeans them.

- Shirks duty.
- Never takes responsibility; it is always someone else's fault.

I am embarrassed to publish these comments. They are historical. I do so only to pose the question, why would any Medical Director not want to investigate a consultant given such a litany of criticisms? And, to demonstrate once again the near impossibility of addressing the problem of a poorly performing consultant, I sent the original forms for the whole exercise to the Medical Director. My argument was never with Dr Walia. He had made a series of mistakes that had cost Kyle Keen his life. There were concerns about his practice amongst consultant colleagues and nursing staff and trainees. Conduct as well as competence was in question. I was not alone in my concerns. My real argument was with the Medical Director.

Then, in April 2008, the Medical Director belatedly took action. On his instruction Dr Walia informed the departmental consultants that he was standing down as clinical lead on the neonatal unit. This had followed some hair-raising criticisms of the way the unit was being run. I was told, by the Medical Director, before the April consultants' meeting that Dr Walia would make a statement. I asked Mike Brown what I, as Dr Walia's manager, was supposed to do with him. "Put him somewhere he can do no harm," was the response. That is quite difficult in an acute unit for sick children. Immediately after the meeting Dr Walia came to see me to ask that I help him get his position as neonatal lead back. He had little insight into his problems.

On 18th April, only days later, I woke feeling unwell, which was not uncommon in those days. I'd only had two hours' sleep: my daughter, a medical student, had been admitted to hospital the previous day with suspected meningitis. Five days earlier I had run the London Marathon with a painful ganglion on my foot. I needed a day in bed. Instead, following the habit of half a lifetime I got up and made a cup of Lapsang. I stepped out into the cool morning air:

the garden was alive with birdsong; a vixen with three cubs strolled nonchalantly across the bottom lawn as though I wasn't there: I felt like Francis of Assisi – "So much in love with all that I survey." An hour later I was in my office.

I saw a few patients on the ward and then did some paperwork. Mid-morning I was teaching medical students about child development. I covered the achievement of head control through to running and playing football, play-acting it out before we went looking for the real thing on the wards and in clinic. I think – I hope – my teaching was always interesting and fun. Most texts on child development are as easy to read as a telephone directory and about as memorable. I was never interested in being comprehensive, only in creating a bit of interest. Somehow, one of the most exciting phenomena in the universe can, in the wrong hands, become tedious. If nothing else I strove to avoid that.

On Fridays I normally attended the adult physicians' lunch-time clinical meeting in the postgraduate centre. The differences between their practice and ours are manifold but I enjoyed the presentations and discussions. It wasn't unusual to see a case where the problem had originated in childhood, and earlier paediatric management sometimes came in for criticism. I was often openly critical of the lack of empathy in some of their presentations: "You've spent 15 minutes talking about this man. It sounds more like you're talking about a lump of meat than a person." I was often surprised, disappointed even, to see how little empathy some of the adult doctors appeared to have for their patients. Their view was that we paediatricians were too soft and mollycoddled our patients, creating over-dependence. I always appreciated the cross-fertilization of such apparently disparate views. I quite often presented a paediatric case myself: I tried to select cases adult doctors might be interested in and was often impressed by their canny ability to contribute. But best of all they put on a good lunch.

As I was about to go into the meeting the Medical Director,

Mike Brown, came in and asked me to meet him in his office at 2pm. I explained my physical indisposition and told him I wanted to get off to Leicester to visit my daughter.

"You need to come and hear something to your advantage."

"Tell me now?"

"It's confidential."

I'd been Clinical Director of Paediatrics at Walsall for more than seven years and I wasn't accustomed to hearing anything to my advantage from the Medical Director. Unsuspecting and full of curiosity, I arrived at his office five minutes early for my appointment.

"There's been a lot of bickering in the paediatric department of late," he said.

He knew the history of the last two years since Dr Walia's arrival. He knew the problems but had been unwilling to tackle them.

"Not bickering, Mike. You know perfectly well what's going on. Get the consultants together and let's thrash it out. You've got a consultant in there who can't hack it."

"Your colleagues Dr Walia and Dr Sinha have been to the BMA and complained that you have been bullying them and telling colleagues that Dr Walia is incompetent."

"That's absolute nonsense. You know I have real concerns about his competence. Half of the department does. But I've never said to anyone that he is incompetent. The process to decide that is your responsibility or NCAS or the GMC." I rehearsed the history.

"An obstetric consultant says you have been gossiping that Dr Walia was forced to resign as neonatal lead."

"He was forced to resign and every paediatric consultant knows it. The nursing staff have expressed profound relief that he has resigned and that we have a good replacement. But I do not gossip. You've known me long enough to understand that."

But there was nowhere to go. Guilty as charged. He told me that the only thing that would satisfy Dr Walia and the BMA was my removal as Clinical Director.

"So, I'm replacing you with immediate effect with Jon Pepper." Jon was Clinical Director in the obstetric department and one of Mike's colleagues there.

"That is barking mad, Mike. Jon's an obstetrician. He knows nothing about paediatrics. And he's got completely the wrong temperament. This will be a disaster for the department. You would be better off putting in any other paediatric consultant rather than Jon."

"The decision's already been made; none of the others is up to it. Jon has agreed to do it."

So, without waiting to give me a hearing, Mike Brown had made his decision and replaced me. I stood and left without saying another word. I looked at my watch. He'd taken sixteen minutes to dispose of me, without a word of thanks for seven years of hard graft. I was shocked at his ruthlessness. It felt like an ambush.

Three years later, at the employment tribunal, I saw a document disclosed by the Trust that I had never seen before. In it, the HR Director stated clearly that *at that time* the Trust recognized that Dr Walia had been in a tight corner and was "playing the bullying card" when he went to the BMA. Rather than be straight, acknowledge this and deal with Dr Walia, Mike Brown found it expedient to shoot the messenger.

I went to my office and hand-wrote a fair account of the meeting. I rang Janet at home. She thought I was joking when I told her what had happened. My first consideration now was our daughter, Rachel. Shortly after I arrived in Walsall in 1992 she had been admitted to hospital with meningococcal meningitis. That was a terrifying experience for all of us but mercifully she made a complete recovery. Even more devastatingly, six months later, having been in good health, she suffered a second episode of the same illness. There is an advantage in having a consultant paediatrician as a father. I asked her consultant to check her C8 complement level: low levels of this important component of the immune system are the main cause for repeated meningococcal infections. Her C8 level was low. Genetic testing showed that Janet and I were both carriers of the abnormal gene but unaffected. Carl Jung claimed that only the wounded doctor heals: these experiences certainly gave me new insights into meningococcal disease and genetic afflictions that must have benefited my patients and their parents. Both brought their own peculiar agonies.

I came back into work on Monday and my colleagues commiserated over Mike Brown's action. My pride had taken a knock but I also had a sense of relief that the burden of management had been lifted. My family claimed this was an answer to prayer! Over the next few days I developed increasing pain in my foot. I consulted Naj Rashid, the A&E consultant who had resuscitated me after my bike accident. He ordered an ultrasound and then performed a minor procedure that only took ten minutes. The local anaesthetic produced an immediate relief. That night I woke with excruciating pain and had to take codeine to dull it. The next morning I was still in pain and could not walk; I slept for two days. Then I went to see my GP: I have a good GP with unhurried listening skills. "You're burnt out, David." he told me. I knew it and Janet knew it but like most doctors I needed a professional voice to get me to act on it. I gratefully accepted a sick note for two weeks.

As soon as I felt able I wrote to Mike Brown to register a protest at his action. He replied expressing surprise, claiming that I had resigned as Clinical Director. This was completely untrue and he knew it. Two years later a Royal College review panel concluded: "The removal of David Drew from the Clinical Director role was not evidenced or articulated explicitly through a diligent process and whether David Drew was removed or resigned remains ambiguous."

I was off work for a couple of months. As a child I found going back to school difficult even when I'd only had a day or two off. I now found myself reliving some of those early anxieties. I went to my GP and asked to be signed off. He urged caution. He had exercised the professionalism required to take a senior doctor firmly in hand. He knew a lot about my experiences through attentive listening and thought it was probably too early for me to return. I respected his view but argued otherwise and he eventually agreed to my going back for a trial period. I returned to work after a week walking in the Cheviot Hills, a week with Jonathan Swift's best physicians, Dr Quiet, Dr Diet and Dr Merryman. On our first day in Northumberland we took the long hike up the College Valley to the mountain rescue hut by the border fence: there are no pills to rival that. Fully restored, I returned ready for anything.

15

Under New Management

*West Midlands Deanery is committed to creating a work environment
free from bullying, harassment or discrimination and the NHS holds
a zero tolerance to such behaviour.*

West Midlands Deanery website

I returned to Walsall in June not knowing what to expect. The office
on Monday morning felt unreal. Everyone told me they'd missed
me – and, by the way, didn't I look well! I'd spent most days out of
doors in the garden. A week in Northumberland had rejuvenated
me and here I stood in ruddy good health. I felt a fraud but had little
time to reflect on that. There was no back-to-work interview and I
took up my workload as if nothing had happened. It was a relief not
to have the Clinical Director duties. If the Medical Director had
accepted my resignation six months earlier none of this would have
happened. Or maybe it would anyway: I was always going to be the
one to speak out when things were wrong, head of department or
not.

At my first meeting with the Divisional Director he
acknowledged the problems in the department and revealed the
Trust's solution:

"Gatrad's going. We're advertising for four new consultants."

"That'll go some way to helping, but it's not just numbers," I
said.

"You can guarantee all four of them will be white."

"Why's that?

"We need to dilute the Asian effect."

"What are you talking about?"

"You know what I mean."

"It's nothing to do with anyone being Asian, Rob. There are two difficult consultants in the department, who don't get on with anyone, including each other. It's nothing to do with them being Asian. They're all Asians except me. It's competence that started all this, not race."

"I'd go easy on competence if I were you, David. You've had enough trouble."

"If you want to rebalance the consultant group make sure at least two of the new consultants are female."

"We'll do that."

Three months later we had four new consultant paediatricians. Three were white and the other doctor spoke a more refined form of the English than I did. I was delighted that two of them were women.

In early March, weeks before my meeting with Mike Brown, the department had suffered a so-called "triggered" inspection by the West Midlands Deanery. For many years the deanery, which had overall responsibility for postgraduate medical training, did quite regular inspections, but these had dropped off and it had been some time since we'd had a visitation. It was a relief to be spared these. We were an under-resourced unit and rather isolated. Things had improved significantly when a few years earlier we had been cleared to train registrars. We found it difficult to fulfil all our training responsibilities but many trainees still reported a good experience. Deanery visits rarely happened without mention of the possibility of training posts and their funding being withdrawn. This would have made it impossible to run the department, with catastrophic consequences for the hospital.

The triggered visit was precipitated, I was told, after one particular trainee made a serious complaint to the postgraduate sub-dean. I was not surprised at this, as a number of trainees had expressed unhappiness with aspects of their training. On one occasion the whole group wrote a complaint about the poor teaching of a particular consultant. I later wrote to the Medical Director: "[He] is quite the worst teacher I have ever observed. I know that other consultants, such as Dr Gatrad, a very experienced teacher, concur." I never had any support from the Medical Director with this.

The deanery team visited and sent a report. It was, needless to say, not good. One of the problems with these reports is that because of "confidentiality" and the need for anonymity the whole consultant body can be tainted by the shortcomings of one or two individuals. There was a very specific reference to the misbehaviour of one consultant in the report. I subsequently wrote to the Medical Director:

> As you say, during the recent triggered Deanery visit (What exactly triggered that visit?) trainee doctors identified a consultant who they were reluctant to call in out of hours. Bullying, intimidation and unsupportive were terms that were used about him at the feedback.

I was always one for tackling problems like this in a direct manner. The consultant should be identified and dealt with, for his (all consultants were male at that time) own good, but especially for the sake of the trainees. Having an unrestrained bully around was possibly the best way of damaging their learning experience. So I wrote to the Medical Director:

> After the Deanery team left I discussed with you the importance of identifying the consultant concerned to protect our juniors and to take remedial action before the deanery re-visit. You asked me if it could be Dr Gatrad. I assured you that Dr Gatrad was fastidious about doing his

on-calls. (He was well liked and not a bully.) About two weeks later I saw you and asked if you had made any progress with identifying the said consultant. You told me the Deanery had been unable to give a name and that we would have to give a general warning to all consultants for the sake of the deanery. I was incensed at that as it meant we were all under suspicion. I therefore spoke to two juniors who had been interviewed by the Deanery. The first told me that Dr Walia was the consultant in question, which, of course, knowing my consultants, I was pretty certain of already. That doctor [name redacted here] gave me a vivid report of junior doctors' views of Dr Walia. This included a statement that no junior wanted to work on the neonatal unit while he was in charge.

As often happened with my letters to the Medical Director, I received no reply.

The deanery visit was the last big issue I dealt with before going off sick. I had addressed the matters of fact in the report but was gone before we had time to draw up a response to improve things. While I was away, in June, the deanery revisited. The report was discussed at the first management group I attended on my return. Management claimed the visit found the situation much improved.

The report is a classic. Section one outlines everything management claimed had been done to remedy the situation. The second section records the deanery team interviews with the trainees. It is quite clear that all was far from well. The two sections appear to be describing two different departments. There are many examples: under "Consultant cover" the Trust view states: "Trainees are encouraged to contact consultants if required." This is the usual bland language that says nothing about what is actually happening. The trainees had their own view. "Consultant cover is very dependent on the individual consultant. Some very easy and supportive. Some very difficult, moody and demoralizing." This section contains quotations from trainees that should have horrified the deanery, with its strict line on bullying.

At the management group meeting, Jon Pepper, who had now replaced me as Clinical Director, told us that at this visit two consultants had been identified as bullying trainees. I was quite relieved that my own absence ruled me out. It was clear that the problems with bullying reported in March had not been dealt with. I had given the Medical Director the name of the consultant reported at that visit but nothing had been done. So we were back where we started. Jon Pepper said he was dealing with the consultants in question. I said it would be better and more grown-up if we faced this as a group, otherwise it would not go away. But there was no chance of that happening and I was certain the problem would resurface before long.

The department had undergone a revolution during my absence. Three managers with no qualification or experience in paediatrics were now running it. They used the complaints generated by trainees against two consultants to label the whole consultant group as "dysfunctional". One of our two paediatric wards had been closed and all inpatients had been shoehorned into one small ward that was unfit for purpose. I asked to see the risk assessment and whether the Board had signed it off. I was told that the decision had come from the top and was irreversible. If I cared for the patients I would do everything in my power to make sure it worked.

It had always been our practice to cancel our consultant clinics when we were on leave. I was quite happy for most of my colleagues to see my patients if necessary but I regarded continuity as very important. During my absence a new rule had been introduced, keeping clinics open during consultant leave. This broke continuity and put pressure on the already overstretched middle-grade doctors who had to provide cover. Within a week of my return I knew we were in for a stormy time: we were managed by a group who made our decisions for us – decisions that often made our work more difficult but had no impact on their lives at all.

At a job-planning meeting in January 2009, six months later, I asked the managers how we were doing with the deanery. "Bad, very bad..." replied Jon Pepper. I later sent an email asking him for clarification. "Informal feedback has been given to the Medical Director. No names have been mentioned. The problems seem to be the same as before," he replied. He also said that there would be a third deanery visit. That was, in my experience, unheard of. It would have been unnecessary if the consultants at fault had been dealt with decisively to begin with.

I found this situation intolerable and I replied to that effect. I also offered to supply him the email address of one of our best SHOs, who had just left. I had done an informal exit interview with her and she had given an outspoken account of how demoralizing her time in the department had been. She named the consultants who had contributed to that. Jon never showed any interest in this contact. I was always puzzled when management showed a complete lack of interest in what, in my view, would help them improve the department — Hear no evil. See no evil. Speak no evil.

At a later date, the Trust, in a document sent to a Royal College of Paediatrics review panel, accused me of the heinous crime of "disregarding hierarchies". This was an instance when I certainly did choose to do that – in the interest of the service. Line management was not working so I emailed Helen Goodyear, the Paediatric Sub-Dean, asking what was going on. She responded:

> We have had mixed reports about Walsall. Some consultants are identified as being highly supportive to junior staff and others are simply not following what they should be doing, leaving staff unsupported. Junior doctors are feeling threatened by some consultants not to speak the truth and

all are reluctant to name names as they fear the backlash from those named.

I found the irresponsibility of this reply staggering. It was general knowledge in the department which consultants this was referring to. This was the third time we had had multiple complaints of consultant bullying from trainees in less than a year. We knew who the consultants were. Nothing had been done to protect trainees or secure their training, and I feared nothing would be done. The deanery had its policy statement on bullying but, as with so many policies, it was not worth the paper it was written on. I responded:

Individual consultants are abusing their position and being allowed to get away with it because no one dare speak out. If true I do not believe this should be tolerated. The allegations need investigating immediately and if confirmed action must be taken to make sure it never happens again. I am afraid this is not the first time we have been in this situation. If I am one of the culprits I will take the hemlock.

In response I received a complaint from the Sub-Dean that I had circulated her reply to the paediatric consultants and managers. In my long experience at Walsall, closing down conversations is the standard way of fire-fighting allegations of wrongdoing. In February, Jon Pepper wrote to say that he and the Medical Director would be investigating the allegations of bullying. A good place to start would have been to contact the SHO I offered to introduce him to or use the names I had provided. This matter was never dealt with decisively to my knowledge and by the autumn of 2009 I was heading for a clash with the Medical Director that would effectively silence me altogether.

Three years later, in an employment tribunal, the Chief Executive, Sue James, was characterizing my determination to free trainees from consultant bullying as "repeated complaints about my colleagues". I was responsible, she claimed, for creating a toxic environment in the department by my serial complaints. That level of spin would put Alistair Campbell in the shade.

This was one of the problems I found in the department on my return in the summer of 2008. There were many others. Under the new management major changes had been effected without the front-line staff having any say. At a meeting with Sue James after my return the managers claimed that the department had been quiet in my absence but now I was back making trouble again. Raising concerns about trainee bullying and patient care was my strength but in the eyes of Sue James and her managers it identified me as a troublemaker. I was being openly fitted up with the so-called disruptive clinician narrative from that point on.

16

Nursing Cuts

How very little can be done under the spirit of fear.
Florence Nightingale

Over the years, as in other general paediatric units, there had been a change in the pattern of admissions at Walsall. Length of stay had fallen and we were now expected to provide a written explanation if this exceeded two weeks. Longer stays were largely accounted for by premature babies and children with neurodisability. On the other hand, there had been a big increase in short-stay patients. Many now stayed in hospital for less than 24 hours. The net effect was to reduce bed occupancy. Paediatrics is to some extent a seasonal activity and as a result we were often full or near full in the winter but half full in summer. The main cost of a bed is the salaries of the nurses, doctors and the many others who service it. We were now less than two years from moving into a new purpose-built paediatric ward; for a year we had been gradually closing down beds but not cutting staff.

The first and most noticeable change on my return was that one of the two paediatric wards had been closed. We had previously had one ward for infants and one for children aged one to 16 years. The latter had been closed and all inpatients shoehorned into the baby ward. This required considerable ingenuity and created immense problems for staff and patients alike. We would have to manage our sick patients on a floor space less than 20 per cent of what we expected in our new unit. And that was two years away. Two long winters away. Teenage patients were nursed in alcoves off the main ward corridor with only a flimsy curtain for privacy and no consideration of gender. Ward rounds were conducted against a steady flow of through traffic. Every conversation was audible to passers by or those who chose to stop and chat in the corridor. Privacy and dignity went out of the window. The managers who were responsible for this were completely unaffected. I rarely saw them on the ward. Our nurses bravely soldiered on and did their best.

There was no bath or shower for older children, it being a baby ward. No one had thought of that. There was no storage space. The overcrowding meant there was little room for parents to stay. There were other problems that took more time to uncover. None of the senior nursing or medical staff seemed to know how this transition had been accomplished in a few short weeks. They had not been consulted. The new managers were full of confidence in their ability to run the department but were ignorant of clinical paediatrics. It turned out to be a fruitless exercise asking the Divisional Director if an option appraisal had been done before the changes had been made. (There was a large ward in the newer west wing that would have been much more appropriate to our needs.) Nor did I get an answer when I asked if any risk assessments had been done. Cross infection was an obvious possibility with so many sick children crowded together, particularly in the coming winter.

In order to look after sick children in hospital you need beds. And that means first and foremost you need nurses. In Walsall at that time we had good paediatric nurses. They were a friendly, down-to-earth bunch, many from the local population. They were highly professional and absolutely dedicated to their patients: Sister Dora, who established nursing in Walsall in 1887, would have been proud of them. She was sent to Walsall by a religious order in the North East and has a fascinating history. She survived all manner of pestilence, including small pox, and achieved virtual sainthood among local people. She is still revered by those with a sense of history in the town and is celebrated by a suitably impressive statue in the hospital. Many pass her by unaware of what they owe her.

Every trainee doctor and student for years, without exception, had eulogized our nurses. They were described on feedback forms in terms such as "the best single experience I had in the department". I knew every one of them by name, and although sometimes sparks flew between us it never lasted. In early 2007, when I was still Clinical Director, the Divisional Director showed me a Trust document anticipating the redundancy of 27 of our nurses. This was underway by the time of my return.

The whole nursing establishment had been put on notice by a circular letter that redundancy was an imminent possibility. This had been done by letters put on the nursing desk by the head nurse without any personal explanation or reassurance. We later reported this to the Chief Executive as something bound to cause unnecessary distress but she refused to take notice. This was unsettling to say the least, and as a result many nurses started to look for other jobs. As a result we lost some of our most experienced nurses, who were snapped up at interview by other Trusts. (I was always careful when making this point to stress that of course many excellent nurses stayed for reasons of their own.)

At the first Hospital Consultant Committee after my return, with Sue James present, Dr Gatrad and I spoke forcefully about the attrition of our nursing establishment and the mismanagement of the job-shedding exercise. We stressed the potentially dire consequences for the heavier winter months. We got little obvious response. The middle managers responsible, (generic managers with little or no experience in clinical paediatrics), had some crackpot ideas. Our paediatric nurse specialist was to be made redundant whatever we thought. Her salary was needed to reach the cost-savings target. She had been in paediatric nursing for 25 years but was offered redeployment as an adult ENT nurse specialist. She went, and found an identical paediatric nurse specialist post at the next-door Trust. We had made a significant investment in her development but that was nothing to the new managers, whose main concern was to meet cost-savings targets.

We wrote as a consultant group to the Divisional Director. He was not a clinician. He replied that he had to take the professional advice of the head nurse. The head nurse unfortunately had no experience herself of paediatric nursing. One problem we encountered was the difficulty in nailing down minimum safe nurse-staffing levels and that remains a problem even now.

The winter, as we had predicted, was hell, both for the patients and for the nurses, who were forced to work in sub-standard conditions. Staffing levels were low and sickness levels consequently high. Management refused to accept that the low morale was in any way related to the redundancy programme. I repeatedly complained that there were not enough nurses on the ward. Sometimes one nurse was left to run a whole ward. On one occasion the one nurse on the ward rang me and asked for help because the orthopaedic surgeons were admitting adult patients to the children's ward as they were short of beds. I rang all three managers to get them to stop this but not one of them was in the hospital. When I did speak to them I was met with incomprehension. I knew of at least two children in my time at Walsall who had been sexually abused while on the ward but the managers lacked any kind of organisational memory. The adult patients being admitted were young men who we knew nothing about. They had to share toilet and bathing facilities with the children while there was only one nurse to keep an eye on things.

The nursing skill mix, damaged by the redundancy programme, led to potentially fatal consequences on the wards. One afternoon I was called in to see a baby with bronchiolitis, a viral lung infection. She had collapsed and needed ventilating and transferring to intensive care. There was not one nurse on duty with the training and skills to support the resuscitation. Fortunately a nurse from the

Admissions Unit next door was able to step in. An hour later he would have gone home. When I drew this to the Divisional Director's attention at a specialty meeting, the Head Nurse blamed the nursing staff for making unauthorized duty swaps. There was never any acknowledgement that the problems had anything to do with the cuts and their demoralizing effects. It was not uncommon to see senior nursing staff still unable to go home hours after their shifts ended. They stayed out of their professional responsibility to the patients. Some of the more junior nurses were inexperienced, and stressed because of the responsibility they were being given. It is part of a nurse's vocation to work as long as their patients need them. But when this is happening on a regular basis because a manager has to meet a financial target vocation wears thin. Nurses who previously had bloomed with health looked drawn and worn out, and sick.

In the New Year my heart sank when Debbie Whittle told me she was being made redundant. The reason the Director of Nursing, Brigid Stacey, gave me for her redundancy was that because she was only a registered general trained nurse "her presence in the clinic would not assist the Trust to meet the OPD1 standard of the Healthcare Commission Report". But Debbie had worked in the department for 25 years and had run outpatients since my arrival in Walsall. She was an old-school nurse with no frills – but numerous skills that management would not have known about. She was not always easy but she ran outpatients like clockwork.

I wrote one of the strongest protest letters I had written at Debbie's treatment. The Trust then failed to replace her with a registered children's nurse. We must have been the biggest paediatric outpatient department in the UK where for most of the time no qualified nurse was present. The work was done entirely by HCAs (Health Care Assistants). Our HCAs were lovely, hardworking staff and using them cut costs, but it was no way to run a service. In my correspondence with senior management about these issues I never failed to be amazed at how people who never visited the clinic believed they knew more about what was happening there than I did. Fortunately management was soon identifying "significant deficiencies" in clinic nursing and the problem was addressed. The concerns subsequently raised over the growing use of unregulated and minimally trained HCAs at the Stafford Hospital Public Inquiry confirmed my concerns.

By late March I was able to tackle the Chief Executive and Director of Nursing about this at the Hospital Consultants' Committee. Low nursing levels and a skill mix weakened by a bungled redundancy programme were having a detrimental effect on care and posed a significant risk to patient safety. The Director of Nursing told us, and it was minuted, that a full risk assessment of the nursing cuts had been completed and everything was fine. I asked the Divisional Director and Clinical Governance Lead if I could see it. They were quite certain one would have been done but they had not seen it themselves, they told me. I made further requests to the Director of Nursing to see it, but without success. The managers were, I believe, quite pragmatic in this matter: cut nursing numbers and no matter how bad it gets we can be certain the nurses' professionalism will get them through and the patients with them. This is no way to run a workforce. Nurses are there to care but they have to be cared for too.

The winter came to an end, and with it some of the stresses. The redundancy programme started to fizzle out and it became apparent that we had lost too many nurses. We started recruiting again. We were never able to get figures for how many nurses we had lost. One Trust document claimed it was only four nurses who actually lost their jobs by redundancy. But many left under their own steam and the posts went with them. Six were redeployed into posts created to expand the special care baby unit. There was continual spin to trivialize the number of nurses lost and the effect it was having on morale.

Later, in October 2009 Sue James, the Chief Executive, and a non-executive director conducted a "Board to Ward" visit, meeting with the nursing staff. I was on holiday at the time but the nurses were anxious to tell me about it when I got back. "We told her it's going to be like Mid Staffs here," one said. Knowing a lot about Mid Staffs, I realized this was hyperbole but in the right ball park. Sue James wrote that at this visit she had heard the nursing staff tell stories of "long working hours, inappropriate practices and general poor morale." These were matters that I had been bringing to senior management's attention for more than a year. She wrote to tell us how very concerned the Divisional Director and Head Nurse were about this. But they were the very managers who, under pressure from above, had caused this crisis. As a result, she had decided to commission an "independent" nursing review – more money wasted in an already cash-strapped department with little hope that it would do anything other than create an illusion of activity.

The consultants were generally cynical about the review but the nurses still hoped it would help them. Many of us met the reviewer, a nurse from Harrogate. I gave her my own account of the mismanaged redundancy programme, the poor morale and the widespread bullying. She told me that more than half the nurses she had interviewed had been in tears, claiming they were being bullied. "This must be the unhappiest paediatric unit in the country," she said. Other consultants and nursing staff heard the same. The review was done at lightning speed and a report produced by November: the nursing establishment was numerically about right (by then) but had an inadequate skill mix; there was a need for senior nurse leadership in the department. There was no word about nurses being bullied by managers, though this had been reported by many. Those of us who knew what was going on were outraged, but when I wrote to the reviewer for information I was accused by Sue James of harassing her. I have the email.

Weeks later, I was told the Trust was bringing in a nurse lead "from Great Ormond Street". The appointee set about knocking our nurses into shape. I was expecting someone who would roll up her sleeves and pitch in, but that was not what I saw. She was always ultra polite to me but apparently subscribed to the principle espoused by Florence Nightingale, "I attribute my success to this – I never gave or took any excuse." And so, over the following months, a good proportion of an exhausted, undervalued, demoralized nursing team came to find themselves on report or under disciplinary measures for mistakes they had made in their practice. And many others lived with the fear of that.

A paediatrician cannot do his or her work without good nurses. No paediatrician should stand by and see the kind of asset-stripping that we saw in 2008 to 2009. It was done rapaciously and contrary to the interests of the department and the families it served. The only consideration was cost saving. I refused to stand by and let this happen. My reputation as a troublemaker was growing.

17

Playing Politics with Child Protection

Nothing we can do will bring back the children who have died at the hands of their abusers. … But we have to be determined to learn the lessons and to act now to make a lasting difference so that more children will be protected in future.

Ed Balls: Ministerial Foreword in HMG Response to Lord
Laming

By October 2008 Kyle Keen had been dead more than two years. Tyrone Matthews, convicted of manslaughter, was in prison. Kyle's mother, Kelly McIntosh, had been given a six-months suspended sentence for cruelty by neglect and lost her other child as a result. The rest of Kyle's bereaved family had disappeared from sight and we had had no contact with them. His father, when I met him again four years later, told me the killer would be in prison for a few years but he had been given a life sentence by his son's death. Kyle had been all but forgotten in the hospital. A number of people preferred it that way. Some of the nurses mentioned him occasionally and it was clear they regretted not having been better advocates. We had still seen no sign of the serious case review.

Towards the end of my career I realized that I had never developed a deep understanding of how child protection services did or did not work. This was possibly because it was only a small fraction of my work. The death of Maria Colwell had dominated the headlines as I was setting out as a children's doctor in the early seventies; even then I remember the local authority trumpeting in the press that "this must never happen again". Following our return from Africa, the press was full of accounts of Jasmine Beckford's killing in not dissimilar circumstances: "It must never happen again." In 2000 one of the most outrageous failures of the child protection services came to light with the death of Victoria Klimbié: "It must never happen again." In August 2007, a year after Kyle's death, Peter Connolly was killed after repeated failures by police and social services and the NHS: in a final and fatal error he was sent home from clinic despite him having a broken back. Three individuals, including Peter's mother, were jailed for their part in this crime. I heard no one saying "It must never happen again." Maybe it is now seen as inevitable, something society has to live with.

At least with all these cases there had been an acknowledgement of abject failure and an open investigation. Apart from the criminal investigation, which I had lost sight of, there seemed to be little or no sign that we were addressing the central failings with Kyle's death.

Late one afternoon I rang Elaine Hurry, the designated safeguarding nurse at the Primary Care Trust, to discuss a difficult case I was dealing with. After giving me the advice I needed, she asked if I knew anything about the appointment of a safeguarding nurse by the Trust. I did not. Most paediatric departments had by that time appointed properly trained safeguarding nurses. We had been requesting funding from the Trust for some years to establish this important post but had been repeatedly turned down: the Trust considered it was not a priority. Elaine was probably the most knowledgeable person on safeguarding in NHS Walsall. She was a quiet, highly competent and – usually – mild-mannered person, but today she was mad. She told me that the safeguarding post had been funded, the job description written and the appointment made without any reference to her or anyone else with expertise. She had written to Karen Palmer, the Head Nurse, who had made the appointment, to register her objections. I asked her to send me a copy of the letter. She did, that same day.

The letter rehearsed the reasons why the appointee, one of our general nurses, was unsuitable for such an important post. Finally Elaine set this in its proper context, Kyle Keen's death:

> The need for this post was highlighted within the hospital in the last serious case review undertaken by Walsall Safeguarding Children's Board. *Catastrophic mistakes* had been made and the review concluded that if hospital staff had *followed basic safeguarding procedures* the child concerned would have survived. This can never be acceptable and highlights the need for a well trained and supported workforce, who could challenge decisions made by senior colleagues.

It would have taken a certain level of experience and assertiveness to face down the particular senior colleague she had in mind, Dr Walia. Having read the letter, my first port of call was the Divisional Director's office. I went through every point Elaine had made and a few more. He told me this was a nursing appointment and he had to rely on the professional advice he'd been given by the Head Nurse.

"Karen can't give you professional advice, she's no paediatric experience and she's an amateur in safeguarding herself." I said.

"Look, David, think about it like this. At least you've got a pair of hands that you didn't have before. We're making progress with this."

"That's nonsense, Rob. You're not listening. This is an important post. You weren't here when Kyle Keen was killed. He'd likely still be alive if we'd had a trained safeguarding nurse. You have that in writing. That means a properly trained nurse who would have overridden Walia's incomprehensible decision not to get social services in. You're just trying to keep the redundancies down with this appointment. That's not helping the service and it's putting children at continued risk."

"Sorry David, we're laying nurses off, if you haven't noticed. Politically there's no way I could have advertised this post externally."

"You mean this is out of your hands? OK, I'll take it to the Chief Executive."

I left frustrated and angry at such bureaucratic stupidity. This was no way to run a dogs' home, let alone a child protection service. It takes a lot to make me angry but I was furious. I spoke to a couple of other paediatric consultants but they knew nothing of the appointment.

I counted to ten and took my time before writing to Sue James. Everything about this appointment was wrong. The nurse appointed to the post was a very good general paediatric nurse, who I had known for years. I did not want to criticize her but she had no safeguarding training or experience and in my view was temperamentally not suited for the role. I concentrated on the fact that Karen Palmer had made the appointment by stealth without reference to the local experts, including Elaine. Karen was delivering the budget cuts. If any of us had been involved the appointment would not have been made.

The post had not been advertised externally. HR failed to provide any evidence that it had even been advertised internally. Three nurses had been given the choice of redeployment into this role or redundancy. The press was beginning to take notice of our nursing redundancies and these had to be minimized. The paediatric matron, who had considerably more experience in safeguarding, had wanted to apply for this post. He had been so badly bullied himself by the middle managers that he was forced to seek redundancy. He was quickly engaged by the largest children's hospital in the country to work as a safeguarding nurse.

Dear Lord, I was still a baby in those days. Naïvely I expected a responsible answer from Sue James by return. Two weeks later having heard nothing from her I asked Rob what the Chief

Executive had made of my letter. He rolled his eyes: "I think you've got a good idea."

Over the next two months a number of child abuse stories were aired in the national media. In nearby Birmingham the Kyra Ishaq case had shocked many who were used to hearing of such tragedies. Birmingham City Council's safeguarding arrangements had been judged inadequate in every way following an Ofsted inspection, a fate Walsall would also suffer at a later date.

We knew that the Health Secretary had ordered a review of NHS hospital safeguarding services. This was about the only thing in my experience that would get those at the top of the organization to take notice. Even then the main concern would be that we ticked all the boxes. So, in December, almost two months after I had written my original scorcher to Sue James, I wrote again to remind her that she had not even acknowledged my concerns. With respect to the anticipated Department of Health review I wrote:

> We are not well placed. Neither the medical lead (a gynaecologist), the head of nursing (a midwife), nor the non-clinical manager has any experience or knowledge of paediatrics or child protection. We have appointed a child protection nurse for the wrong reasons. The person in the department who best understands Laming has been bullied and taken redundancy.

Sue James's PA emailed me to say they had not received my letter. I was able to respond immediately that this was not true. I had considered this letter so important that I'd had it hand-delivered by my secretary. The PA then emailed to say sorry but the letter had been lost, could I re-send it. The final story I heard from Sue James's office was that the letter had arrived when she was on holiday and so it had been sent to the Divisional Director to deal with. I am afraid that story did not check out either. In the context of a child protection investigation we tend to get suspicious when the story keeps changing in this way. It would of course be unthinkable, possibly fatal, to challenge the integrity of a Chief Executive in these circumstances.

It was not until July the following year, nine months after my original letter, that I got a definitive answer. This letter was possibly one of the finest examples of spin I have seen and relied heavily on information from the middle managers I had with justification criticized for this mess.

Elaine had not been involved in the appointment, Sue James informed me because "Karen Palmer was unaware that Elaine wished to be involved." The post was, she said, a "good redeployment opportunity for interested nurses". Everything had been done in line with Human Resource Policy at the Trust: "It is always pleasing to note that our own staff are highly qualified to be able to apply for such posts and that it is not always necessary to search outside for such talent." I laughed aloud at the utter folly of this self-justification. "The successful applicant had extensive knowledge and skills within the field of child protection," she claimed, presuming I was some kind of dimwit.

This was all untrue, and even a superficial reading of Elaine Hurry's letter would have shown this. Sue James preferred, as Rob Hodgkiss had, to take her advice from Karen Palmer, advice that was wrong, but so much more comforting. "Thank you for your interest in this matter, and apologies again for the delay in responding to your letter. Yours sincerely, Sue James"

I began to have a recurrent nightmare at that time. I was in the sea, being carried on the outgoing tide and waving desperately for help. A woman strolled along the beach. She took no notice of me for a while. When she finally did spot me she smiled, waved back and turned to go up the beach. "I'm drowning," I called out. "Drowning."

After six stressful months and many tears the foundation

safeguarding post holder admitted defeat and with some relief went back to general nursing duties. She had, no doubt, benefited from the experience, painful as it had been for her. But the service had not developed and a replacement was needed. Sue James may still have believed the department was bursting with native talent but I was pleased to see the post advertised externally. None of our own nurses were qualified to apply. I had contributed in a small way to developing the service and made enemies in the process. There followed a time of quiet but it would not be long before I found myself in a pitched battle to ensure the Trust was forced, once again, into taking its responsibility to protect children seriously.

18

Cold Babies

Systematic reporting of 'near misses' (seen as an important early warning of serious problems) is almost non-existent across the NHS.

An Organisation with a Memory, Department of Health, 2000

In the Trust's 2004 outline business case for replacing Manor Hospital's East Wing, including the paediatric wards and paediatric assessment unit, there is an unusually pithy background note:

> Current building is of Victorian stock, of inadequate standard to provide modern clinical services, cannot provide appropriate accommodation to Health Building Note (HBN) standards; suffers from considerable backlog maintenance of approximately £3.3m and fails to meet fire regulation standards. Total replacement is required.

Five years later the building was still in use for the care of seriously ill children. Shoehorning all our patients into the baby ward in the summer of 2008 without consulting clinical staff had made things much worse.

A further problem arose in the winter of 2008/9 that we had not encountered before. Towards the end of November a cold northerly wind blew in. I was on call over the last weekend of the month and the county was shrouded for much of the time in freezing fog. I rarely wore a coat to work even in winter, but was forced to for those three days. On the Saturday morning ward round parents were complaining that both they and their children had been cold overnight. We checked all the charts and twelve patients in all had been recorded with temperatures between 34 and 36 degrees Celsius. The ward was busy but fortunately there were no children with critical illness. Parents and patients had passed a miserable night but no one had come to serious harm.

After the ward round was finished and we had discharged a few patients, I asked switchboard to find the Medical Director for me. I explained the situation to him and asked for his help. He promised to speak to the engineers; I heard no more from him. The next morning things were improved but far from perfect. The Medical Director had been out to a shop and purchased four domestic electric convector heaters and some wall thermometers out of petty cash. I rang him after the weekend to ask about the engineers' report. He could give no clear idea of the problem. I explained that the heaters were inadequate, and in any case produced a very dry atmosphere that was inappropriate for small babies with breathing difficulties. "Your own nose will tell you there is a problem when you walk into the room," I said. Respiratory illness was the main cause for hospital admission at that time.

By Monday the steam-driven heating system was maintaining a steady temperature and the auxiliary heaters were put away. The nurses were diligently recording room, as well as patient, temperatures. The Medical Director asked me to ensure that clinical incident reports were submitted on each patient who had become cold. At that stage there was widespread cynicism among the consultants that anything was achieved by filling these forms in, and it was generally left to nursing staff. For years the clinical governance committee had been run at departmental level, chaired by the Paediatric Clinical Director. The Trust at some point reorganized this and it was now convened at divisional level, so that most of us rarely heard anything of it. I copied Risk Management in on my emails, but never at any time, then or subsequently, was the Trust willing to look at the root cause of the problem. I was convinced that this would have resulted in moving paediatric inpatients elsewhere in the hospital.

The weather improved and the ward temperature remained fairly constant over the next few weeks. The responsibility for monitoring this fell on our matron and, although he was the most diligent of nurse managers, he was clearly distracted when I spoke to him about it. He looked ill. He was leaving in a few weeks, he told me. He had been bullied by both his managers and could take no more. I felt bad as I knew about this, having heard the Divisional Director referring to him as "that idle bastard Simon". I had defended Simon as a diligent and capable nurse but had done nothing practical to help him. He had accepted a voluntary redundancy package and was thinking of leaving nursing altogether. Two weeks after the incident I sent him an email asking him to check the nurses had completed the incident forms.

We had at that time a couple of quite sharp medical students with us. I had spent some time talking to them about risk in the context of the heating failure. We discussed proximate and remote causes of events and different models of risk. The babies had become cold because the outdoor temperatures were very low and the antiquated heating system had either failed or been unable to cope. We had quite a discussion about why we had allowed this situation to arise. My email to Matron ended with this: "Today, patient XX had pressure sores acquired in a care home. We have reported the home to Social Services for child protection reasons. Hypothermia and pressure sores are both symptoms of neglect. On the ward round, one very sharp medical student asked me if our cases of hypothermia were in any sense due to negligence."

Before Christmas I met one of the engineers responsible for maintaining the steam system. Mike Brown had written to me about the fall in ward temperature. The secretaries upstairs, he explained, had reported that their offices were uncomfortably hot. The adjustments to correct this had resulted in the temperature in other parts of the building plummeting. The engineer was dismissive of this. No, he told me, the system was ancient and clapped out and it could not be guaranteed. I should expect further trouble.

I have little memory of December and almost no documentation. My diary notes stored on the desktop of my computer were destroyed by the Trust after I was dismissed. Before Christmas we held a leaving party for Matron, who was hired shortly afterwards to work in safeguarding at the regional children's hospital.

On New Year's Day the cold returned and the heating began to fluctuate wildly. There were no critically ill babies and the nurses were coping. I wrote to management and clinical staff about the situation:

> The cold weather is back. Once again babies and children on Salisbury Ward are dropping their body temperatures. The first four babies I checked this morning had dropped their body temperatures to between 35 and 36C. This is once again down to environment. The nursing staff say that the heating has been very variable, sometimes hot and sometimes cold. We need to be able to ensure the ward's thermal environment if we are going to nurse sick infants on it.

The Divisional Manager emailed everyone to ask that he be informed next time there was a problem; the Risk Manager emailed to ask if nursing staff were monitoring room temperatures; the Medical Director was of the opinion that the problem had been fixed. "My understanding is that the root cause has been identified and fixed," he emailed. My understanding was that the root cause had been identified as a clapped-out heating system in a Victorian workhouse past its sell-by date. It was beyond fixing. When I raised the issue of cold babies at the paediatric specialty group meeting I was taken aback by the response. The Clinical Director, Jon Pepper, cut me dead: "You're not still banging on about that, are you?" That was the attitude I had to contend with.

I subsequently put my opinion on record:

The medical care of these babies was compromised. As soon as a small baby (a 2.5kg baby born prematurely, in one case) moves into a temperature below its thermal neutral environment there is a metabolic cost. Oxygen consumption increases. Work of breathing increases. If you are a little baby with pneumonia your medical care has by definition been seriously compromised.

A year later when I made a public statement about this problem on TV I expressed it as simply as I could:

"If a healthy baby is kept in a cold environment it will become ill. An ill baby will get worse. A seriously ill baby's chance of survival will be compromised."

I came on to the ward one morning over this period to find, ironically, a child admitted with signs of cold injury: red, shiny, grossly swollen hands and feet and chilblains. Earlier in my career I had seen many such cases but in recent years they had become rare. These signs are recognized as generally being due to neglect. This child had been kept on the coldest part of the ward for more than two days and his temperature, which had been 34.7 degrees Celsius at admission, had not budged. Social Services became involved. No mention was ever made that we, with all our knowledge and resources, had been unable to do any better than the parents at keeping him warm. The parents were investigated. Our failings passed unnoticed.

I was a rather old-fashioned doctor. Although I worked hard to keep up with new knowledge, my approach sometimes reflected the less evidence-based age in which I had been trained. I was acutely aware of risk, having seen so many things go wrong in my working lifetime. I was not by nature a cautious person, but I was always alive to the possibility of risk to my patients. The heating failures on Salisbury Ward presented a significant risk to them. I intuitively estimated this as potentially severe. At some point during the following winter the nursing staff produced a formal risk assessment. There is an NHS template for this: the likelihood of an event occurring is ranked 1 to 5, that is, from rare to almost certain; the likely consequences of the event, 1 to 5, from negligible to catastrophic. The product of these numbers is a score indicating low, moderate, high or extreme risk. The risk for further heating failure was calculated at 15. My intuition said it was 25. This was academic. A score of 15 to 25 is classed as extreme. This is an oversimplification of how patient risk works. James Reason had argued 20 years earlier that risk is more like a piece of cheese.

A British professor once visited us in Nigeria at a time when it was impossible to find cheese of any kind. Before he left he reached into his rucksack and pulled out a large piece of Emmenthal, our favourite cheese. "I won't be needing this; can you use it?" Our kids were delighted and we ate it in the evening on warm Lebanese flatbread bought in the town. "My piece is more holes than cheese," complained our daughter, Rachel.

The Swiss cheese model is one way of looking at clinical risk and has found a place in NHS thinking. Imagine six slices of Emmenthal, each with differently located holes in it. Put the slices together and there is no point at which it is possible to pass a pencil through from one side to the other. But jiggle the slices, align the holes and it will pass through with ease. A series of risks that individually cause little or no harm to the patients may, in conjunction, prove fatal. A cold night may pass uneventfully. But if the heating is on the blink that night some effects may be noted on the temperature charts. And patients, parents and staff may experience some discomfort. If there is a sick small baby on the ward, risk increases. If there is a nursing shortage or the doctors are busy elsewhere, a blood test is not done, a chemical imbalance not corrected or a drug not prescribed, the holes move into alignment with potentially catastrophic consequences. I have seen it. All too often the progress of this alignment is only seen with the aid of the retrospectoscope. Near misses give us a glimpse of possible unhappy futures. If acted on they can help us to change the future.

The winter passed with only one significant and several minor recurrences of the problem. Then we enjoyed one of the warmest springs in a hundred years. No patient had died as a result of our inability to provide a safe environment. It may have been that some had more severe illness than they would otherwise have had or took longer to recover but this was unprovable. There was no doubt that we had caused many of our charges and their parents discomfort. The nurses, at a time when they were under-staffed and harassed, had been given extra work to do. There had been some heated exchanges in the department and I had personally suffered continual anxiety – which, of course, I was well paid for.

We had one more winter to survive in the "workhouse" and I was determined that our patients would not be put to further risk.

19

Excluded

Someone must have been telling lies about Joseph K for one morning without having done anything wrong he was arrested.

Franz Kafka: *The Trial*

The 23rd of April 2009: a day that was to become deeply etched in my memory. I'd finished my morning clinic, dictated my letters and was having a cup of Lapsang in my office, a rare interlude. I was reading a short newspaper obituary of J. G. Ballard, who'd died a few days earlier. We'd just returned from a weekend in Paris and had visited Père Lachaise Cemetery, mainly for Janet to put a rose on Chopin's grave but also to visit the graves of Maria Callas, Jim Morrison and Héloïse and Abélard. Ballard had once written that a visit to Père Lachaise would add a year to your life. We found it strangely invigorating, so perhaps he was right. Happy days. The phone rang and my reverie ended. It was the Medical Director's secretary asking me to meet him in his office at 5pm.

"What's it about?" I asked.

"He wants to talk to you about the complaint."

I'd made a written complaint to the Medical Director the previous day about the Head Nurse, Karen Palmer's, rude and unprofessional behaviour. It was uncharacteristic of Mike to engage so promptly. I must have caught him on a good day, I thought. I arrived promptly and was kept waiting for 20 minutes outside his office. It was Thursday night and I was on call right through until 9am on the Monday morning. I was not happy at being kept waiting: I had things to do. When he called me in Sue

Wakeman, the Head of HR, was sitting beside his desk. Another ambush.

"There's been a serious complaint against you by the Head Nurse and I'm suspending you on NCAS advice, initially for two weeks." He blurted it out as though it were something he'd wanted to get off his chest for a long time. It is mandatory for NHS Trusts to discuss all intended consultant exclusions with NCAS, the National Clinical Assessment Service, a branch of NPSA, the National Patient Safety Agency. I was a stranger in this territory with no map or compass.

"Sorry, can you run that past me again?"

He did, ad verbatim. From his diction I guessed he'd been rehearsing his lines. Sue Wakeman scribbled an occasional note. I sat quietly for a few de-realized moments to allow this strange news to sink in.

"OK, so what's the complaint?"

"You've been harassing her."

"That's a joke. This is what's called a counter-allegation, Mike. I sent you a written complaint about Karen's unprofessional behaviour yesterday. So what am I supposed to have done?"

"I can't give you any details. They're confidential for the time being."

It would be months before I discovered that Karen Palmer had made a verbal complaint that day. She had put nothing in writing, nor would she until after my exclusion. According to a Royal College investigation of this incident published a year later, Mike Brown and Karen Palmer had had "an emotional encounter" in his office earlier that day, and this had resulted a few hours later in my exclusion. Details of this encounter were never forthcoming.

"As I said, your exclusion is for two weeks and it will be reviewed before expiry. In this time you are not to enter your workplace or any premises under the control of Walsall Hospitals NHS Trust without my permission. NCAS has also advised me to refer you to

Occupational Health. You should leave the hospital now." He read it from a scrap of paper.

At least I did not suffer the indignity that many of my whistleblower friends have of being escorted off the premises by a burly security guard.

"It's Thursday evening, Mike, I'm the paediatric consultant on call through to Monday morning. I'll have to leave arrangements for cover to you," I said.

He was clearly irritated but asked me if I could go and arrange my own cover. I was inclined to refuse but, as that would obviously have been against my patients' interests, I went down to the Divisional Director's office. He was in a meeting with one of that growing number of people whose job title you can't remember and whose role is a mystery.

"'Night, Rob. See you sometime, I've just been suspended."

"What for?"

"Don't know."

"I'm sorry to hear that."

"I'm on call. You'll need a locum to cover 80 out-of-hours of my on-call starting in 30 minutes, when I have been and locked my office."

"Shit."

I went up to my office. The whole floor was deserted apart from Jackie, our cleaner. I knew her troubles were much greater than mine. She didn't look well enough to be at work. That didn't stop her asking if I wanted a cup of tea. I sat down and sent an email to my consultant colleagues. I told them I was suspended, using the old-fashioned word for exclusion they would understand, and the little I knew about why. I reassured them that I was quite certain I had done nothing to deserve it but apologized for any inconvenience I would cause them. I reminded them that the next day there was an important meeting with the Divisional Director over job plans. I warned them to be firm: "If I do come back I don't want to find myself stuck with a crap job plan." I signed off with a touch of flamboyance: "Love you all to the stars and back." I locked up. Jackie had gone. I went out into the night; it was starting to rain. And so I entered the world of Kafka's Joseph K., a man prosecuted by an unknown authority, never to be told and unable find out what he had done wrong.

I arrived home more shaken than I cared to admit and Janet could see something was wrong when I walked through the door.

"You're as white as a sheet."

I explained what had happened in detail.

"We'll have to make the most of it. If they don't want you I've got plenty of work for you here."

We had something to eat, lit a roaring log fire and watched our favourite film, Franco Zeffirelli's cheesy musical biopic of the life of St Francis. Soon we were out of our own skins and innocently engaged with the marvellous lyrics:

Brother Sun, Sister Moon,

I seldom see you, seldom hear your tune,

Preoccupied with selfish misery.

Like a couple of ageing hippies we sat on the floor, lost in a simpler world than our own. We turned our back on selfish misery and determined to make the most of what must surely be no more than a minor reverse.

I have little memory of the next day other than that I walked a lot, probably 20 to 30 miles. I think and pray better on the move. I did quite a lot of both, but by the evening I was worse rather than better. I didn't sleep well and lay in bed the next morning, a Saturday. I heard the post drop through the letterbox and Janet open the hall door to collect it. Then I heard her yell, "David, come and look at this." I ran downstairs and found her in the hall, crying, with a letter in her hand. We've been married 40 years and we mostly open each other's post. We've got no secrets. I read the letter: it was an appointment to see a psychiatrist in Birmingham at 9am on Monday.

"What's the matter with them, David? What are they trying to do to you?" she asked me.

I had no need of a psychiatrist and decided not to keep the appointment. I contacted the BMA to confirm this was OK. At 9am on Monday I rang the consultant in his clinic, as a matter of courtesy, to say I was not coming. I asked where the referral had come from, what the objective was and what information had been given as a context for the consultation.

"It was a secretary at Manor Hospital who rang our secretary. No information was given. I assumed it would be the usual scenario for NHS consultants, drink or drugs."

I'd been told by Mike Brown, the Medical Director, to expect an appointment with Occupational Health, not a psychiatrist. The Monday midday post brought a letter from Mike Brown reiterating what he'd said at the exclusion meeting. That included the need for me to see the occupational physician. No mention of a psychiatrist. I had been excluded, he stated, on NCAS advice, etc. When I contacted NCAS at a later date, with a Data Protection Act request, I learned that this was untrue; no such advice had been given. This was quite typical of Mike's idiosyncratic way of getting things done. I was beginning to learn that he was a law unto himself.

I sent a letter by return asking him, among other things, for an explanation for the psychiatric appointment. As so often happened, he ignored it. I have always been an industrious person so within a few days I set out to try to understand what exclusion was and how it worked. This was my first experience of any kind of disciplinary process. It immediately became obvious that this was no level playing field. Hospital management know the territory. They have full HR and administrative support, besides the services of the Trust lawyer if required. The suspended doctor is likely to be demoralized and demotivated. It's often the case, as it was in mine, that exclusion is sprung on the unsuspecting doctor or nurse without warning.

Little explanation, advice or genuine support is given. The standard line from HR is that exclusion is a neutral act. In my case it felt like a hostile act of retaliation and I know that has been the experience of many.

There are a number of advisory and support groups for excluded doctors and I came to learn of the reality behind the claim of "a neutral act". Death from heart attack is four times more common among excluded doctors than comparable doctors at work; depression and other mental illnesses are more common, as are relational breakdown and divorce. Suicide is perhaps the most tragic consequence. I set about addressing some of these issues. First, I gave Janet a big hug to make sure all was well in that department. Then, since action is probably the best antidote to self-pity, I rang the BMA. I was put in touch with Mr Ian Mckivett, an Industrial Relations Officer (IRO), and he visited me at home a few days later. I have heard the IROs criticized by some whistleblower doctors, but the advice and support I had from Ian up until my dismissal two years later – and beyond – could not have been better. I would not have survived without him.

20

Quarantine

That's all there is to it. You are arrested! And you'll find nothing
better to respond with than a lamblike bleat. "Me? What for?"
Alexandr Solzhenitsyn: *Gulag Archipelago*

After the first few days at home I was overwhelmed by the enormity
of what had happened to me. Perhaps the most difficult thing to
cope with was the certainty that I had done nothing wrong, rather
the opposite. Moreover, I had been given no indication of what the
allegations against me were. That information was three months
away. I wrote to Mike Brown asking permission to visit my office
to write two outstanding child protection reports and collect
personal items. He refused and it was two weeks before I was
allowed in. I had been in my office five minutes when he rang me.

"David, Jon Pepper's just rung to say that you are in the
hospital."

"Yes?"

"You're not supposed to be here."

"You sent me written permission to come in today. I'm doing
child protection reports."

"Oh, right. You ought to let people know you're coming."

"It's not my job to let them know, Mike, it's yours. I don't want
to be harassed like this next time I come in."

A week or so later, once again with the Medical Director's
written permission, I went to my office to sign the typed child
protection reports. My experience this time was considerably more
traumatic. I met one of my running pals, Martin, the hospital

postman, in the entrance to East Wing. We stood chatting about what races he was doing when Sue Wakeman, the Head of HR, came up, stridently demanding what I was doing in the hospital. I had no right to be there. She was going straight to the Medical Director to report me. Martin was shocked at her tirade, especially as it was delivered in front of staff and visitors. Shortly afterwards, he wrote a witness statement describing Sue's behaviour. I sent this to the Medical Director but it was ignored. I sent it with my supporting documents to a Royal College review the following year. I did not receive so much as an acknowledgement of this complaint. It was one more example of senior management being above the law.

This experience made me feel like a criminal, and although I kept in touch with many of my colleagues, from then on I couldn't face going to the hospital again.

A book turned up in the post around this time. It was *Your Right to Know* by Heather Brooke. An inscription in the front cover read: "To Davey. You are a legend. Thanks for all your ongoing support, bro'. David Cremonesini." Heather describes her book as a citizen's guide to the Freedom of Information Act. It was more than that to me: it was a book that baptized my curiosity; I already knew information had been withheld from me; here was one way of getting it.

When I read the Trust's disciplinary policy, it was clear the Medical Director had breached it at every point. That was where I started.

On a website run for excluded doctors I came across NCAS (the National Clinical Assessment Service) and read its online handbook. Hospital trusts must consult with NCAS before excluding consultant staff. I emailed NCAS an account of what had happened to me. This led to a phone conversation, with an adviser who was a consultant psychiatrist. That was not particularly useful. I then sent in subject access requests to NCAS under the Data Protection Act. I was rewarded with a ream of documents, all relating to my exclusion. Best of all were the records of phone conversations between Mike Brown and the NCAS adviser. These told an astonishing story: an account of my recent history at the Trust that anyone who knew me would have recognized as a shameful fabrication.

Mike Brown, the documents recorded, thought my exclusion necessary because serious allegations had been made against me, and he believed I might interfere with the investigation. At a later date, he had requested an extension of my exclusion on the grounds that I was a "danger to staff and patients". I knew, and so would any of my colleagues, that this was an outright lie. In a Trust document also obtained later by DPA, the Head of HR admitted that the real reason for the extension was that the Trust needed more time to investigate my case because of administrative delays. Normally an investigation should be completed in two weeks, but after two weeks the Trust had not even appointed investigators. This was the level of sheer dishonesty that I was to become used to. But again, senior management are above the law in these matters.

The transcript also contained Mike Brown's account of my misbehaviour: he referred to my "persistently obstructive behaviour" and to managers having found me "unmanageable". He alleged that I had written a large number of unpleasant and potentially defamatory letters to Karen Palmer, Head Nurse, and had upset most of the nursing staff. He claimed that I exhibited signs of major psychiatric illness and that one colleague believed I was hypomanic. (The Medical Director preferred "mood swings", apparently meaning bipolar disease.) And, in a clear reference to the Kyle Keen case, he suggested that I had leaked confidential information to the press.

I learned all this as a result of reading Heather Brooke's book. Thanks, Babe.

There was no truth in any of these allegations. The Divisional Director had sought my help and advice on practically every important matter in the department up to the day of my exclusion. I had emails from him thanking me for my co-operation. I had written only one email (no letters) to Karen Palmer in the ten months since I returned to work. I was on excellent terms with the whole nursing establishment. The Occupational Physician later wrote to Mike Brown reporting that even after months of exclusion and illness my mental health was good. I am blessed with a sunny disposition and my mood is constant, as Mike Brown well knew. Never, until after I began to investigate the cover-up of Kyle Keen's death in 2012, did I contact the press about him. That would have been unprofessional and unethical.

Performance management, according to disciplinary policy, is a continuous process. Problems must be drawn to the employee's attention and remedied. If the remedy is ineffective, there is a process leading from verbal to written warnings and disciplinary procedures. None of the things Mike Brown reported to NCAS had ever been raised with me beforehand. Nor were they afterwards. Ever. He obviously believed his phone conversations with NCAS were private. I don't suppose he thought that under UK access-to-information law I would find out the porkies he had been telling about me. When I wrote to him asking for an explanation he ignored me. He has never acknowledged his dishonesty or apologized.

After I recovered from the initial shock of exclusion I tried to adopt a routine. I spent time gardening, talking to Janet and going for long walks. I found it hard to settle. I'd always loved reading but had no inclination to read anything other than material relevant to my case. I tried running but easily became short of breath. The centre would not hold. Six weeks into my exclusion we took a week's holiday – I had booked the time off months earlier. On Saturday we drove to Padstow in Cornwall to do some coastal walking. I was under the weather when we left and wheezy. We enjoyed two lovely days walking up the Camel estuary and around Rock and Port Isaac.

On the third night, at 2am I woke in agony. A severe blistering eczema had erupted over much of my body; my hands had swollen to twice their normal size; the only way I could get any relief was by putting them into the deep freeze compartment of the fridge. I had to repeat this through the night. Next day I rang a dermatologist friend in Walsall and booked an urgent appointment in his clinic. I had a long history of allergies, including hay fever and asthma, and had a permanent patch of eczema that was always exacerbated by stress. It had been active since my exclusion but I had ignored it. We drove home abandoning our holiday.

Dr Bazza, my dermatologist, was extremely helpful and prescribed high-dose oral steroids, which I needed for many weeks as each time I stopped them the eczema relapsed. I valued Bazza's kindness as much as his methodical way of dealing with my illness; he was a Muslim and I a Christian but there was a genuine spiritual connection between us that made an important contribution to my care.

When we arrived home I found a voicemail from Mike Brown: "I've decided to end your exclusion. Ring my PA and fix a time to come in for a back-to-work interview." Instead I sent in the sick note Dr Bazza had written out for me. Two weeks later I received a letter confirming that my exclusion had ended. That was the level of inefficiency I usually experienced at Mike's hands. It was difficult to decide whether his behaviour was accidental or deliberate – probably a bit of both. The Trust disciplinary policy required Mike Brown at the time of my exclusion to arrange an appointment with the occupational health consultant in case I had underlying medical problems. This was one of his duties of care to me. As in every other area, there was no care and I received no appointment. After I had seen Bazza, I self-referred to the occupational health consultant. I'd met Dr Cathcart before, following my bike accident and after my illness the previous year. He was pleasant and plain-speaking. When I entered his clinic he was anxious to get something off his chest:

"David, I can only apologize for the psychiatric appointment you were sent. Mr Brown contacted me after suspending you. He told me that you had personally requested a psychiatric appraisal. I was shocked when I got your letter saying you hadn't made that request. I'm so sorry." He wanted to hear the whole story and told me he was well acquainted with the consequences faced by clinicians raising concerns about patient care.

Some weeks later I developed severe arthritis in my shoulders, elbows and wrists. I rang my rheumatologist friend, Trevor Constable, at Manor Hospital for help. "I'm in clinic this afternoon, David. I'll put you on the end of the list so I can spend some time on you. Come at 7:30." I arrived on time but he was caught up with a patient. At 8pm, when I went into his room, he looked old and drawn. There is an urban myth that consultants have an easy life and get well paid for it. Maybe some do but many definitely do not. He dealt with my problems in the same methodical, kindly, way that Bazza had. He took the bloods himself and aspirated one of my joints. I winced but he told me not to be a baby. "Get this prescription tomorrow but here are a few to get started," he said considerately, pushing a blister pack into my hand. I was grateful that I wouldn't have to wait until the morning to get relief.

I stood up to leave. "Let's go and get a pint," he suggested. "Fine by me." He wanted to drive me there for some reason, so we walked to his large Mercedes in the car park. He sat silently at the wheel, then, quite gently, as a theatrical gesture, banged his head against the steering wheel three times. Trevor was a lovely colleague given to swearing. He did it in such an inoffensive and hilarious way that so far as I know it never offended anyone. But now he let rip with a string of forceful expletives that were completely out of character.

"What's up, Trev?" I asked.

"Mike Brown called me to his office today about a trivial complaint."

"I think I know what's coming."

"Some trivial complaint from a patient."

"So?"

"He told me he would have to suspend me while it's investigated."

"What did you say?"

"I told him he'd have my resignation tomorrow."

We went and had a drink together and talked of happier times. His resignation went in the next day, and when I rang him to ask if it had been accepted he told me the Trust didn't even want him to work his notice. So, off to Spain for a holiday he went. This is the way an illustrious career can end at a place like Walsall Manor Hospital.

In July, exactly eleven weeks after my exclusion, I was called to meet Naj Rashid, an A&E consultant, and Sandra Berns, an HR officer, who were investigating Karen Palmer's allegations against me. I was worn out with my illness and had put weight on with the steroids and lack of exercise. Ian was his usual avuncular self and gave me confidence to face the investigators – and, even more important, to stay calm.

My life over the last three months had exploded the myth of exclusion as a neutral act. In my case it was a declaration of war. I'd been ripped from the work I loved. I was not allowed to enter hospital premises without permission and even when I had permission in writing I was harassed by senior managers. I was referred against national policy for a psychiatric assessment. The stress had caused real physical illness. The distress it caused my family cannot be told. And it was all done without reason. The following year, a Royal College panel would conclude that even if all the allegations had been true they would not have warranted exclusion.

The investigators asked me a number of specific questions, which I answered. I had still at this point not seen a list of the allegations Karen Palmer had made. Both investigators looked and sounded indifferent. After a while, Naj Rashid asked Ian and Sandra Berns to step outside. "Its bollocks, David," he said as soon as they'd gone, "There's nothing in it. No case to answer." He told me that he didn't want to be there all afternoon and suggested that I give short answers to any remaining questions. "Just yes or no or I deny that. That's all we need." He brought Ian and Sandra back and we were able to finish quickly and leave. Afterwards Ian told me that Sandra Berns had said the same thing to him. She too did not want to waste her time any further.

It took ten more weeks for the Medical Director to meet me and officially confirm what I had already been told, that I had no case to answer. The summer should have been a rest and a relief but it was not. My own health continued to be poor, though I put on a brave face and even managed to stagger through a couple of half marathons. One of our grandchildren was critically ill and thought unlikely to recover. My dad had a hip replacement after walking round and driving with a fractured neck of femur for six weeks. I was distracted temporarily from the injustice of my exclusion by family concerns. It was my nature to remain optimistic that all could still be resolved.

The summer drew to an end. I had a couple more visits with Dr Cathcart. His advice was to return when the Trust had sorted things out. Though I was anxious to get back after so long an absence I took his advice.

21

No Case to Answer

The things people say of a man do not alter a man. He is what he is.
Oscar Wilde: *The Soul of Man*

On Friday 25th September 2009, five months after my exclusion, Ian Mckivett and I met Mike Brown and Sue Wakeman to hear the outcome of the investigation of Karen Palmer's allegations against me. We had known from June of course that there was no case to answer; the investigators had told both of us as much when we met them. Ian had warned me that in his experience the Trust would take advantage of any criticism of me heard in the investigation that could be used as leverage in future: "They're not going to let you walk away scot-free, David." And there was I thinking it was all over!

We sat in a small office I hadn't been in before. Irene Lemm, the HR secretary, was present to take notes. It was a complex discussion and would have been almost impossible to précis. I could see she was struggling to take minutes. I'd been acquainted with her for years and had always found her pleasant and unusually helpful. She was a diligent soul and the difficulty she had keeping up was written on her brow. I felt for her. It took me six weeks to obtain the minutes of this meeting and then it was only after three requests, which cannot have been anything to do with her efficiency. Timely availability of minutes enables corrections to be made. By the time I got these it was too late for that. They omitted important parts of the discussion and mangled some of the rest.

The room was narrow and not designed for meetings. Mike

Brown sat facing Sue Wakeman. I was looking directly into his right ear. He made no eye contact throughout the meeting. He began with a rambling speech of no relevance; he wasn't nervous, this was just his style. Sue Wakeman called the meeting to order. The purpose of the meeting was to feed back on the investigation and "complete the process", she told us in pristine HR speak.

Mike Brown knew I had been away from work for months; he had been sent details of my illnesses by the occupational physician. He knew that there had been no truth in the allegations made by Karen Palmer and that my exclusion was unnecessary. I had expected at least an expression of regret for these things, but there was none. I had once been on friendly terms with him but he now withdrew — silence, and space, and strangers separated us.

Ian and I began to point out the irregularities in the procedure Mike Brown had adopted in excluding me. I quoted the outrageous suggestions he had made to NCAS: that I was "obstructive" ... "unmanageable" ... that I had defamed Karen Palmer ... that I was possibly suffering from psychotic illness ... that I had leaked information on Kyle Keen to the press. These allegations were all more serious than those made by Karen Palmer. Mike refused to comment. "This is not what this meeting is about."

We then came to the investigators' five recommendations. One, intended to sharpen up communication within the department, was uncontroversial. Three concerning my alleged communication difficulties resulted from the investigators' failure to understand the problems with the department's managers. We were managed by people who, in my opinion, were not just singularly unqualified but were bullies as well, (and this was later supported by the Royal College review). Every time I addressed one of my concerns with the divisional managers I was put off. They were unable to take a senior paediatrician seriously. I was instructed by the investigators to use the standard line management for raising concerns but that simply did not work. Against all the evidence, Sue James would later claim, to the Trust Board at tribunal and in the press, that these toxic relationships were of my making.

The investigators recommended that I see a personal profiler. Ian asked what evidence there was that I needed this kind of help. In fact all the paediatric consultants in our department had had two days of profiling done by Westminster Associates Ltd less than a year earlier, and quite coincidentally I had my profile with me. The picture this painted of me was entirely different from the image the Trust tried to impose on me:

> David deals imaginatively with social relationships. He is a "networking" expert. He is a particularly good communicator and uses his gift of verbal expression often and effectively. A creative thinker, David is generally warm, enthusiastic and confidant of his own abilities. He makes stimulating company with his witty and interesting conversational style. He focuses his attention outwards and is skilled in understanding the needs and motivations of others. He attracts many friends and acquaintances.

There was universal agreement that this expensive profiling exercise had achieved nothing. The results were filed and never referred to by the Trust again. Taxpayers' money was wasted because senior managers were poor at sitting people down and having a sensible conversation. An interesting corollary to this was that in later correspondence with the independent review of paediatrics Sue Wakeman claimed that at this meeting I had refused the help of a profiler. More spin casting me as one of the awkward squad.

The fifth recommendation (later to become famous as recommendation 6.5) was a complete shock: "Dr Drew should accept that his own wider personal views and religious beliefs should be kept to himself and should not be imposed on others."

"What's this?" asked Ian. "This is the first we're hearing about religion. It wasn't in the allegations. We weren't asked about it at the investigators' meeting. Where has this come from?"

He told Mike Brown there was no evidence to base this recommendation on, and if there was we needed to see it. I asked where on earth it had come from. We were working in a multinational, multi-religious department where such behaviour would be catastrophic to staff relationships. Mike Brown, staring into the middle distance, said that as he didn't do the investigation he didn't know. I asked him to find out. He said he would. As I had come to expect, he showed no interest in doing that and never did.

I then raised the issue of whistleblowing. I said quite clearly that I would continue to blow the whistle when I saw patients at risk – as with the child protection failures in the Kyle Keen case and the recurring problem of hypothermia patients. I gave notice that I intended to report the Trust to Social Services and the Local Safeguarding Children's Board if there was a serious recurrence of the heating failure over the coming winter. I said I had been in post for 18 years and Clinical Director for seven. I was the best-placed person to critique the current situation in the department. I was surrounded by a management team with no experience in paediatrics who would not listen to senior clinicians. This was an opinion that was fully supported by the Royal College panel only six months later.

Mike Brown then rather surprised me by recording that my motive was clearly "deep concern for the department". He went on, "It's essential that we develop a framework to allow Dr Drew to voice his concerns without causing problems." He had fallen for the classical stereotype of the whistleblower: a whistleblower is a person who causes problems. A whistleblower is a problem. There was no understanding that a whistleblower is responding to problems that everyone else is ignoring. What I wanted to hear was "We want to ensure that when our most senior paediatrician says something is wrong we listen and fix it." There was little understanding of the importance of this kind of professional feedback. In management circles it generated undisguised hostility.

Finally we came to the important subject of relationships: my communication style was fundamentally unacceptable. But no one could or would tell me what was wrong with it. Communication skills had been acknowledged as a major strength throughout my career. The simple fact was that I was the best communicator in the department and one of the best in the hospital. What was wrong with my communication was not its style but its content. When I saw a consultant who appeared to have difficulties doing his job properly I said so. When I saw a child die as a direct consequence of this I said so. When I saw the nursing establishment being decimated and doctors being made redundant purely to cut costs I said so. When I saw the safety of vulnerable sick children being put at risk on freezing winter nights I said so. When no one would listen or respond I turned up the volume. This was what the Trust in its upper reaches did not like about my communication style. They did not like whistleblowers.

Some months later, the Trust compiled a 16-page document largely to discredit me with a Royal College panel. I was not allowed to see it. It was not intended that I should see it. That I did so was once again down to Heather Brooke's guidance on information access law. There is a delightful complaint in this document about me: "He disregards hierarchies. He goes to a higher and higher authority until he gets the answer he wants." I thought that was a pretty good description of a whistleblowing consultant when his patients are at risk and he is being ignored. Senior management was too far removed from the reality of clinical practice to appreciate this.

My communication was poor and I had relational difficulties I was told repeatedly. I did not recognize this description and nor would any of my colleagues. Nowhere were my personality difficulties more in evidence, it seemed, than in my relationship with Karen Palmer. I had upset her grievously, according to her complaint, by casting doubts on her ability to manage the nurses in the paediatric department. The Trust was later instructed by the Royal College panel to remove Karen from her post for the very reasons I had specified. But at this point I was going to have to work with her for the foreseeable future. So, Mike Brown promised to meet with the Divisional Director and formulate a plan for repairing the working relationship between Karen and me. I asked Irene specifically to minute that and thanked Mike. —"Blessed are the peacemakers for theirs is the kingdom of heaven."

We left. I felt slightly better but not optimistic. Mike Brown had promised to find out how I had been imposing my religious opinions on others, how I could report my concerns in a protected environment and how I could be reconciled to Karen Palmer. In fact he failed to take any action on any of these issues, which again was entirely consistent with my past experience of him as Medical Director.

It was lunchtime. I went straight home to Janet but found it hard to give a coherent account of what had happened. We had a quiet day discussing our various family troubles and went to bed early. The next day we went for a long hike along the upper Dove in our beloved Derbyshire. The ancient coral reefs at Chrome Hill and Parkhouse Hill were clearly visible at the northern extremity from miles away; I had seen these countless times and they had never failed to thrill me. But that day I sensed the quagmire at Manor Hospital sucking me in and I was left unmoved.

It is not now as it hath been before,
Turn whereso'er I may, by night or day,
The things which I have seen
I now can see no more.

There had passed away a glory from the earth. I should have been reassured by a meeting that affirmed I had no case to answer. Instead I was troubled and went home to prepare for Monday morning and my return to work. —*Dear Diary: My heart misgives.*

22

The Prodigal's Return

*To move into the lead means an act requiring fierceness and
confidence. But fear must play some part. No relaxation is possible,
and all discretion is thrown into the wind.*

Roger Bannister – he ran the first sub-four-minute mile.

(People forget these things.)

By Monday (28th September 2009) my mood had shifted. I drove to
the hospital early and was the first in the office. I closed the door
and sat wondering how things were going to work out. Then I
prayed the Richard Harris prayer from *Cromwell* (the movie). "Lord,
today I am a busy man. If I forget thee, forgetest not thou me." And
so, to work. My secretary had managed my mail while I'd been away
and almost everything relating to patient care had been dealt with
by my generous colleagues. The room was dusty, and for some
reason the windows had been nailed up while I had been away.
Seriously, they had been nailed up. Not screwed, *nailed*. To stop me
climbing in at night, perhaps?

The secretaries were the first in. Each one gave me a big hug. I
asked if I had any clinics or rounds planned but no one had been
told I was coming back. At about nine I rang the Divisional
Director's personal assistant. I asked what time my back-to-work
interview was scheduled for. She didn't know but offered to ring
Rob and get back to me, which she did ten minutes later. "He says
he can't fit you in today. Is 11am tomorrow OK?" It was fine by me.
I did some paperwork and then went to visit the new consultants.
They shared one large office and made me coffee from an

expensive-looking espresso machine. A happy enthusiasm filled the room as we chatted about paediatrics in Walsall. Their obvious level of engagement assured me of the service's future. I went home in the early afternoon. I had answered a couple of letters, disposed of the spam, chatted to colleagues and drunk coffee. That had cost the taxpayer £400 – small beer compared to the £50,000 the Trust had paid me in the last five months for doing nothing. All, as we would later be officially informed, for no good reason. And no one would ever be held accountable for such waste.

I left home late the next morning, arriving just in time for my appointment with Rob Hodgkiss, our Divisional Director. As Clinical Director I had frequently held back-to-work interviews, and even if they were done informally I believed them to be important. I expected as a senior clinician absent for five months something quite structured. What it amounted to was little more than "Let me know if there are any problems." I expressed my main concern. How could such an obstructive, unmanageable, disruptive doctor, who was possibly mentally ill, be allowed back into the workplace? Rob claimed to know nothing about any of this.

"Forget all that and let's get back to working together," he told me. That was exactly what I wanted, and in the face of the widespread denial of why I had been excluded I saw no alternative. Rob explained that we were only months away from the great move to the new unit in the PFI hospital. He was full of ideas and some of them were very good. He'd visited the Evalina Hospital in London and wanted to replicate their life-size helter-skelter in our own children's unit. In his opinion I was best placed to act as clinical lead for the move. His enthusiasm was infectious and I did catch a dose of it – but not enough to take on the role. I politely declined the offer. My health was not fully recovered and, whether anyone believed it or not, my self-confidence was badly shaken.

Within a week I was working normally. Clinics, ward rounds, on-call duties, and everything else that makes up a jobbing paediatrician's daily life, ran smoothly for me from day one. I was refreshed by the work, particularly by clinical problem-solving and the contact with children and parents. I realized also how much I had missed my colleagues. Sue James seemed to relish describing us as a dysfunctional group; this suited her as it took the spotlight off the executives' responsibility for our troubles. The truth was she had little or no direct knowledge of the consultants. As a group of professionals we had been quite happy and worked well together 95 per cent of the time – better than many departments I had worked in.

But the storm clouds were gathering; morale was low. Dr Sinha had replaced Jon Pepper as Clinical Director but Jon continued as Associate Medical Director with responsibility for our paediatrics. This meant effectively no change in leadership. There were still problems with patients being crammed into a ward that was not fit for purpose. The cuts had resulted in nurses being overworked in understaffed wards. As one nurse told me, "There's no time for personal development, Dr Drew. There's no time for a break even. It's work, work, work." But the worst problem was managerial bullying. Bullying is a difficult subject. There are policies about it. There is no law against it. Bullying can be highly subjective but it can be overt and objective. It saps everyone's energy. Managers, even if they are not the perpetrators, are loath to deal with it decisively. Absence due to sickness escalates; productivity suffers; in a hospital, that inevitably means patients suffer. In my experience it becomes increasingly difficult for staff to run a safe service where there are high levels of bullying.

Realistically I knew that the Trust would probably try to get rid of me one way or another. One consultant had rung me a few weeks into my exclusion to ask me to write him a reference for a job application. "I'm not sticking around in a place where they can treat someone like they've treated you, David." On my return he was getting ready to leave for his new post. I have kept in touch with him and he now has a happy and productive life elsewhere. He still waxes lyrical about the bravery and professionalism of the paediatric nurses in 2008/9. We all knew how they suffered. Three other consultants spoke openly about leaving: one, after long service, was considering going to Saudi Arabia; two, only recently appointed, told me they were thinking about leaving and were soon asking for a reference before moving to new jobs in 2010. Two years later, at the employment tribunal, Sue James under cross-examination said that she had to get rid of me "to save the department". She would never admit – even to herself, I guess – how much damage she did to the department by pursuing me and condoning the bullying culture. This contributed to the loss of four excellent consultants in one year.

In October Janet arranged to go to Kent to help out with some of our grandchildren. I intended to run the Snowdon Marathon that weekend, so she went alone. I drove to Wales after work on Friday. It was a glorious afternoon, and as I approached Betws-y-Coed the hills were on fire. I'd booked in at a small hotel and taken a huge tub of pasta for dinner. I went to bed but, unusually for me, could not sleep. I was not worried about the run, which I had done several times before. I found myself ruminating on everything that was wrong in the department. The details assembled themselves. I was resentful that good hard-working doctors and nurses were having to work in an environment that distracted them from their real business of caring for sick children. And also that, Red-Queen-like, they had to stressfully run faster and faster to maintain the same level of care.

I arrived early next morning at the assembly point in Llanberis. The Snowdon Marathon is unusual in that the whole field has to be bussed some distance up the pass to the start line. We were queuing for the buses when the heavens opened. Within minutes everyone was drenched. Even worse, the buses were delayed by an "administrative error". I was wet, cold and about to quit when, after

40 minutes, the buses arrived. I ran with a heavy heart; I ran with a burden. I always enjoyed running, even when it was a struggle, but I found it hard to finish. I picked up my goody bag, got into my car and drove home without stopping.

When I arrived home I was so stiff I could hardly get out of the car. I drank two cups of black coffee, took three paracetamol and ran a scalding hot bath. You will not find this in any running journal but it prepared me for my intended mission. I climbed into the bath with a phone (in case Janet called) and a dictating machine with six tapes. For the next two hours I poured my complaint onto the tapes: "Dear Sue…". I am not an especially intelligent person but I have, or rather *had* – the gift is fading, an uncanny ability to remember ad verbatim at length. I dictated the whole letter, quoting chapter and verse throughout. The angst flowed out of me. I experienced a palpable relief. I got out of the bath, dried off, cleaned my teeth and went to bed. I slept like a baby and woke feeling so fresh I wondered if I had dreamt the previous day.

23

"Dear Sue"

There is no greater agony than bearing an untold story inside you.

Maya Angelou

On Monday morning I felt transparently well. DOMS – Delayed Onset Muscle Soreness – is at its peak on day two after a long run. I normally suffer to some extent, increasingly as I have got older. On this day I was symptom-free. I was so relaxed that I lay in bed until 8am and by the time I arrived at work everyone was hard at it. "I dictated a letter over the weekend. Can you type it up please, Sue?" I asked my secretary. I casually dropped the six tapes on her desk, labelled and in order. We had our own little language that depended mainly on facial expression. The look on her face said, "You're joking, Dr Drew." She was a prodigious worker though and by late morning emailed me the whole document. I was disappointed with myself: I'd got a number of dates and quotations wrong and missed one issue completely. I did the corrections myself and then printed off ten copies and signed them.

The letter detailed my grievance against the Medical Director and was a comprehensive disclosure of my concerns about the department's mismanagement; it was addressed to Sue James. I sent copies to the Trust Chair and one of the non-executive directors. It also went to the Chief Executive at the Primary Care Trust and the Director of Public Health, Sam Ramaiah. I believed him to be a fair man who would want to help. He had recently brought a small team from the PCT to inspect the department. (I had conveniently been excluded from this.) And I sent a copy to the Director of Children's Services at Walsall Metropolitan Council.

Only a month earlier I had been told that my communication style was unacceptable and that lines of communication within the department should be agreed. Since in that time I had heard nothing from Mike Brown, the Medical Director, about his offer to facilitate this, and had good reason to suspect that I never would, I felt free, obliged even, to write directly to Sue James and copy in the parties who had a responsibility to the department. I also sent a copy to Bruce George, the Labour MP for Walsall South, who I'd been writing to for some time. He was very helpful but, I sensed, tired – he stepped down at the next election, in 2010. Finally I sent a note to all my consultant colleagues advising them the letter was with Sue and could be obtained on request. I knew some were nervous and I did not want to involve them against their will.

I had no response from anyone other than Sue James and Bruce George.

The story that was bursting to get out of me was that a service of vital importance to the health of Walsall families was being jeopardized by managers who did not know what they were doing. Attempts to bring about cost-cutting service change by force and bullying were resulting in a disengaged, demoralized workforce and were putting patients at risk. Senior management was living in a bubble and relied entirely on middle management for information.

On more than one occasion I sent articles written by the well-known management guru Gerry Robinson to Sue James.

I understand how this culture of multiple managers develops. I think Chief Executives get to a point where it is easier to manage other managers than it is to deal with medical and nursing staff, especially consultants, who can be resistant to being told what to do by those with no medical background. Instead, Chief Executives surround themselves with a safe set of managers who tell them what they want to hear, and perhaps they look to hire more – for business development or finance or new initiatives. Increasingly, the man or woman at the top of the tree is distanced from the reality of leading doctors, nurses and other staff, and delivering care to patients.

He expressed the problem perfectly. This was exactly what Sue James and her executive officers had achieved.

My letter was long and went into great detail; nothing was superfluous. I received criticism later in my disciplinary hearing and at the employment tribunal for writing at such length: I stand by what I wrote. I quoted from a recent letter Sue James had written to me.

I am saddened by your lack of willingness to share the optimism that is now pervading what has been a very challenged department in the past and look forward to a time when you too are able to share the promise that the future holds for Walsall children at Manor Hospital.

I responded,

I am equally saddened by this statement, which shows you are completely out of touch with the true state of affairs in the department. You do not have sufficient direct personal contact with the department to have formed an accurate first hand opinion. You rarely if ever speak to the consultants but have depended on your middle managers to build up this illusory picture.

A year or so later, at my disciplinary hearing, I was castigated by the Trust lawyer for having dared to speak to the "most important person in this organization" in this way. The lawyers are a problem. They do not realize that patient safety requires flat hierarchies. Situations involving patient risk require plain speech. Politeness, but plain speech. Mrs James did not like plain speech.

I was mainly concerned to provide her with a detailed account of how bad things were in the department and how much of this related to the managers she had put in place.

Her managers were actively damaging the Trust's ability to carry out its statutory obligation to protect children. The PCT designated officer and I had both informed her of this but we were ignored. For four years the Trust had put off financing the safeguarding nurse post that we all knew was essential. It took more than two years from the death of Kyle Keen to create this post. It was recognized that this would probably have saved Kyle if it had it been done earlier. The first appointment to this post was largely determined by a need to save face on nurse redundancy numbers. The second nurse appointed was ideally suited to the role, but she was incessantly bullied by managers and eventually, after being sworn at by the Divisional Director, resigned.

I reminded Sue James that when this nurse had come to her for an exit interview she had told her "not to take the swearing to heart. This is the way people behave under stress." I expressed concern at how Sue had tried to redefine the reason for the nurse's resignation: "To then suggest that you understood how difficult safeguarding work was, implying the nurse was not up to the job, is inexcusable. You also commented on how difficult it must have been working with consultants 'who do not work together', implying this may have contributed to her decision to resign." Sue James absolved herself and her profane, bullying managers of responsibility and instead blamed the nurse herself and the paediatric consultants. I have found this to be a typical management strategy throughout my difficult years. "I am very disappointed in you, David..." was standard. Managers make underlings feel bad about themselves and shift the blame for their own failings: it is a specific technique. I was alive to it and never let it come near me. And I tried to defend others from it.

Sue James was rarely seen on the wards but in the autumn she had conducted a so-called 'Board to Ward' visit with a non-executive director. At this point she claimed all that I had been reporting to her for the last year as her own discovery. She ordered an independent nursing review. I distrust such processes. This one was particularly poorly done: morale was low amongst the nursing staff; bullying was rife. I reported a conversation I had had with a good and previously bubbly nurse. When I asked how she was she replied, "You don't want to know, Dr Drew." When I told her I did want to know she continued, "I only come here now to pay my mortgage. I used to love my work but now I do it for the money. You can't say anything. It's not safe." I made it clear that the level of demoralization and staff disengagement was a result of mismanagement.

I went on to give Sue James an account of the resignation of an excellent consultant who was promptly signed up by another Trust. Sue James had been quick to tell us "One of the key members of staff who has resigned is Dr Satish, who has made it clear to me that he has no problem with managers." But Dr Satish had written widely to say that it most certainly *was* the managers who were responsible for his departure: "Dear Sue, I agree with David Drew that my resignation is a silent protest against the events that have happened in our department. Indeed, I had suggested at the end of our meeting that you should find out from the new consultants about their satisfaction or the lack of it straight from themselves." Sue was living in her own hermetically sealed world. She was dangerously blind to what was happening on the ground.

We had a delightful doctor working in the department, Dr Mittal. He was unable to do the rigorous out-of-hours calls for health reasons, but was hard-working and a very safe pair of hands in normal working time. Management decided to make him redundant. This was in a department that on a daily basis had difficulty finding enough doctors at his level. His redundancy was planned against the advice of the consultants and purely to cut costs. Information we obtained from the BMA was that he was the only paediatrician being made redundant in the country. The "marvellous thing" was, the Divisional Director explained, that there was a ring-fenced pot of redundancy money at the PCT, so the savings would be felt "the day we are rid of him". Dr Mittal was needed and he would find it difficult to find a similar job elsewhere. I described the attempt to remove him as being down to a heartless, aggressive management style. Sue James made no response but allowed the redundancy to proceed. She was heavily backed by the head of HR on this. Here was an unequal clinician–management balance of power: they were going to do what they wanted; that was the end of it. Dr Barathan was hustled down the redundancy route and the managers were able to claim his salary as immediate cost savings. His years of loyal service were invisible to the cost-cutters.

Our long-serving and long-suffering Matron, Simon Langford, had been badly bullied by managers, and rather than carry on had taken a voluntary redundancy. On two occasions I heard the Divisional Director, who had only recently arrived in the hospital, refer to him as "that idle bastard Simon". Apart from this being totally unprofessional, it was untrue. Perhaps Sue James thought this was also behaviour that could be excused on the grounds of work-related stress.

Four new consultants had been appointed a year earlier. I had insisted that job plans, with scheduled ward and clinic duties and out-of-hours rotas, be ready for their arrival in February. Eight months after their start date, job plans had still not been agreed. This was entirely due to managerial intransigence: the Divisional Director was trying to insist on consultants agreeing to plans that were in breach of the Consultant Contract (2003). The consultants, including me, signed a letter asking the BMA to negotiate on our behalf. The Divisional Director had been given a deadline to meet and settle with the consultants before the BMA was asked in and I was suspended the day before that meeting: an uncanny coincidence. Other consultants said of the meeting afterwards: "David, we are ruled by gangsters. The level of aggression at the meeting was unbelievable. They did nothing but shout at us. David, if you had been there they wouldn't have spoken to us like that." Sue James subsequently cited the consultants' failure to agree job plans as evidence of their own dysfunctionality.

My experiences over the previous 18 months at the hands of the Medical Director were what constituted my grievance against him, and was the subject of the second half of the letter. There was nothing I claimed in the grievance that I did not have documentation to prove.

I knew this letter in its entirety constituted a protected disclosure and finished accordingly: "If, having digested the contents of this letter, I do not receive written assurance from the Chairman of the Board that my concerns will be dealt with as seriously as they deserve I will consider my responsibility to the Trust under its own Whistleblowing policy fully discharged." That was my bottom line. The whistleblowing policy was a bit of a joke really. I had written to the Head of HR asking that one of her officers brief me on this and got no answer. I had tried to find the policy on the Trust's admittedly chaotic intranet and failed. I had rung the department – to be told it was there somewhere. I was not even sure the Trust had a policy. But I used the BMA policy, which must have approximated. Once a staff member refers to their raising concerns as "whistleblowing" there should be a conversation to ensure that this is managed on both sides to ensure the policy is followed. I am sure that at that time neither Sue James nor her executive officers understood my report as *whistleblowing*. They only saw a troublemaker.

Sue James never again referred to the spirit of optimism that was pervading the department. From then on the references were to departmental dysfuntionality and the toxic environment I was creating by complaining about my colleagues: to repeatedly ask that a consultant colleague's competence be looked at was troublemaking; to aver that the department was being mismanaged by three aggressive individuals, without adequate qualifications if any, was troublemaking – troublemaking not whistleblowing.

My secretary delivered the letter as hard copy – I was painfully aware of how easily correspondence was lost by senior management. I spent the rest of the day with my little patients, who neither knew nor cared about any of these troubles. Later, David Cremonesini caught me as I was on my way home.

"What you doing, dude?"

"I just lit the blue touch paper and now I'm retiring."

"Night, dude."

24

I Appeal to Caesar

When the Lord sent me forth into the world he forbade me to put off my hat to any, high or low.

George Fox, founder of the Quakers

A few days later I received an invitation: "The Trust Chairman would be pleased to meet you with your BMA representative." On the first Friday morning in November Ian Mckivett and I sat in the management block waiting to meet the Chairman, Mr Ben Reid. I had no idea what to expect as we had never exchanged a single word in the time he had been with the Trust. "It's Fireworks Night," said Ian.

Mr Ben Reid OBE was, in his professional life, Chief Executive of the Midcounties Co-op; he had also, for some years now, been Chairman of the Board at Walsall Hospitals NHS Trust. This was the first time I had met him although I had seen him at a distance on odd occasions.

He invited us in, explaining that Sue James would be joining us shortly. Ian and I sat in comfortable chairs and he sat at a desk. I asked what we should call him. "Ben will be fine." I was wearing, as I often did, a badge with "RESPECT YOUR MUMS" printed on it.

"What's your badge for, David?"

"It's to encourage people to respect the mums we work with."

"Why? Don't you think they do that already?"

"Some do – some more than others. It's hard to respect people if you've got no idea what the world looks like through their eyes.

The badge is to stimulate people I work with to think about that. And to affirm the mums. I know the mums appreciate it: they tell me so. It makes a point."

"Is that why you're wearing it today?"

"I've just come from the ward, Mr Reid, that's all."

"Call me Ben."

He was totally pleasant but regarded me with a quizzical expression: what have we here? We were from different planets. Sue James walked in and sat in the corner. There had been all kinds of change in the NHS over the previous 30 years, accelerating under Tony Blair after 1997. Managerial posts had expanded by 78 per cent in the past ten years, while medical posts had increased by only 48 per cent in the same period. The wholesale transfer of organizational and management methods from the private sector, barely noticed by many of us healthcare workers, was now well underway. There was good and bad in that. Sue James and Ben Reid were icons of this new corporate ethos. Sartorially elegant and immaculately groomed, they seemed to me distant, and, while not hostile, somehow unreachable. To my mind there was a curious dissonance between them and our patients, some of whom came from the most socioeconomically deprived families in Britain. (But that was my own origins speaking as well.) I wondered if they spent much time with patients, and if they had any ability to identify with them. I didn't really wonder that at all in the Chief Executive's case: I had almost never seen her on the wards – except perhaps for a photo opportunity.

Sue James's predecessor was John Rostill. In his time, I would bump into him in different parts of the hospital at least weekly. He always wanted to know what was going on in paediatrics. He was not always able to help when we told him but he was on the ground and interested. The same went for past Trust chairs. Mavis Foden was a Black Country woman and proud of it, as was Barry Blower, another chair. He'd rescued the Saddlers, our local football club, from bankruptcy in the 80s. Sadly, he came to a sticky end, caught in a recorded sting making unfortunate comments about some of our nurses. This was shown on television and his comments were denounced as discriminatory. In my experience, what he said was absolutely wrong but completely out of character for him. It was a fatal error; he had to go. I wrote and thanked him for all the help he had given me.

The old guard was always around the hospital, chatting, picking up the local intelligence. They sat on appointments committees with us from time to time and were wise and good fun. The same went for middle management in those days. Ben and Sue had shown little interest in what was happening in the department until the trouble kicked off. I suppose they must have had the overall interest of the hospital at heart, but they were too far removed from the coalface to translate that into action.

Ben Reid started the meeting. He told us it would be digitally recorded and transcribed.

"The Trust recognizes your concerns but personally I find the issues in your letter overwhelming. There's too much colour. I want the core issues. This meeting is my serious attempt to get to the bottom of things."

I immediately detected a note of criticism. My letter to Sue James was in fact a carefully worded and detailed description of the current mismanagement of the paediatric department. If Ben had read it carefully he would have known exactly what the core issues were. Anyone who had read it would realize something was alarmingly wrong in the department. And if there was a little colour that would hardly be surprising.

"We may not do everything you want us to do," he said. "We may not do anything you want us to do, but I want you to understand at the end of this that we want to take you seriously." He recognized, he said, two main issues: there were the things that might be affecting the quality of the paediatric service that we were offering and there was the matter of getting me "settled".

That was fine but he apparently failed to recognize any connection between the two. It was precisely the myriad ways in which things were going wrong and the mistreatment I had experienced trying to address these that had caused me to be unsettled.

This was one of the occasions when I found Ian Mckivett's presence invaluable. He steered the meeting in the right direction and helped me to get the main personal issues off my chest. There were four: the psychiatric appointment sent after Mike Brown misled the occupational health consultant, the instruction by Naj Rashid that I stop imposing my religious beliefs on others, Mike Brown's failure to observe Trust policy in suspending me, and his failure to answer the majority of my letters.

"It's not possible for me to respond to the issues you've raised," Ben told me. "I haven't seen the documents. I haven't heard the other side of the story."

Our objective for this meeting was to secure an *unbiased* hearing of my grievance, and an investigation of the mismanagement of the department. Sue James knew perfectly well that a major element of my grievance was *her* implementation of the Trust's harassment and bullying policy, under which I had been excluded, and so it was disingenuous, I believed, for her to offer to hear my grievance herself. The bullying policy ("The Chief Executive will take responsibility for ensuring the Policy is correctly implemented and that the Trust takes effective action to tackle harassment/bullying in the workplace.") had been disregarded (as had the disciplinary policy and NCAS advice). For *Sue James* to hear my grievance constituted a conflict of interest: she was hardly likely to find against herself.

And, as Ian pointed out, it was a failure on Sue James's part that we were talking about. There had been no valid reason to suspend me in the first place. Nothing in the allegations could have been construed as misconduct. The investigators had recognized that.

They had shown no real interest, realizing that there was no case to answer at an early stage. Ian mused that one had to wonder if someone had an "agenda" in taking this action against me. We were fairly certain this was the case but were unable to prove it.

I then turned to the core issues affecting the department and its staff. I pointed out that Sue had entrusted running the department to three managers with no experience of paediatrics and a disinclination to listen to the front-line staff. I also raised the problem of endemic managerial bullying. I had given specific vivid examples of this in my letter. Ben assured me that those points were "noted". My heart sank when he used that word.

Ian pressed for an independent investigation of my concerns. Ben told us that he knew of no precedent for this and would like to go away and think about it.

Finally, because any investigation was going to look at my removal as Clinical Director, I gave Ben Reid an account of the problems with Dr Walia. These had been core issues for me for four years now and I knew other consultants in the department were in broad agreement with me. I described the case of Kyle Keen, who had become Child K, and Dr Walia's removal as clinical lead in the neonatal unit. I left Ben Reid in no doubt that there were serious questions about this doctor's competence that had not been addressed and may even have been covered up:

> I said (to the Medical Director) look, this is the guy who you know to have competence problems and you are not dealing with it properly. Now, I have never documented this because it is too sensitive but this was the person who sent a baby home to be murdered by his stepfather in which we were seriously criticized in the serious case review, and if you look very hard at that case and in my opinion, there is nobody who has any responsibility for that being done apart from the consultant (Dr Walia).

Ten days later Sue James wrote to confirm the main conclusion of the meeting:

> We agreed to an independent investigation of your grievance and, following discussions with the Registrar of the Royal College of Paediatrics, we have commissioned the College to carry out a Review in line with some terms of reference that I shared with you on 11 November, which are also attached to this letter.

"We have commissioned the College to carry out a Review..." At that point I relaxed, knowing that my own College with all its experience and gravitas would adjudicate my case and investigate the problems, particularly the mismanagement of the department and the child protection irregularities. Ben Reid continued to refer to this as the "Royal College Review" in emails. But it was not.

Following my dismissal a year later I approached the Registrar of the RCPCH about the Review. He informed me that the College took no responsibility for it. A certificate of indemnity had been drawn up between the College, Walsall Healthcare and Nadeem Moghal, the review panel chair, to protect the College from future loss. This certificate was subsequently used by Nadeem to refuse to co-operate with a College investigation of the review. None of this could have been known when the review was being commissioned. We assumed the College's Royal Charter guaranteed a certain level of integrity.

I told my colleagues about the Review and that it could only bring good to the department. It did indeed bring good but it was also to become the instrument the Trust used to dismiss me.

25

Bullies: Challenging the Culture

I was never a bully. I was a hard man.
Roger Daltrey of The Who

Years ago our youngest son came home with a badly broken nose. He'd come between a bully and his victim on the school bus and suffered the painful consequences. I was proud of him. He had been true to our family's zero tolerance of bullying. I have always challenged bullying myself, and more than once suffered physical injury in doing so. When it erupted in the paediatric department in 2008 I found myself on a collision course with the bullies and those who sheltered them. Bullying is a difficult problem to grapple with. Bullies often do not recognize themselves for what they are. And they never admit to it. There is no badge that I have seen anyone wearing that proclaims, "A bully and proud of it".

On 26th October 2009 I had written my comprehensive disclosure to Sue James. In it I asserted that over a period of about 18 months "a culture of institutionalized bullying" had developed in the paediatric department. I went on, "Although some of this may have escaped your attention I will present evidence that you have to some extent been aware of this and for reasons which are hard to understand have chosen to ignore it. I believe that in certain instances, which I will also refer to, your actions have compounded and even given sustenance to this culture." At this point, I still believed that evidence was the solution to the problems we were experiencing. I gave many examples of this culture. Here is one from the same letter:

Take for example one of our nursing staff, who the Divisional Director rang at home. This nurse's husband overheard the Divisional Director speaking to his wife as the phone was on loudspeaker. The Divisional Director's conversation was so aggressive and peppered with expletives ("effing and blinding", as it was reported to me) that her husband told her that he was going to the HR department the following day to report this manager. The nurse begged her husband not to go as it was likely to cause her more grief. I am afraid this is how institutionalized bullying works. The bullied come to tolerate that kind of behaviour. They try to keep their heads down. When they are bullied they fail to take any action because they believe that it can only produce more difficulties for themselves in their work environment.

Following the Fireworks Night meeting with Ben Reid and his agreement to an independent hearing of my grievance by the Royal College of Paediatrics, I experienced a surge of relief. I wrote to Bruce George, the Labour MP for Walsall South, who had agreed to meet me, and cancelled. I had total confidence that the College would send its team in and the impasse would be resolved.

But within days of that meeting there was an outcry from senior nurses in the department over bullying, particularly by the head nurse, Karen Palmer. I therefore arranged for the senior paediatric nurses, supported by the paediatric consultants, to meet Sue James and the Nursing Director. It was obvious that it might take six months for the College to do the Review and for its report to be implemented. That was too long for nurses who were in tears every day to wait. Sue James was clearly fed up with me and did not want me to attend. I withdrew in order to let the nurses speak for themselves. But they lacked the confidence to go to the meeting without me being there to support them. I informed Sue James that as a result I would be attending after all. "I regret that you have gone back on your word..." she emailed me. I was by this time immune to these barbs designed to make me feel bad about myself, regarding them as another manifestation of the bullying culture I had complained of.

We met on Friday 20th November. Sue James and Brigid Stacey, the Director of Nursing, were faced with the two paediatric matrons who had suffered the brunt of the bullying and six consultants. Sue James had made no provision for the meeting to be minuted. I asked for this to be done. She told us she did not want minutes taken. I took extensive notes anyway and circulated them as minutes afterwards. It is not safe to have such meetings with no agreed record.

The matrons were invited to describe their experiences of bullying. These included being shouted and sworn at and being subjected to physical threats. Some had received emails from their manager, the head nurse, Karen Palmer, in which they were told to toe the line or their jobs would be under threat; in the same emails they were told to be grateful that they had a job. They complained of being ignored by management (a recognized form of bullying) and even the consultants had experienced that. The head nurse had changed the ward nursing rotas without consulting them (the matrons) and had made derogatory comments about them at a meeting with human resources. They also raised the problem of how impending redundancies had been dealt with in the department by the head nurse in 2008. Individual nurses had not been told of their possible redundancy: the whole establishment had been informed by what was essentially a circular. Management had made no attempt to mitigate the consequent widespread anxiety. This was not an exhaustive list of allegations. Bullying is often trivialized. In this case the level of distress it was causing, either deliberately or by thoughtlessness, was near intolerable.

The Chief Executive and Nursing Director did not engage with us. Detachment was written on their faces, although from time to time they gave each other an anxious look when a particularly horrible experience was being described. They promised to meet with the managers concerned, and scheduled a meeting with us to report back. This was later postponed.

I missed the second rescheduled meeting through illness. Ironically, it was minuted by our safeguarding nurse, who had recently resigned after being sworn at by the Divisional Director. It was clear at this second meeting that no formal investigation had been carried out, nor would it be. No action was to be taken against the managers – they were not even to be given a warning. Sue James mused on why it should be that others who worked under the same managers were not experiencing the problems we were. Of course, why hadn't we thought of this? It must be *our* fault! This was the response that I encountered every time I tried to address a serious problem in the department. What was *I* doing wrong? What were *we* doing wrong? Senior and middle management were always in the clear and always tried to deflect the blame onto the clinicians. This culture of managerial cronyism was deeply frustrating to all of us on the front line. It was absolutely unassailable. The dice were loaded.

Sue James told the clinicians that the paediatric department was thought to be a "basket case" and that the PCT and Walsall Council had lost faith in it. She went to some lengths to create further insecurity by saying that a number of paediatric units would be closing. We'd heard this repeatedly and would hear it again. The nurses had already heard the head nurse telling them to toe the line or lose their jobs. The matrons were then warned by Sue James not to register formal grievances against management. She later told the employment tribunal that she had done this "in the interest of the paediatric service".

This was a disappointing outcome. The nursing staff in particular had put their necks on the line. The Trust had a harassment and bullying policy that clearly stated "The Chief

Executive will take lead responsibility for ensuring the Policy is correctly implemented and that the trust takes effective action to tackle harassment/bullying in the workplace." But here we were, eight of the most senior clinical staff in the department, with allegations of bullying so serious that we had gone to the Chief Executive herself, and she had blatantly disregarded the policy she was responsible for.

The policy also gives a specific instruction: "Where it is clear there is a pattern of unacceptable behaviour within a particular area, a full investigation will be carried out." What could possibly have been clearer than the allegations made by these clinicians? Again, the Chief Executive was able to breach the policy for which she had executive responsibility with impunity. There was no investigation.

In my experience, such policies are a waste of paper. Most employees are insufficiently familiar with them to make use of them. HR departments, on the other hand, are often well acquainted with them but disregard them. I imagine that it was unusual if not unique for Sue James to be on the sharp end of one of her policies in the way she had been at these two meetings. Later, under cross-examination at my employment tribunal, she demonstrated her flimsy knowledge of her own policies. But these policies contained some useful and often wise words. The Trust policy at that time had a section describing the damaging effects on individuals and organizations when bullying is tolerated: employees are unable to work effectively; team work is damaged; absenteeism due to stress increases; motivation and morale are damaged; staff lose confidence in the organization; staff leave. But here was Mrs James actively tolerating managerial bullying reported en masse.

We all knew the nurses were being badly bullied. At the employment tribunal four senior witnesses (three, consultants) named the head nurse, Karen Palmer, as a serial bully, giving graphic descriptions of the support they had had to give to nursing staff as a result. The hospital's head of HR, Sue Wakeman, was present throughout that testimony, but sat unmoved. Those within the managerial clique typically enjoy a startling level of immunity, so no one expected anything else.

At the second meeting, David Cremonesini, a new consultant and the husband of Louise, the safeguarding nurse, expressed incredulity at Sue James's refusal to take any action. His comments were disregarded and he resigned shortly afterwards. The Royal College of Paediatrics review, which reported four months later, instructed the Trust to remove Karen Palmer from line management in paediatrics. The report referred to her "aggressive managerial style". On the evidence presented to Sue James this should have been done when the bullying was first drawn to her attention. Her failure to act resulted in months of unnecessary suffering in a group of golden-hearted nurses who wanted nothing other than a protected environment in which they could do their work.

Following the meeting there was an atmosphere of doom and despair. Sir Ian Kennedy gave his last interview as Head of the Health Care Commission to the *Health Service Journal* in April that year. He chose to speak on bullying. It was, he said, the most important problem facing the NHS: surveys of NHS staff regularly showed a high level of bullying. Of course no trust ever admits to this problem. Few that I have heard of deal with it decisively, and in some it is a management tool. In our own department it was sapping energy and destroying morale, but the Chief Executive, whose responsibility it was to enforce the Trust's bullying policy, could not have cared less. That was the only conclusion we clinicians could reach.

I suppressed my inclination to react immediately, but after two weeks wrote to the Chairman and a non-executive director. I described the content of both meetings and the unsatisfactory outcome. I tried to get to the heart of the problem and wrote:

Sue James on both occasions has told these nurses effectively not to cause any more trouble. She advised them at the second meeting against any more complaints and against lodging a formal grievance, as this was likely to cause more problems and would hazard the unit's future and jeopardize their jobs. She also used me as an example of how unpleasant lodging a formal grievance could get. I am afraid that this approach is tantamount to intimidation of our senior nursing staff.

His reply was unhelpful. I complained about too many things, he wrote. That spoke eloquently of the organization and its culture, which had its fountainhead in its Chair and Chief Executive.

The postscript is that the two matrons who made those complaints were later replaced by an outside appointment. They were both excellent paediatric nurses, and with the right personal development plans would have risen through their profession. They both left hospital paediatric nursing soon afterwards. The limited opportunities provided and the stress of workplace bullying took their toll: two of the consultants present at the meetings would soon resign and leave. As for me, the bullet with my name on it was already being loaded into the breech.

26

A Clinical Incident on the Ward in the Night-Time

All clinicians must speak up for patients when they witness poor quality care. It is our overarching duty.

David Colin-Thomé:
Report on Mid Staffordshire NHS Foundation Trust:
Recommendation 5 on Clinical Leadership

I wrote my email to Ben Reid on Sue James's supine attitude to bullying in hope and sent it on 17th December. But hope was fading. It was Thursday night. I was on 24-hour call and the frantic winter season was in full swing. I was late home and late to bed, only to be woken by an urgent phone call in the early hours: a very premature baby was about to be delivered and the registrar asked me to come in to help. Five minutes later I was out of the door into a bitterly cold December night. My car was iced over. I cleared the windscreen as quickly as I could and set off. The road was deserted and thick with frost and snow; driving conditions were treacherous. Five minutes into the journey I heard a police siren and saw a flashing blue light in my rear mirror. I stopped and wound my window down. A policewoman leaned over, sniffing for alcohol.

"Are you all right, sir?

"I'm fine, why?"

"You're all over the road."

I apologized, explained my mission and asked not to be delayed any more than necessary.

"On your way then, doctor. Take care now."

I was sixty-two, tired and cold to the marrow. This was a young man's sport, and although I had always loved it there were times when it became too extreme. I imagined Ben Reid, Sue James and her managers tucked up warm in bed with not a thought in their heads of what it actually takes on the front line to ensure a safe service.

I had become an expert at distracting myself from such negativity and soon found comfort in *Love's Labour's Lost*:

When icicles hang by the wall
And Dick the shepherd blows his nail
And Tom bears logs into the hall
And milk comes frozen home in pail,
When blood is nipped and ways be foul...

And in the twinkling of an eye the car park barrier was saluting my arrival as I drove into the hospital. On the unit everyone was waiting for the baby but she was running to her own timetable. After half an hour, labour slowed down. It was a false alarm and the delivery took place later in the safety of the mid afternoon. I could have gone home, should have gone home, but instead I left the modern maternity block and went to my office in 'the workhouse'. I wanted to re-read the email I'd sent to Ben Reid. This obsessional side to my nature manifested itself almost exclusively in my professional life and I'd always counted it an advantage. My office was freezing. The wall thermometer was stuck at zero. My experience during the previous winter was that a freezing office meant a freezing children's ward, which was located directly below and supplied by the same antiquated steam heating system. I went down to the ward.

My fears were confirmed when I walked through the swing doors. It wasn't as cold as my office but it was cold. The nurses were wearing extra clothing, cardigans and scarves. One had an outdoor coat on. They explained that the heating had failed some hours earlier and though the engineers had been informed it had not yet been fixed. I asked about the babies. Quite a number had dropped their core temperatures, some to as low as 34 degrees Celsius, which can have serious consequences for an ill baby.

The nurses had responded to the situation quickly and correctly. A few electric convector heaters kept on the ward since the previous winter's problems for this very contingency had been turned on. Babies lose a great deal of heat through their heads, so the smaller patients had been dressed in woolly hats. Two babies with particular problems had been put in incubators. Most of the patients had a parent staying with them and the ones I spoke to complained that they were cold themselves and had asked for blankets. The reception area and most of the rooms had wall thermometers and I made a note of their readings.

Next door, the Paediatric Admissions Ward, which was closed overnight, was as cold as my office. We were unable to reopen it for use for another two days. After ensuring that the situation for the babies was safe I went back to my office. I emailed the Divisional Director, who had managerial responsibility for the ward, with details of the incident. I told him that unless he could give me a good reason why I should not, I intended to blow the whistle by contacting Walsall Safeguarding Children Board. My intention was to report the Trust for repeated failure to provide a safe environment for its small patients. I was by this time more knowledgeable about the Public Interest Disclosure Act, and knew the list of qualifying disclosures under section 43B off by heart. I knew that once again "the health and safety of an individual [actually lots of little individuals] was being or was likely to be endangered". I was clear that my report would constitute a protected disclosure.

Back on the ward everything was being done for the patients and their parents. The nursing staff reassured me that the engineers had promised steam pressure was coming up but that it would be hours before the temperature normalized. I drove home, lay down for a while, had breakfast and went back to work. By 10am, when I started the ward round, the engineers had done their work and the ward was warm again. It was in fact too warm. Some of the rooms, at 35 degrees, were far too hot. This can be as bad for a sick child as being cold. I did my rounds and made a detailed record of all patient and room temperatures, plus other clinical information from the charts. I knew I was going to need precise data about this incident. I asked the nursing staff to make sure a clinical incident form had been completed. In truth, I had little faith that we would ever hear of it again.

I received no response to my email to the Divisional Director. When I finished my clinical duties I drafted a letter to Pauline Pilkington, Chair of Walsall Safeguarding Children Board and Head of Children's Services at Walsall Council. I wrote a detailed history of the heating problems over the previous winter and of the latest incident. I reported my meeting with Mike Brown and the BMA in September at which I had warned him that I would blow the whistle on any serious repetition of heating failure. With a degree of prescience I wrote:

> I have previously raised concerns about patient safety as you know. The Trust may try to trivialize the seriousness of this incident and is likely to ascribe negative motives to my action in reporting it. The only reason I am writing following Friday's incident is that I am desperately concerned about the welfare of patients on our ward.

I sat on the letter over the weekend; on Monday I sent it. By late afternoon I had an email from Sue James that, despite my office wall thermometer reading only just above zero, made my blood boil. In it she claimed to have sent the Medical Director to the ward on Friday morning to make sure the patients were safe. She told me that she knew I had gone outside the organization (a warning word from Ms Pilkington I presumed) and judged that to be "inappropriate". She had asked the Medical Director to write a report on the incident, which she had attached to her email. Reading his report made me even angrier.

The Medical Director had arrived at work on Friday morning and was told about the incident on Canterbury ward. He then wrote a report for the Chief Executive that was inaccurate and misleading in practically every detail. He had not spoken to me before writing his report, although I had been on the ward in the night and all morning. The night sister later told me he had not spoken to the nursing staff; he had arrived after they had gone home. He did not check any of the patient information I had carefully documented. This is the kind of wilful blindness that enables managers to cope with the difficult situations they encounter when things go wrong: to maintain his ignorance it was important for him to deliberately avoid speaking to me.

According to his report I had visited the ward during the early hours of the morning and "assessed it as inappropriately cold". I usually laughed at these preposterous managerial euphemisms but today I was in no mood. That the heating had failed did not appear to have been noticed by the ward staff, he claimed. Furthermore, no manager had been informed of the heating failure. Then he added, "Despite Dr Drew's concern neither he nor the nurses took the obvious step of plugging in the auxiliary electric heaters." He wrote all this without speaking to any of us. In his view, despite our many years, experience we did not know how to look after the most basic of our patients' needs. I found it hard to read that report without feeling angry.

According to Mike Brown, this had been a minor problem that the consultant and nurses had failed to deal with. To add insult to injury, he concluded that both doctors and nurses had "left their common sense out in the cold that night". It is hard, as a senior and very experienced paediatrician, to have someone like Mike Brown write a report to the Chief Executive stating that you don't know what you are doing. Neither at the time nor at any future point was he prepared to discuss this with me. That was in my opinion cowardly and unprofessional behaviour on his part. It demonstrated the avoidance tactics that I was to witness again and again.

Two days later I wrote to Pauline Pilkington again, this time about Mike Brown's false account. I reported the simple, unadorned facts as an eyewitness. I had been on the ground in the ward at 5am. Mike Brown had been tucked up in bed. I had seen and spoken to the nurses on duty. He had spoken to none of them, nor to me. I had seen the patients and their parents, and collected all the data, including ward, room and body temperatures. He had reported the ward temperature as 19 to 21 degrees Celsius, but I had taken the reading from the thermometer myself. It was 12 degrees Celsius. In fact, throughout his report, Mike Brown described the situation in the ward as he found it some five or six hours after the incident and with a new set of staff on. He knew that was misleading.

In two or three letters and emails over the following fortnight I provided Pauline Pilkington with an eyewitness account and all the data. I made it clear that Mike Brown's account was untrue, either deliberately so or due to incompetence. I said this amounted to attempted concealment of a potentially serious clinical incident or at least trivialization. I expressed my opinion that this might have constituted a criminal act. I asked for an investigation.

There was no investigation. And so it was that on an appropriately cold January day, a month after the original incident, in an email headed "Imminent Public Disclosure", I wrote to Pauline Pilkington and copied in the Trust Chairman, Ben Reid:

Unless you take immediate steps with the Trust Board to address this matter with me face to face with a BMA representative present I will be taking action under the

Public Interest Disclosure Act 1998. I have now given a three-hour verbal briefing to the BBC on the situation and unless I get a proper response by 5pm Friday 15th January 2010 I will be handing over all correspondence and documents relating to the most recent incident and its history to them.

It did not occur to me that the Trust would refuse to meet me with the BMA. I considered that this had now become a matter of patient safety, not just in my department, but across the Trust. If the Medical Director had been prepared to produce a false report about one incident; what guarantee was there that he wouldn't do the same about others?

I received no reply indicating a willingness to meet. At one point Ben Reid advised me to think about my colleagues and the Trust's reputation. I responded that it was my responsibility to think about the babies.

I was now locked into a course of action that could not be avoided.

27

Risky Management

As an NHS manager, I will observe the following principles:
* *Make the care and safety of patients my first concern and act to protect them from risk*
* *Respect the public, patients, relatives, carers, NHS staff and partners in other agencies*
* *Be honest and act with integrity*

Code of Conduct for NHS Managers,
Department of Health October 2002

Pauline Pilkington had failed to take my concerns about the heating failure, cold babies and Mike Brown's attempted cover-up seriously. She was, I considered, in breach of her duty as head of safeguarding children for Walsall. Only a few months earlier she had been awarded an MBE. Ironically, two years on, in 2012, following a disastrous Ofsted inspection that showed widespread inadequacy in the service she was responsible for, she "stepped down". In reality, someone who has "stepped down" has usually been given the choice of "going quietly or being sacked". It looks like an ignominious end but it's not. Failure is often rewarded in public life: honours are retained; there is usually a generous settlement that we are not allowed to know about because of a compromise agreement; other well-paid work is often available if it is wanted. Patients and their families who have suffered as a result of this cry "Shame!" but little changes.

I had asked Pauline Pilkington to meet me. I emailed her my mobile number so she could contact me to discuss the incident and subsequent developments. She showed no interest in direct contact. Here again was the familiar pattern of avoidance that well-informed doctors meet when reporting serious concerns to insecure or inadequate senior managers. What Ms Pilkington actually did was talk to Sue James about the incident. That sits much more comfortably. It may not help the babies but it does ensure the organization is positioned to defend its reputation. That is the priority. We have no record of the conversations they had but the outcome was that Walsall Safeguarding Children Board refused to conduct a proper investigation of my concerns about the ongoing risk to patients, in particular my allegations that there had been a cover-up. This was unacceptable and resulted in my ultimatum to the Trust Chair, regarding imminent public disclosure.

Ian Mckivett was, as I remember, more in favour of my going to the Strategic Health Authority (SHA) or the Care Quality Commission (CQC). A senior colleague outside the Trust gave me different advice in confidence. Ben Reid, he reminded me, was an OBE, Pauline Pilkington, an MBE, Ian Cumming at the SHA, an OBE, Cynthia Bower at CQC, an OBE. There was little chance that the great and the good would break ranks with each other. In any case, I learned that CQC does not get involved in individual cases, a fact confirmed in writing to me by Jill Finney, the deputy CEO, at a later date. I could speak to an adviser to provide general background information about the Trust, I was informed, but no more. A little earlier, serendipitously, I had met Michele Paduana at the BBC. He was helpful and always, of course, on the lookout for a good story. I rang him and he came to see me at home. I gave him a detailed briefing of what had happened. My concerns were the ongoing safety of patients over the rest of what promised to be another very cold winter and the dishonest report written by the Medical Director.

I had no wish to appear on TV to express these concerns. I expected a reasonable response from the Trust Chairman but was disappointed. On 18th January 2010 I made a short appearance on *BBC Midlands Today*. In preparation for it, Michele did extensive filmed interviews with me. These would have provided an explosive news item. On the day of the broadcast, however, a story of huge local interest blew up, the Kraft takeover of Cadburys. This dominated the local news all day and my television interview was cut to the bone. It concentrated on the heating failure and the Medical Director's false report was not mentioned.

I have kept a recording of the interview on my hard drive. I looked ill but nevertheless spoke quite clearly about what was wrong. Sue James gave the Trust's response, which was itself a masterpiece of spin. She relied, she said, on her Medical Director, who had assured her that though some babies had been "cooled" (she made it sound almost therapeutic), none had come to harm. At a later date I wrote to the Trust about this:

> Ben Reid has written to me to say that no child has suffered harm. Since he is a layperson he can only be making such statements on the basis of medical advice given to the Trust. Here is a lay analogy. A teacher on a school trip allows all 30 of his charges to walk along the top of an unfenced cliff. When questioned about this by a concerned parent he replies that no one fell to their death so what is the problem. We would rightly question that teacher's judgment and would certainly not want him in charge of children again until there was evidence of an attitude change. This is not the model we should be following in risk management. It is a model that says at the bottom line "We got away with it."

There was an air of excitement in the ward as the lunchtime news came on. I watched it with the staff. That was a surreal experience. The nursing and domiciliary staff were delighted that someone had had the balls to speak up about this issue: they all understood perfectly well the dangers and difficulties with our current arrangements for inpatient care. Many thanked me for taking a stand. I had no expectation that any of them would support me openly when it came to engaging middle or senior management. And I never blamed them for that.

Despite the support I'd been given I was stressed that afternoon. I had an appointment to see a clinical psychologist paid by the Trust to work with the whole department. This approach had been used in other departments by Sue James – I am not sure it ever achieved anything. It was, in my opinion, a coping mechanism for poor leadership that consistently failed to deal with the real issues. Anthony, the psychologist, was charming and non-judgemental, and let me talk most of the time. "I'm 99 per cent sure I've done the right thing," I told him. I felt better in myself after our session and more confident in the course I had taken. I'm not sure that is what Sue James intended.

The Trust, for the first time, as far as I could see, began to take the problem seriously. The nurses told me that engineers were physically present on the ward at least three times daily. "Bit like a TPR (temperature, pulse, respiration measurement) round really," one nurse joked. More heaters were brought in. Email notifications of planned maintenance requiring steam shutdown were sent out for the first time ever. As a result, there were no further major breakdowns over the rest of what proved to be a very cold winter. I am not by nature a worrier, but over those two winters I lost a lot of sleep knowing the risk to our little patients. My sleep pattern began to improve.

Following Michele's broadcast, the Trust, through its Press Officer, wrote to the BBC to complain about alleged factual inaccuracies in its content. In a telephone conversation around this time the Trust Press Officer told Michele Paduana, "Everyone knows that Dr Drew is doolally," attempting to discredit my account of the incident. I subsequently wrote to Ben Reid, the Trust Chair, to complain about this but he replied to say he would be taking no action. In retrospect, it seems to me extraordinary that a press officer could be allowed to be so rude about the most senior children's doctor in the hospital with impunity. It is the experience of so many whistleblowers that once a line is crossed it becomes open season. Bang! Bang! Bring the Mad Hatter down.

Of course the BBC was not in a position to respond as the news report was based on information I had provided and opinions I had expressed. Michele sent the complaint to me and I replied to the Press Officer. I was very direct: this is silly; let's talk to each other. Why talk through the BBC? I answered all the Trust's allegations of inaccuracy. I asked who was giving medical advice to the Trust. I requested a face-to-face discussion with their "expert". I received no response: avoidance behaviour that was by now the norm. The Trust never raised any aspect of this incident with me again. As this drama was unfolding, the Head of HR was writing to a Royal College Review panel in a secret document that I obtained a year later by FOI. The Trust, she informed the panel, regarded my appearance on TV as gross misconduct. "We have decided to take no action on this at present but reserve the right to do so in future," was the Trust's stated position. I was not told this. How can a good doctor who has raised honestly held concerns about patient safety under the Public Interest Disclosure Act be guilty of gross misconduct? How could a senior manager report this as an act of gross misconduct to a Royal College panel, secretly and without telling him? My future was being written for me.

After this I tried to get on with my work. I experienced a lot of support from colleagues but realized that not all of them would have been happy with my action. A consultant colleague told me of a story doing the rounds that described me coming in in the middle of the night on the off chance of finding a cold baby. So, I wrote an email to the whole consultant body at the hospital describing the background to the heating problem and explaining why I had made a public statement about it. I closed as follows:

> We are due to move into a new unit in four months. The current level of monitoring of ward temperatures and maintenance of the heating system is unprecedented. If there is no further heating failure no one will be happier than me, apart from the babies, who will be sleeping safe and sound. It is a pity that it has taken such extreme action on my part to ensure this happens. I am personally still uneasy about the department's future. This attitude to risk management (lack of transparency, wilful ignorance of the facts, refusal to communicate, defensive positioning) on the part of senior management causes me as much anxiety as the heating failure.

Staff from other departments who I'd never seen before greeted me like a long lost friend. "You might not know us but we know you, Dr Drew." Several nurses who had seen me on TV rang me to ask for help. One told me of conditions on the then new "modular block". "We don't have time to give drugs properly or feed or wash patients. We're permanently short of staff." I reported this in a letter to Sue James but she showed no interest and did not respond. She probably thought I was troublemaking again. In a better culture all of these concerns would have been valued as an opportunity to improve patient care, but not in Walsall under Sue James and Ben Reid.

The Trust started an investigation into the heating failure incident immediately. Two weeks after it occurred I saw a nurse who had been on duty that night writing her statement at the nursing station. I was not told of the investigation or asked to contribute. I eventually wrote to the Medical Director asking for a copy of the completed investigation report. He replied to say that since it was a nursing report he did not have the authority to give it me and I should request it from the Director of Nursing Services. He promised to send the engineer's report, which was a part of the investigation, to the Clinical Director, Dr Sinha. I was told to ask him for a copy.

This was disingenuous: anyone reporting a clinical incident has a right to be involved in its investigation and to see the final report, with its analysis and recommendations. That is common courtesy but, more importantly, is enshrined in policy. The BMA's "Advice to Whistleblowers" states "Any matter raised should be investigated thoroughly, promptly and confidentially, and the outcome of the investigation reported back to the worker who raised the issue." The Medical Director had an executive right to let me see the report. I wrote to the Nursing Director asking for the report. I got no response. Dr Sinha never received the engineer's report.

The Trust failed to engage with me on this incident and no one ever met with me or spoke to me about it. To this day I have not seen the investigation report or learned its conclusions. I wrote to Mike Brown complaining that this was no way to practise clinical governance and that it gave me little cause for optimism about patient safety at Walsall in future. No comment.

28

The Independent Review of Paediatrics

The Review's guarantee of non-attribution of comments to witnesses
allowed people to say things that would be too sensitive to voice openly
to David Drew.

Nadeem Moghal, Independent Review Chairman
(in his statement to my disciplinary investigation,
19th August 2010)

The months after the Fireworks Night meeting with the Chairman were packed with activity. The department was still in serious difficulties with nurses being bullied by managers. I had tried to address this with Sue James but to no avail. Consultants, as they testified at my employment tribunal, regularly encountered nurses in tears and had to take time out to counsel them. The heating failure recurred and I was engaged with Ben Reid, trying to get him to understand its potential seriousness. Mike Brown's untrue report made my job much more difficult. A new Clinical Director, Dr Sinha, was in post. He was ill-equipped to stand up for the department and would soon be removed on the review's instruction. Then, there was the work the NHS was actually paying us to do, looking after sick children and their families. There was no end to that over those winter months.

The review was approaching but I had little time to think about it. Sue James wrote up the terms of reference and sent them to me. She claimed in them that I had been incompletely vindicated by Naj Rashid's investigation. At the time that seemed no more than churlish. In retrospect I saw this as part of a wider strategy to discredit me with the review panel. I objected but the Chief Executive rules: my objection went unheeded.

I wrote to ask her if I could provide supporting documentation for my statement of case. My case had been made in my letter of 26th October, she replied. It was, "not usual to allow new issues to be raised at Review stage". This was in spite of the fact that the Trust continued to produce its own statement of case for three months after it had received mine and, with all the administrative and legal resources at its disposal, assemble a mass of supporting documentation. I saw none of this until after my dismissal. Mrs James never intended competing on a level playing field. Later, the review administrator accepted most of my additional documentation.

In February I was given the names of the three panel members. Nadeem Moghal, the chair, and Peter Heinz were both Fellows of the Royal College of Paediatrics: they came with the full recommendation of the College. Sarah Faulkner was an HR consultant who had been invited onto the panel. Their potted CVs bristled with qualifications, evidence of experience and testimonials. Neither of the two Fellows, however, gave any evidence of previously conducting a Review nor of being trained to do so.

I had a brief email correspondence with Nadeem Moghal on issues relating to my case. On 1st March I responded to an email in which he referred to my "difficult journey".

What you refer to as my difficult journey is a direct result of the behaviour of senior managers, some of who are Trust Board members. This is the fundamentally difficult position whistleblowers are in. The GMC has reiterated this week (in the wake of the Mid Staffs Inquiry) its existing guidance on the responsibility of doctors to speak out when they see poor quality care. The report on Mid Staffs says, "The few instances of reports by whistleblowers of which the Inquiry was made aware suggest that the Trust has not offered the support and respect due to those brave enough to take this step. The handling of these cases is unlikely to encourage others to come forward, and the responses to the investigation of the concerns raised have been ineffective." The whistleblowing doctor finds himself in the hopelessly Kafkaesque world that I have lived in for two years now.

On the 4th and 5th of March 2010, the Independent Review panel sat. They had read the documents provided by both sides. Reading time was charged at £300 an hour. The timetable began with a briefing session from the Chairman and Sue James at 8am. At 8:30 Sue James was interviewed alone. We will never know what either of them told the panel. They were given, in line with the Review's warped methodology, a guarantee that nothing they said would ever be attributed to them. I would never be able to find out what the two most senior people in the organization, who had plenty of reason to wish me harm, had said about me. To ensure this no written statements were made; the panel took notes of interviews but these were subsequently destroyed. Considering that the Review was primarily an independent hearing of my grievance the panel had a strange way of conducting itself. That methodology would be more at home in North Korea or Stalinist Russia.

Next, two focus groups, made up of paediatric nurses and consultants, met the panel. After that came the Nursing Director, Brigid Stacey. Ben Reid was given a further hour at the end of the day.

I was interviewed for 40 minutes at one o'clock. The morning ward round had overrun and I'd missed lunch. I arrived with Ian, agnostic about the whole process, given my correspondence with the administrator and Nadeem Moghal. I am acutely sensitive to "set", partly because I have no binocular vision. By set I mean the spatial disposition of participants in an interaction. (That's management speak for where we all sit or stand.) I outraged orthodoxy when I first arrived in Walsall by moving my clinic desk so that it did not come between me and the children. It took years for other consultants to catch on to this and some never did. The set today was wrong. The physical divide between the panel and us was too great, adding to the air of unreality I already sensed. Nadeem Moghal took a central position and Peter Heinz and Sarah Faulkner sat to either side in such a way that it was not possible to focus on or address the whole panel at one time.

Nadeem asked the questions. The other two may have made an occasional comment but if so I do not remember. As Chairman, Nadeem not so much led as dominated the interview. I had provided a detailed statement of case for my grievance against both Mike Brown and Karen Palmer. I had also submitted 20 to 30 supporting documents. These included press cuttings about Kyle Keen's death. I had brought with me a long letter sent to Mike Brown two years earlier expressing serious concerns that I and others had about Dr Walia's competence.

Nadeem's questions were tedious, and largely related to the department's history. I probably knew this better than anyone in the Trust and tried to be helpful. After a while I asked what this had to do with my grievance but only got more questions: Nadeem wanted to know about the Black Country Review, (an earlier attempt to reconfigure services in the Walsall), and about our relationships with the PCT. I was asked about conflict between consultants: the truth was that most of us got on very well but there were strains between two consultants and the rest.

Then, with no context, he asked me about my use of religious references at work. I had to ask him to clarify before I could answer. As it happened, I had that morning been asked by a trainee about an expression I had used on the ward round. It was "going the extra mile". A trainee had said he had not heard that expression and asked what it meant. I told the panel how I had briefly explained this phrase going back to the Roman occupation of Palestine. It was impossible, I explained to Nadeem, to escape the English language's rich heritage of religious and mythical reference. And why would I want to? Many of our trainees had English as a second language. It was my role as a teacher to explain the idioms I used, especially when asked. It was one aspect of communication training. Besides, the juniors and even my consultant colleagues seemed to enjoy these snippets. It did not occur to me that this had anything to do with Naj Rashid's recommendation that I stop imposing my religious opinions on other staff. Sue James had written to me before the review to say the Trust had dropped that matter altogether.

I tried in vain to raise issues with the panel but without success. Nadeem seemed to have no interest in discussing the concerns central to my grievance. My dismissal as Clinical Director was raised briefly. Nadeem told me the Medical Director claimed I had resigned. I made it clear, as had my correspondence at the time, I had not. Why would I have? My removal related to my concerns over Dr Walia's competence, which I had often discussed with the Medical and Divisional Directors. In private they agreed with me, but that was as far as they took it until Dr Walia was removed as lead consultant in the newborn unit. I told the panel, as bluntly as I had told Sue James and Ben Reid, that Dr Walia had sent Kyle home to his death contrary to the child protection policy and against the specific advice of his medical and nursing colleagues. Nadeem put his hand up to stop me. He had an imperious manner that was hard to oppose. "The panel has seen the press cuttings on that incident," he told me. Foolishly I trusted that there was enough in the documentation for the panel to come to its own conclusions about Dr Walia and Kyle Keen.

I wanted to discuss my other disclosures, I said.

"Disclosures?" asked Nadeem, quizzically.

"The Trust's failure to remedy the mistakes leading to Kyle Keen's death. The safeguarding nurse's appointment. Nursing and medical redundancies. Heating failures and hypothermia. Bullying."

"We've read your statements about these."

"What about the NCAS disclosures – the untrue statements Mike Brown made about me clearly believing I would never see them?"

"We have all the emails."

The panel members were inscrutable. Our 40 minutes expired and Ian and I left. I felt disappointed and unsatisfied. The panel seemed to have little interest in pursuing my concerns.

The next day all the main players in my grievance were interviewed: Mike Brown, the Medical Director; Karen, Jon and Rob, the middle managers at the height of the troubles; Naj Rashid, etc. All spoke knowing they could say whatever they wanted and I would neither be told nor able to challenge it. In addition, Elaine Hurry, the head of safeguarding at the PCT, was interviewed. There can have been no other reason for her appearance than to give evidence about the Kyle Keen case. There is no record of what she said, and, to avoid being accused of interfering with the review, I never asked her. I am still curious, as I believe she knew everything there was to know and must have told the panel.

I had a further 30-minute interview on Friday afternoon. "Have you been satisfied by the review so far?" asked Nadeem. Not wanting to antagonize him I said that in the main I had. My question at this stage was what the panel had concluded about my repeated harassment by Mike Brown. And what about the untrue statements he had made about me in his reports to NCAS? What about the psychiatric referral? What about my disclosures? What about Dr Walia? What about Kyle Keen? I knew I was in danger of looking obsessional but I wanted answers and I could feel the situation slipping away from me. We were told that all this had been covered with Mike Brown and would be in the report.

"I wrote to you, David, telling you not to expect any answers today," said Nadeem.

"I'd expected that there would be a face-to-face meeting with Mike Brown to thrash this out," I answered. The most basic grievance procedure worked in that way.

"That's not going to happen," said Nadeem.

Finally, Nadeem asked me what I wanted, what I expected of the review. I replied that after the last two years I was too raw from the way I had been treated by the Trust to give a proper answer. But I was able to give the main points. I concluded with what for me had always been the bottom line, "I want closure on the last two years. I want an end to the managerial harassment I've suffered. I want to settle back down to my clinical practice before retiring. This all hangs on your final report and the Trust's response to it."

29

The Report

"And what's the use of a book," thought Alice, *"without pictures or conversation."*

Lewis Carroll: *Alice in Wonderland*

Three weeks later, on Friday 26th March, we met the panel again to receive its report. Sue James and Ben Reid represented the Trust. I half expected Mike Brown to be present but was disappointed. There had been no direct encounter between us in the whole process: more institutionally mediated avoidance. It was clear that this was not, as formally scheduled, my grievance against two Trust officers so much as a contest between me and the Trust. The review's original "Framework of engagement" specified that for reasons of "confidentiality" the report would be given only to the CEO and Board Chairman. This would have been understandable had the original purpose of the review not been my grievance and had its subject not been a matter of *intense public interest*. At some point, I presume, the panel had agreed that they had no choice but to give me a copy.

Nadeem was in charge. He raced through an unmemorable introduction. Then he picked up from the table two copies of the report. One he gave to Ben Reid and the other to me. He held a further copy on behalf of the panel. He assured me months later that no other copy had been produced. "The Independent Panel Review of the Paediatric Service, its Management and Issues Specific to Dr David Drew, at Walsall Hospitals NHS Trust" was a slim volume in a plastic sleeve with an artist's impression of the new PFI hospital on its front. It was never intended that more than half a dozen individuals should set eyes on its full contents, despite its relevance to patient care across the Trust.

"I am going to read out the parts of the report that refer to you, David," said Nadeem. And before I had an opportunity to ask him why this was necessary he was off. Once again, he spoke at a speed that I found hard to keep up with. I had, by the time he finished, caught enough to know that I had won my grievance against both Mike Brown and Karen Palmer. "Do you have any questions?" he asked. Ian smiled wearily at me. "I don't," I said, "Not now." Ian answered for me: it was difficult to say anything about the report until we'd had an opportunity to study it and discuss it together in detail, he said. Nadeem told us that would have to be done with the Trust as the panel was leaving that afternoon. Past experience left me less than hopeful about open discussion with the Trust in its present incarnation.

There was nothing more to say so Ian and I left. I went back to work for the rest of the day. I took the report home with me and spent most of the weekend trying to digest it. That was not easy. The actual report was only sixteen pages long. It was written in a pithy style but I found it hard going. There was neither evidence nor explanation for any of the opinions expressed. What were listed as conclusions were, without evidence, little more than opinions. The same went for the recommendations. This was frustrating. I had seen no evidence presented to the panel by way of documentation. I knew nothing of the oral evidence gathered. All records of this had been destroyed and could not be reconstructed. I was quite certain this was unsafe. I kept some notes of my interviews, obsessional recorder that I am. I doubt anyone else did.

The report was peppered with misjudgements. It generalized the poor working relationships between consultants. I had made it clear that most consultants got on very well. This had been even better since our four excellent new colleagues arrived a year earlier. Reports of unsupportive consultants and bullying by trainees in the deanery report were subsumed into this narrative again as a generalization. There were only two consultants that trainees complained about. The failure of job planning for more than a year was cited as further evidence of consultant dysfunction but this was entirely due to the intransigence of managers wanting to squeeze blood out of a stone. The spin about our consultants as a dysfunctional group can only have come from the managers, including Sue James.

In its central analysis of the recent troubles, however, the report got a lot right. The obvious context was the change programme. This had been necessitated by the cost reductions required to prepare us for Foundation Trust application and the high mortgage costs of the new PFI hospital, due to open later that year. The board and executive had overall responsibility for this. The change programme, the report informed, was not focused on service improvement. It was focused on cutting costs. Frontline staff were reported to be unreceptive to change.

[But the mismanaged redundancies, the understaffing, the patient-safety issues, the cramming of patients into a ward that was not fit for purpose and the managerial bullying that had been required to achieve this were not mentioned. It was entirely right that the clinicians rebelled against changes that were so obviously damaging to the service. It was our professional duty to be unreceptive to such change.]

Starting at the top, the report analysed the genesis of the crisis. The Trust board had "no way of interrogating the system for detail of what was happening in one of the hospital's core services". There was "a gap between what the board understood of the Trust's performance and the reality". The board was living in fairyland, to put it in paediatric language. If that was true of one service it was likely true of others. In a nutshell, the board, apart from being able to balance the books, was seriously underperforming in its oversight of the hospital.

The executive had played a major part in the crisis by making "inappropriate appointments to divisional and departmental leadership roles". There was no word of explanation as to why the executive had done this, though I believed those appointed were seen to have the muscle to force the changes through. "The executive was reactive rather than proactive in managing paediatric issues". The executive had surrendered its leadership responsibility. That had been my feeling for almost two years of trying my best to engage with senior management on matters of crucial importance: they did not want to engage.

Senior management was seen to be of the view that "problems would be quickly solved by the move to the new hospital". The panel had to remind Sue James and Ben Reid that "people and teams deliver healthcare not buildings". With a board possessed of such naïve views and no idea of what was going on at ground level effective leadership was impossible. The report told me nothing that I did not already know, nothing that I had not told senior management and the review panel.

On middle management, the report was damning and explained, I believe, the rift that had developed with the clinical staff. None of the three managers appointed had any paediatric qualification or experience. They "lacked the knowledge to modernize the service". Their management style had contributed to the change programme stalling. All three had shown themselves aggressive. Sue James had referred to this in one version of the terms of reference as a "new management style". I had called it what I believed it to be, bullying. I had provided graphic examples of this. The nurses, who had suffered the brunt, were said, patronizingly, in the report not to really understand what bullying was. There was no evidence, said the report, that divisional management actively engaged with front line staff. [The front liners had vast paediatric experience and the managers had none but they went ahead and acted without consultation.]

Frontline staff came in for criticism too: the consultants were a dysfunctional bunch; they resisted change. The nurses came out rather better: the department was old-fashioned and needed bringing into the 21st century. The current Clinical Director, Dr Sinha, did not have the skills for this role [prompting, once again, the question as to why, when everyone else in the department knew this, the executive had appointed him]. The report wasn't unkind enough to call him a management puppet but the consultants knew this was the truth.

I received my own share of criticism. It was accepted that I was and remained a respected and effective clinician: "Managers, consultants and nursing staff spoke of David Drew as a very good and passionate doctor," but I did not have the skills to modernize the service. This, I told the panel, was why I had offered my resignation more than two years earlier in an attempt to concentrate on clinical work. Seven years as clinical director had almost broken my will to live.

The report contained some profound criticisms of my behaviour but no attempt was made to link this to the circumstances I found myself in or my claims as a whistleblower. I was said to be contributing to the demise of the paediatric service. It had been "inappropriate" for me to go on the BBC about the heating problem. This precisely echoed the senior management view but ignored my own account, including a written disclosure made under PIDA before acting. The concluding sentence on this incident was "Evidence suggests that David Drew is not a whistleblower." I was angry when I read this. I had written to Nadeem stating that I was a whistleblower and I had provided documentary evidence but the panel had shown no interest in interrogating me about my disclosures. Now the panel claimed to have evidence that I had not seen and never would see that I was not a whistleblower.

There were criticisms once more of my communication style: the panel did not like it, but apart from the fact that my emails were long and detailed could cast no further light on the problem. The length and detail of my emails were, in my opinion, commensurate with the situation we found ourselves in with so many things going wrong. The recipients of my communications had been upset the report stressed, and I did not appear to recognize this. Any half-decent senior manager, rather than being upset by my serious and detailed critique, would have seized upon it to improve the service. But it was their hurt feelings that they and the panel seized upon. I was quite certain that it was the professionally reasoned content of my concerns and the way it reflected on management up to and including Sue James that was the real cause for offence. The panel did not recognize this. I was being prepared for the firing squad.

Finally, the report concluded that my "use of religious language was not appropriate in a professional setting". This had become "normalized behaviour, tolerated within the organization and not made clear as an issue early in David Drew's career". I had no idea where this had come from. It was the most nonsensical contrivance in the whole report: there was no truth in it and my colleagues of many years would have confirmed this if asked. I was a well-read and expressive person, delighting in language, metaphor and myth; people, including my patients and their parents, took pleasure in this. I know I was always interesting, humorous, provocative and memorable: colleagues told me so. What did Nadeem Moghal and his panel know about me? They had shown no interest in an open conversation on this subject during my interviews.

Mike Brown came in for flak. He had mismanaged my removal as Clinical Director. He had followed no diligent process, had no evidence and no documentation to support his action. This reflected my consistent experience of his behaviour as Medical Director. Excluding me as a result of Karen Palmer's allegations was judged to have been wrong. The allegations, even if true, did not warrant exclusion. NCAS did not advise exclusion as he had claimed. An "emotional exchange between Mike Brown and Karen Palmer" had influenced his decision to act. No details were given of what this exchange was. The strong implication was that Mike had allowed his emotions with respect to a female colleague to cloud his judgment. My treatment during the period of exclusion had intensified the breakdown of trust between Mike Brown and me. This included his failure to respond to my letters and in particular the psychiatric referral. The significance of this referral was acknowledged but the panel made no attempt to verify my account.

The panel's findings unfolded in five short pages. Most surprising of all for me was that Kyle Keen was not mentioned once. In line with the Trust's dealings with this little boy, the review panel airbrushed him out of history. Nor was there a single word about the concerns expressed over Dr Walia's clinical competence in this and other matters.

There followed five pages of recommendations. These were framed as "required outcomes". This turned out to be, in my case at least, required in the most rigorous sense of the word. Agree to this or face dismissal. Sixteen requirements were listed against my name and were given first priority. The rest of the large cast in this drama attracted only 22 required outcomes between them. I was the one in the dock.

Practically everything required of me was negative. There was a long list of the people I had upset: I was instructed to apologize to them. I was to use business etiquette in my emails – but I was a paediatrician, not a businessman – I was pretty familiar with email culture in the Trust and it was often far from businesslike. I was instructed to withdraw my grievances. That was a puzzle to me as the report upheld them. Only later did I receive BMA advice that this is incompatible with any official grievance policy. But again in terms of the review it was something I would not be allowed to challenge. In the hands of the Trust solicitor, Mr Martin Brewer, this would become a sackable offence.

Most of the rest was clearly aimed at controlling me, and

preventing me from exercising my professional responsibilities. This was all the more galling when I had made it clear that I was asking the panel to investigate my claim that I had made protected disclosures and it had failed to do so. I was instructed to accept the report as final. Within days I came to understand that meant exactly what it said. There would be no questions or answers, no explanations. No conversation.

And tucked away in the report was an instruction that I "refrain from using religious references in professional communication, verbal or written – regardless of past apparent acceptance of this style". As with the rest of the report, this was to be accepted as final. No evidence was presented that this was a problem or even that it was true. No complaint had been made that I knew of. I had little doubt that this had originated with the divisional managers I had been in conflict with. But I would never be able to find this out. I scribbled "Never" next to this instruction in preparation for my discussion with Ian Mckivett.

Mike Brown was instructed to acknowledge his mishandling of my removal as Clinical Director. Likewise he had to recognize he was wrong to exclude me and had mismanaged my exclusion and failed to communicate with me properly. He was told to provide me with a verbal and written apology for these errors and to work to rebuild his relationship with me. I had provided irrefutable evidence that he had repeatedly lied about me but the panel concluded that it saw no reason why he should not continue as Medical Director.

Two of the panel's "required outcomes" to ensure the department's survival were that the Trust remove the current Clinical Director as unfit for purpose and replace him by an outside appointment with someone who had the necessary skills. Presumably this meant leadership skills, and training in quality improvement and service development. These were the *very* skills that the panel's Chairman, Dr Nadeem Moghal, had been developing. Sue James testified under oath at a later date that

Nadeem was at that very time looking for a position where he could apply his talents and had made his availability for this role known. I noted with interest that all the major players involved in the department's troubles and interviewed by the panel were named in the report *with the exception of Sue James and Ben Reid*. Anyone who understands the rules of patronage will admit at least to the *possibility* that Dr Moghal was strengthening his position for what was to come.

Jon Pepper and Karen Palmer were to be removed from any responsibility for the paediatric department. That would be a relief to many.

The executive was told to get to grips with the paediatric department and its staff: the failure of middle management in this task was the result of executive blunders in the first place so that seemed fitting.

The board was instructed to develop governance structures capable of interrogating the executive team and to get out a bit more in the form of ward visits: that must have been pretty humiliating for them.

The HR Director was told to take her responsibilities seriously and to follow Trust procedures, including recording evidence and reasons for decisions.

The whole senior management team was being told to do what they were being paid by the taxpayer to do but were not doing.

Finally the panel gave clear instructions on the dissemination of the report. The Trust executive team was to ensure that "the key findings of the report are communicated to staff within the paediatric department and the wider hospital community within two weeks from March 26th 2010. The urgency is necessary to avoid the build-up of gossip and assumptions." I was instructed to "allow the Trust to share this report as advised by the independent panel with the relevant staff and not to pre-empt or interfere with the reporting process". Since the review primarily concerned my grievance I considered I had a perfect right to be involved in communicating the report and intended to challenge that. Besides, on first reading of the report I was certain that everything possible would be done to conceal this account of senior managerial failure.

Only three months earlier, Dr Martin Ward Platt, also recommended by the Royal College of Paediatrics, had completed his report, "Review of Services for Neonates and Children at Heart of England Foundation Trust (HEFT)". This Trust bordered Walsall and had significant problems with its paediatric services. In contrast to the Walsall report, which was delivered into the hands of a CEO and Chair that had already failed us badly, the HEFT chief executive published his report on the internet. This was despite its containing such alarming statements as "some of the relationships between consultant staff at Good Hope Hospital, Birmingham, are so dysfunctional that there is potential for patient safety to be compromised." Nothing was confidential and there was no scope for a cover-up.

By Sunday evening I had read the report several times and made notes. It became clear to me that rather than being an independent hearing of my grievance it had put me on trial. It took me three more years to discover how this had been achieved. My intention was to meet Ian over the next fortnight to discuss my misgivings. I was not allowed to take this considered approach. On the next working day I was caught up in a firestorm resulting in Sue James asking for my immediate resignation.

30

Indecent Haste

I am a man of peace; but when I speak, they are for war.

Psalm 120:7

The report of the Walsall Independent Review of Paediatrics was hot off the press and must have occupied Sue James and Ben Reid, as it had done me, over the weekend. I developed a migraine on Sunday night and arrived at work on Monday nauseated and unsteady. Waiting for me was an email from Sue James informing me that she had discussed the report with Ben Reid. They had agreed to accept the panel's findings and were planning implementation. "However we cannot progress any action until we have received your own view on whether you are also prepared to accept the panel's findings." She had asked her PA to fix a meeting for Wednesday.

The only thing I wanted to do at that stage was to get back to work as a clinician and forget the whole thing. I hoped that if the Trust implemented the review in good faith most of the concerns I had raised would be dealt with. Looking back, given the report's shortcomings and my recent experiences of Trust senior management, that was pretty optimistic of me. My next act should have been to ask for time to meet the BMA. Instead I made a tactical error. I wrote a conciliatory response to Sue James by return, expressing my general satisfaction with the report and my willingness to accept it.

For the reasons I have already explained, I refused to accept the instruction on the use of religious language in my verbal and written professional communication. I had worked with Sue James for seven years, five of them as Clinical Director. She had never once in that time known me use a religious reference – as she witnessed at the employment tribunal two years later. I pleaded the case for common sense on this. "This recommendation is unnecessary. I do not believe you are likely to have difficulty in this area if you are willing to trust me." I hoped that would do it.

The only other real difficulty I had was with the review's instruction for the report's dissemination. I accepted the instruction, I wrote, but would "have difficulty with any account (especially given to the department or hospital consultants' committee) that obscures the review's quite precise analysis. We have a duty to learn from this unfortunate experience." I did not know at this point that Sue James would not even give the Trust board an unabridged copy of the report. I did not know that she would alter the review's instruction with regard to dissemination in the précis she gave them or that she had no intention of letting the hospital consultants' committee see the report at all. What I did know was that both she and Ben Reid would want as little of the report's content known as possible. The failings of the board and executive that had been identified in paediatrics, particularly with respect to middle management, affected other departments too. I offered in my response to meet Sue at the earliest opportunity without BMA representation. An olive branch.

At nine o'clock the next morning I received an email telling me to accept the review in full or resign. The review had been commissioned in response to my grievance against the Medical Director; my grievance was over my removal as Clinical Director for raising legitimate concerns about a consultant's competence and about my exclusion following the serious concerns I raised about patient safety. As the panel at my disciplinary hearing later concluded, my grievance was upheld at practically every point: yet here I was, three days after the report was published, being asked to resign. Most reasonable people will understand what this was about.

A week later I responded, apologizing for the delay: I had been working continuously and had done four nights on call into the bargain. I wrote a holding letter asking for time to meet my BMA representative since it appeared my job was on the line. In response, Sue James sent me an appointment for a disciplinary hearing, with date, time, and venue, even naming the disciplinary panel. The letter contained three allegations against me.

This was in complete breach of the Trust's own procedures: there can be no disciplinary hearing without an investigation showing that there is a case to answer and there had been none. It was this failure to follow Trust policy that had been criticized by the review and which the Trust had been instructed to remedy. Mrs James had, with the Chairman, accepted the review in full but was, only weeks later, showing that this was lip-service. They were already in breach of a required outcome. The truth is that senior management do what the hell they please.

I then met Ian Mckivett: "My God, David, they can't wait to be shot of you." He wrote to Sue James pointing out her "error" and the disciplinary hearing was stood down. Months later, when a further disciplinary procedure was started against me, I obtained a copy of the Trust Statement of Case prepared for the cancelled hearing. It was dated 23 April. It would have taken some time to compile. The internal evidence was that it had been written before the Trust had received the review's report. "They've kettled you and the charge sheet had been written out before they made a move," a journalist friend told me when I showed him the documents. Sue James's indecent haste to move on was to me a clear indication of her premeditated decision to dismiss me. I cannot be certain whether this was conscious or not, nor can I prove it, but I find the conclusion inescapable.

The review had clearly recognized that the Trust board had no idea what was going on in the paediatric department. But how do boards get information about what is happening on the ground? In my own case their main source of information was Sue James. In early May she informed the board that she had written to me asking for my complete unequivocal acceptance of the report on 29th March but that it had taken me a month to give a proper response. There was no mention of my emails or my request to meet her. She reported that I had been instructed to attend a disciplinary hearing but forgot to mention that this had been stood down after BMA complaints. "David Drew has created a toxic environment which will impede the successful development of the Paediatric Department," she wrote in her position paper on the review. This was nowhere to be found in the review or anywhere else. It was Sue James's own spin on the situation to make her case for my dismissal that much stronger. "David Drew's continued presence in the department is therefore the highest risk we will face going forward." And so on.

Later, Sue James informed the employment tribunal that when the board was not sitting she and the Chair *were* the board. She referred repeatedly to herself and the Ben Reid as "The Board in Action". The general account was consistent with a board that was ill-informed and not particularly concerned about being informed. Supine, in fact. But the Vice Chair, Nigel Summer, at the May board meeting, breaking out of that mould, "felt that there were also actions and outcomes for the Chief Executive to lead on as a result of the review and these related to developing an organization that is fit for purpose which would require constructive challenge from the Chief Executive to Non Executive Directors, the Board and the Senior Management Team to implement a fair and consistent culture". Wow! Mrs James had been in post for seven years. It was a bit late to address an agenda that should have occupied her attention from the start.

I must again confess my naïvety. Throughout this period I was convinced that I had done nothing wrong, rather the opposite. I had a false confidence that this would all blow over and in six months things would be back to normal. Ian Mckivett, with a more cynical realism born of many years working with hospital management, knew different and told me so. We heard around this time that Mike Brown was taking early retirement, and that Sue James was applying for other Chief Executive posts. I kept on looking after the sick babies and hoped for the best.

31

An Irregular Appointment

Outcome 5b: Bring in paediatric medical leadership to build internal
consultant leadership and support innovation in the service
Required Outcome of Independent Review of Paediatrics
(Chairman: Dr Nadeem Moghal)

Two weeks after we received the report, Sue James wrote to the paediatric consultants to communicate its key findings. This consisted of a list of the thirty-one outline conclusions and ten sets of required outcomes. Must do's. Much of the embarrassing detail of the original was airbrushed out of her version; even the sparse detail given in the report itself as to what had actually gone wrong went missing. Perhaps most telling for me was her tinkering with the instruction in the report that the key findings be "communicated to staff within the paediatric department and the wider hospital community within two weeks". She had erased the reference to the wider hospital community being informed about the review. The target group became "paediatric staff and management team". The Trust board, having no access to the full report, was unaware of its obligation to inform the wider hospital community within a specific time frame, two weeks. This was an early confirmation of my suspicion that Sue James would try to bury this deeply embarrassing report.

A few short weeks later, on a quiet Friday afternoon, Mike Brown turned up unannounced at the paediatric consultants' meeting.

"Yesterday the Trust appointed Dr Nadeem Moghal to head up the department and help us all move on," he announced.

The consultants expressed surprise and wanted to know details. When would he start? What would his role be? Would he do clinical work? Would he work on the out-of-hours rota? What about his lack of experience in newborn medicine? Mike Brown told us he had not been on the "appointments committee". "I have no details of what Dr Moghal will be doing," he told us. "Why not?" we asked. "I've not been told." But he was the Medical Director.

The appointments committee had in fact consisted solely of the Chief Executive and the Trust Chairman. This was later confirmed in writing by Sue James herself. Every consultant present knew this was fixed and several said so. I knew it better than any of them. I had the full report.

I was outspoken about the appointment. Mike Brown was embarrassed and did not want to hear. But I rehearsed the problems: the review had been quite clear about the failings of the board and executive in mismanaging the paediatric department: "There is a gap between what the board understands of the Trust's governance and performance and the reality. The board did not have the capability to interrogate the system for detail as to what was happening in a core service in the hospital," I quoted verbatim. The board was chaired by an able businessman, Ben Reid. For some reason he had less concern for what was happening on the hospital shop floor than he must have had for the one in the Co-op, where he was also chairman. Following the review, the board minutes show that its members had enough insight to recognize that it had become "unsighted" with respect to the paediatric department. Those funny little managerial words somehow gloss over the seriousness of failure at the most senior level. Unsighted? Blind you mean.

It was exclusion of the senior clinicians that had got us into this mess in the first place. "The executive made inappropriate appointments to divisional and department leadership roles," I continued to quote. It was the executive's responsibility, by using its middle managers, to keep the board informed of problems in the department. The divisional and departmental managers had been ready to tell Sue James more or less what she wanted to hear. Sue had wilfully put herself in a very dangerous position.

Many of our problems had arisen from the change programme, as every consultant was aware. The review concluded that this was focused on cost cutting and not improvement. I had written to Sue James on this subject months earlier, "You have conceived this change under the banner of 'More for Less' but what we are getting in fact is less for less." The review had concluded, I told Mike Brown and the consultants, that managers "felt there was limited time to test the model before the move to the PFI. Paediatric staff felt rushed through the change with consequent tensions and poor relationships between the department and the divisional management. There was little input to the necessary adaptive change in people needed to make the technical change engaging and sustainable." This top-down reorganization of the department without consultation had cut costs but had put patients at risk and resulted in a demoralized workforce. It had been achieved by managerial bullying. That this was sanctioned by the CEO herself was fully documented and witnessed to by most of the consultants present. Everyone involved in this change, including the managers, had felt the heat.

The appointment of Nadeem Moghal by Sue James and Ben Reid suited all three down to the ground. It certainly suited Nadeem. As chair of the review panel, and first (dominant, in my opinion) among equals, only weeks earlier he had written the two "required outcomes" to "secure the department's leadership and development". That involved the removal of the current Clinical Director as not fit for purpose and an outside appointment to fill the role. It is hard to avoid the conclusion that Dr Moghal was helping create a post that precisely fitted his own professional development needs at that time, and then making known his availability to fill it. He used this to ensure his own career progression.

The Chief Executive and Chairman then made themselves exclusively responsible for his appointment. This may have been seen as good practice in Walsall but it was cloaked in secrecy and almost certainly breached equal opportunities – to say nothing of the review's specific requirement that we consultants be involved in this process. It exposed senior management's willingness to abandon good governance in the pursuit of what was ultimately self-interest. A quick fix. It posed a huge conflict of interest for Nadeem himself. He would be responsible for implementing the review and at the same time defending Sue James from my charges that she was suppressing the report.

Mike Brown had little else to say other than that our failure to co-operate would probably result in the department closing. We'd heard these threats on so many other occasions, most recently from Sue James herself, that no one took any notice. We were keen for Mike to go so that we could talk amongst ourselves. Finally, he gave a long turgid account of what he thought was coming to the NHS and our hospital: its main objective was to create insecurity in us to ensure our compliance. Having done as thorough a job of this as possible he left.

Everyone was keen to express an opinion. The general conclusion was that Sue James would use the report to label the consultant group dysfunctional as a smokescreen for her own failings. We agreed that Nadeem Moghal was hardly likely to get into conflict with his new patrons over that. The meeting broke up with a sense of foreboding.

A colleague who had read the signs warned me as we left. "You do realize he's coming for you, David, don't you?" I did. And so did everyone else.

Nadeem Moghal arrived in the hospital a few days before his official start date. He was anxious to get on with the business of saving the department. This would later enable him to publish the feat on his LinkedIn website as "Turning around a troubled clinical service". He met with as many consultants as were around to outline his mission. Six paediatric departments in the West Midlands were going to close, he told us. It was up to us whether Walsall would be one of them. Once more we felt the same old rod intended to beat us into submission. Good leaders begin with strengths: we had many. He began with our weaknesses.

Our greatest weakness, he told us, was that we did not have enough middle-grade doctors to run the out-of-hours rota. These registrars or staff-grade doctors had enough training and experience to work on-site without consultant supervision outside 9 to 5 on weekdays and at weekends. We knew from our Royal College's annual manpower report that this was a longstanding, widespread and intractable problem. The European Working Time Directive and work permit restrictions had conspired to make the problem even worse. In any case Manor Hospital had never been the place to work to advance your career.

In providing a consultant-delivered service we were the most progressive department in the hospital. We already guaranteed 9 to 5 on-site consultant cover every day of the year; that included weekends and bank holidays. This was part of our job plans that we had agreed years earlier. We were a hard-working group of consultants and recognized this provided high-quality safe care for our patients. We were also present in the hospital for as many hours outside those times as our patients needed us.

Nadeem had not only identified our main problem of which we were already painfully aware; he also had a solution. All consultants would have to cover the rota weeknights and weekends from 5pm till 10pm, working as registrars. He paused, waiting for a response from us. No one spoke.

"Someone's going to have to speak to this."

No one else would so I did.

"Nadeem, I'm almost 63. My health hasn't been good over the last year. Some enlightened countries don't expect consultants to do on-call work at all past 60, and for good reasons. I have difficulty putting cannulas in the very small babies. That is essential for the middle-grade role. This is no country for old men. We've been discussing consultants doing registrar work for a year in job-planning meetings. The consultant contract stipulates that out-of-hours residency is optional. Speaking for myself, it's not that I will not, I cannot do it."

A colleague of similar age, Dr Sinha, also said that he would not be doing it. A couple of the younger, recently appointed, consultants said they would be willing to go on the registrar rota.

Nadeem looked at me disapprovingly. "It wouldn't be fair for some of the consultants to have to do this but not others, would it, David?"

"It's not a matter of fairness, it's about common sense. You haven't been on the ground in the department. We would still need another consultant on call at home. It's common, almost usual, to need three doctors for the acute paediatrics and neonates to be physically on site at night during the busy months. You need to show us in detail how this will work with those consultants willing and able to do registrar duties. Show us your proposed rota."

The meeting fizzled out with no general agreement. Nadeem was not happy. Here I was holding back the department again. Outside the meeting a consultant colleague suggested, "One-nil." But I wasn't competing.

Nadeem was in a strong position: he was a bright doctor, full of energy, and, unlike most paediatricians, he had formal training in management, quality improvement and service development. He also had the ear of the Chief Executive and the Chairman. Previous Clinical Directors had been given four hours a week to manage the department but, apart from a four-hour clinical session, all his time was reserved for managing – or "saving the department", as Sue James referred to it. The consultant body was highly experienced and assertive and would resist Nadeem's attempts to foist any half-baked ideas on their job plans. But, as one consultant pointed out, he could make our lives as difficult as he wanted to as our manager without it affecting him: he had no on-call commitment. Nadeem had become our manager and was already acting like one of those his own review had instructed the Trust to remove.

32

Mistakes were Made (but not by me)

… a hyperactive learner and keen citizen observer who does not take the sense of Britain's civilised order lightly or for granted.
Dr Nadeem Moghal: Self-description, Newcastle University
Business School website

Nadeem arrived in June. He came to modernize the department as a part of implementing his review. I was his first priority. He instructed the Divisional Director's PA to fix an appointment with me in his office on the 8th of June at 2pm. He could have asked me himself but he chose to do it formally. It wasn't going to be a friendly chat. I arrived promptly, fully prepared for what was to come.

"Come in and sit down, David. Right, we are meeting today to secure the implementation of the report's recommendations. You know what the objectives for you are and they are now going to be time-linked."

I found myself uncharacteristically irritated from the onset. This was not the language colleagues address each other in. It was the language of the hierarchy. I was a naughty schoolboy about to be read the riot act.

"Can I say something, Nadeem?"

"Of course you may."

"Have you seen my correspondence with Sue James about the recommendations?"

"Yes, I have."

"Then you'll know I've accepted the recommendations but I've asked for clarification on two points."

"David, the point of this meeting is to get your acceptance of what is required of you without reservation or caveat."

"Just a minute, Nadeem, I want to discuss some of the thinking behind those recommendations."

"David, the review is finished. It's over. It is now time for you to accept your responsibility."

"I've never tried to duck my responsibility. There are two issues I want to discuss. We can't get any further without that. You know very well there's nothing in this allegation that I'm some kind of religious fruitcake. I've been told not to impose my religious beliefs on staff. I've never done that and no evidence or example has ever been given that I have. No complaint has ever been made against me. You instruct me to desist from all religious reference at work but, apart from what's common to most well-educated native English speakers, I don't do that. I deserve an explanation. What's behind all this nonsense?"

"The panel gave a cast-iron guarantee of non-attribution to everyone who gave evidence to the review. I'm not at liberty to talk about what witnesses said."

I found myself tumbling again into the world of Franz Kafka's Joseph K. I was being treated like a criminal but was unable to find out what my crime was. I subsequently discovered that in his statement to Julia Hollywood, the investigator for my eventual disciplinary procedure, Nadeem had said, "This guarantee enabled people to say things about David Drew that were too sensitive to say to his face." He had also said that if more than one person made the same statement it was considered credible by the review. He refused to say where that principle came from but I recognized in it an ancient Jewish law, "In your own law it is recognized that the testimony of two men is true." John 8:17. Nadeem, ignoring the irony, denied that this was his source.

"More than one person said that you habitually came to meetings, put your hand on your heart and said 'I am a Christian therefore…',", he explained.

223

"Therefore what?"

"I really can't remember."

"Do you have any religious belief, Nadeem?"

"We're not here to discuss my beliefs."

"Most people here know I'm a Christian. I'm out as a Christian like Bashir and Rashid are out as Muslims. I don't think anyone would have much idea what I believe as a Christian. If any allegations have been made against me they've come from Rob Hodgkiss, Karen Palmer or Jon Pepper. You clearly understood from the review why they might want to make negative statements about me."

"You may be right or you may be wrong. The assurances we gave mean I am not at liberty to discuss witness's evidence."

I repeated my position: I could not, would not, accept the instruction of the review without stronger evidence that I had done wrong and been given an opportunity to refute it. I also had BMA advice that this instruction was discriminatory.

"I've told you, David, the review is over. We are here today to secure your agreement, that's all."

"OK, I want to discuss the dissemination of the review."

"Fine."

"As soon as I saw the review was very critical of the board, executive and middle managers I knew that Sue James would not want it widely circulated. Did you know that last year she was threatened with a vote of no confidence by the hospital consultant committee?"

"I may have known that."

"Her failures, highlighted in your report, are the same ones that precipitated the consultants' committee's concerns about her leadership."

"These problems are universal."

"But your review has clearly analysed the problem: Sue James was happy to put a bunch of unqualified amateurs in charge of a core service. You prescribed a remedy: you said that the management needs to change; you said that extra resources are needed. Don't these other consultants in other departments need to know about this if the problem is so widespread and you have come up with the answer?"

"Please stop calling it my review."

"Did you know that Sue is currently looking for a new job?"

"I may have known that."

"Do you understand then why Sue has a serious conflict of interest when it comes to disseminating this report?"

"I couldn't possibly comment on that. The dissemination of the review was put in the hands of the Chief Executive who commissioned it, and it is nothing whatsoever to do with you."

"Hang on. The review was commissioned at my request and supported by the BMA. The substance of the review was my grievance against the Medical Director. The rest related to my complaints about the mismanagement of the department. You upheld my complaints on this. How come it's nothing to do with me? If it was a straight grievance the conclusions would be mine to do with as I pleased."

"This was not a grievance procedure, David. In any case, when I write to you tomorrow I will be instructing you, as you were instructed in the report, to withdraw your grievances against Mike Brown and Karen Palmer."

"That's outrageous, Nadeem. The review supported my grievances at practically every point and you want me to withdraw them. In the interests of peace and quiet I wrote to Sue James agreeing to do that but I am advised by the BMA I cannot be required to. By you or anyone else."

"You *will* withdraw the grievance."

True to his word, inexplicably, he confirmed this in writing the next day."

"This is now my final word on the matter, David. You have to accept the review, and if you don't you will soon find you are not working in Walsall."

"That's it then."

"Yes, that's it…you can go. You will be meeting with the Chief Executive to discuss your options shortly."

Ian had been telling me for months that the Trust would find a reason to dismiss me. I had just provided Nadeem with that reason. I walked out into the corridor. A colleague hurried up to me and with a conspiratorial flourish ushered me into a nearby empty room.

"Good God, David, I heard the whole thing! I was in the toilet by Nadeem's office. The walls are so thin you can hear everything going on in there! How many times did you say "no" to him?"

Another consultant colleague later gave evidence at my employment tribunal. He testified under oath to the widespread belief that Nadeem had been brought in to get rid of me. He told the tribunal Nadeem had been on my case from the time of his arrival, ignoring me, cutting me off mid-sentence and telling me he'd heard enough of me. He also referred to multiple occasions when Nadeem had been heard shouting at me in his office. I heard that evidence with relief. There were times when I thought that I had imagined the whole nightmare.

The following day I received an email from Nadeem. He listed and even extended the things I had to agree to. No other person involved in the review was required to give more than verbal assent to their instructions. No-one was ever held to them. Now I was required to give written assent by an immediate deadline otherwise I would soon not be working in Walsall. I replied in line with our conversation. I was unable to accept instructions that were unreasonable, unlawful and against my conscience.

After that I didn't get on with Nadeem too badly. I have never been able to bear a grudge. I thanked him at the hospital consultants' committee for the work he was doing updating the department on quality improvement, etc. He told me more than once that I was the natural leader in the department and that others knew it. When I did work such as drawing up the morning safety check and implementing it, he was generous in his praise. But we had further skirmishes. Some weeks after our first meeting Nadeem summoned me again to his office

"David, you are the most extreme case of cognitive dissonance that I have ever encountered in my life. You need to read a book." It was, he told me, *Mistakes were Made (but not by me)* by Tavris and Aronson. I checked the title on Amazon when I left his office. It was subtitled, *Why We Justify Foolish Beliefs, Bad Decisions and Hurtful Acts*.

"What does cognitive dissonance mean?" I asked. "I've come across it but I don't see how it fits me,"

"I'm not going into that."

"You recommend a book based on a psychological dysfunction it describes. You reckon I suffer from that dysfunction and yet you refuse to discuss it with me?

"I'm not going to be drawn, David. Read the book"

"OK, since we're on the subject let's discuss my mental health. Two gynaecologists claimed I had a major psychiatric illness. That went to NCAS. Mike Brown lied to the occupational consultant, who then sent me a psychiatric appointment. "

"Mike Brown didn't lie."

"I made a written request to your panel to take evidence from the occupational consultant. He told me personally that Mike Brown had asked him to arrange the appointment at my own request. Why didn't you interview him?"

"We did not feel it necessary."

"I had a right to have my witnesses heard. It wasn't for you to pick and choose. There were three other important witnesses I asked you to speak to. They had information about how this situation has developed and who is responsible. Two of them left their posts because they were bullied. Why did you not hear the witnesses I listed?"

"It was a panel decision."

"That would be a breach of any grievance policy. I gave you an opportunity to get to the truth and you ducked it. I was stitched up with a psychiatric appointment by the Medical Director who lied to the occupational health consultant."

"Look, David, you may or may not have a psychiatric diagnosis but some of the most senior people in this organization refer to you as unhinged. That's the word they use, David, "unhinged". I mean, look at you."

I knew a lot by this time about whistleblowers being smeared: search out their worst cases and get them to the GMC; run through their expenses; check for porn on their computers. But the very worst thing that I had encountered in the whistleblowers that I had now met was that many had been smeared over their mental health. I'd had enough and was about to leave but Nadeem asked me a question.

"What do you think about the way that Dr Muhammad dresses for work?" Dr Muhammad dressed (and still dresses) in traditional Islamic clothes with a hat and robes.

"It's interesting you should ask that. When I first met Bashir I thought his sartorial choices strange in a hospital setting. A manager actually told me, after his appointment, that the people of Walsall would not accept a consultant who dressed like that. Yet, only a few months later a nurse came in to my clinic and said 'Dr Drew, you'm been passed by Dr Muhammad as most popular consultant here.' (I always loved Debbie's Black Country brogue.) Walsall people know a good doctor when they meet one, Nadeem. That's more important than what he wears"

"I believe we should have a professional dress code. I wouldn't allow a consultant to dress like Bashir does."

Nadeem's views on diversity were self-evident. I'd clocked his views on dress, religious identity and freedom of expression. I thought about telling him that the English were quite laid back about most of these things but held to my general rule of keeping the peace. He was English himself after all.

"So, for interest, Nadeem," I asked, "You concluded that I wasn't a whistleblower. What about the Kyle Keen saga and the safeguarding nurse? What about the hypothermia? It was all tightly documented."

"It was a panel decision. You've got to stop living in the past. David. You haven't got a Baby P. You are not a whistleblower. If you try to go down that route you will die. I'm telling you, David, you will become ill and you will die. That's what happens to people who think there is a conspiracy."

I was left helpless. Like a baby. Frustrated. Nowhere to go. No one to turn to.

Skirmishes continued on an occasional basis. Over the August bank holiday Janet and I went to Kent to visit our son and his family. Ian Darwood asked me to swap duties with him and do his Bank Holiday Monday on-call. As the consultant out-of-hours rota had originally been written (by me), the Bank Holiday Monday consultant came on at 5pm. The consultants who habitually did the Mondays had changed this and they started at 9am. I had never been made aware of this. There was a system error in the rota, which went unnoticed until this swap uncovered it for the first time since its implementation two years earlier. As a result I arrived at 5pm and this left an eight-hour gap in the cover.

The next day I was summoned to Nadeem's room. He was furious. I tried to explain the rota problem but he was having none of it.

"It's not just this, David; I'm picking up noise about you in the system."

"Speak English, Nadeem. Speak plainly or I can't help you. What noise?"

He claimed that I had failed to do two of my clinics recently. I had in fact cancelled the clinics and submitted all the appropriate leave forms, but somewhere in the Divisional Director's office these had got lost. It was the first time such a thing had ever happened to me in 18 years. The Divisional Director had written a letter questioning this at the time and I had given him a full explanation. He had written to all consultants at an earlier date saying that they were in the habit of taking leave that he had not approved. This was a direct result of his own faulty system for approving leave. I had been head of department for seven years and was obsessional about such administrative matters.

Nadeem wasn't interested in an explanation. He intended conducting a formal investigation with the help of Human Resources. Nothing came of this and he eventually accepted that it was a rota error. The whole thing could have been settled with a short informal discussion. I had always thought of myself as an extra-mile doctor and these allegations that I was trying to avoid work upset me immensely. I was on my very best behaviour from that point on. Nadeem and I then enjoyed a fairly business-like relationship until my dismissal.

33

The Choice

Now, I give you fair warning, either you or your head must be off.
     The Queen of Hearts in *Alice in Wonderland*

The meeting with Nadeem confirmed one thing: unless I agreed unconditionally, without caveat, to accept the whole of the review I would, in his words, "soon not be working in Walsall". And I could not in good conscience, with the advice I had, do that. We generally behaved professionally towards each other, although he was occasionally rude to me in front of my secretary and juniors. I always saw this as diminishing him, not me. He told me to wait for an invitation from Mrs James, who would be making me a financial offer to leave my post. This duly arrived and Ian and I met with her on 25th June 2010. She had Sue Wakeman, Head of HR, present to advise her.

We met in the Chairman's office. Before the meeting I had asked that it be properly minuted. I was surprised when Sue James told us the meeting would be digitally recorded. She later claimed that the meeting had been "without prejudice", that is, off the record. That had not been agreed. Why would anyone digitally record a meeting that was off the record? The Trust subsequently gave copies of the transcript to at least six other people, showing it felt no obligation to treat it as such. I was able to obtain an ad verbatim transcript so there is no debate as to what was said.

The Chief Executive and the Head of HR were ill at ease. There was a lot of initial nervous laughter – it can be heard as the recording starts. Sue James quickly got her business hat on and explained the purpose of the meeting.

"We need to move on. You have said that you cannot accept the recommendations of the report without reservation. You have told Nadeem that you do not accept. That leaves us in a position where your place in the organization is untenable."

I reminded her that agreement to everything in the review without reservation had never been a condition for either side.

Ian McKivett: "The vast majority of recommendations that affect David are accepted. The rest was not a matter of him not accepting but asking for clarity. There's been a lot of movement on his part but there are some bits that put restrictions on David beyond any other employee. We cannot accept that David's continuation in post is untenable."

Ian was referring among other things to the instructions that I stop imposing my religious and other beliefs on colleagues and the restrictions on religious language. These were in my opinion blatant discrimination and a denial of my freedom of speech and conscience. In any case there was no basis in fact for these restrictions. I had it clearly in my mind now that these were the result of managerial machinations and bullying.

Sue James then claimed to have the Trust board on her side.

"Whilst you might not accept that it's an untenable position, I feel, and the board feels, that it is an untenable position."

The truth was that the board did not know about this decision. I rang one of the non-executive directors shortly after this meeting. He told me, "Sorry, David, we were kept in the dark. I knew nothing about it." At the tribunal two years later, Sue James referred to "the board in action" several times. When the board is not sitting the Chief Executive and the Chairman *are* the board, she explained. This was pretty convenient as it gave the two of them authority to speak for the board more than 99 per cent of the time. What she meant in this meeting was that she and Ben Reid had decided it was time for me to go. She was behaving more like a second-hand car salesman than an NHS Chief Executive. I pressed her hard to get the truth.

"Did you say the whole Trust board is behind this and is in agreement? Is that correct? Does the board know about this? Are they unanimous?"

"They haven't taken a vote on it. They wouldn't take a vote on something like this."

"But are there any dissenting voices on the board? At all?"

"No. The time has come for us to end the relationship. We need to do that in a way that reflects your long and distinguished career."

She had clearly made up her mind that I was going, so I asked her to get to the point. The proposed offer was that I leave as soon as possible with four months' salary in lieu and two years' extra pension. The BMA lawyer's written estimate of the value of this package, with my terminal bonus was £247,000. In addition she added that I would be able to draw down my pension immediately. I would also be given a reference that would enable me to continue working in the NHS if I wished. Anywhere, that was, other than Walsall.

There was one other condition: "Because the SHA is involved and because this is now considered a kind of extraordinary expenditure, we'd also need a compromise agreement as part of the deal." She writhed in her seat as she said this. Her body language radiated untruthfulness. She cast an occasional glance at her HR adviser as though looking for immoral support.

I had been prepared for this moment by Dr Peter Gooderham. Peter was an academic lawyer in Manchester; he was also medically qualified. I had met him earlier that year and familiarised him with my case. Before the meeting he had briefed me on all aspects of compromise agreements. I didn't need any explanation as to what Sue James was suggesting; the consequences of signing a gag were clear to me: everything that I had blown the whistle on would be swept under the carpet. One of Sue James's favourite phrases was "the past is the past." It was clearly her intention here. The whole Kyle Keen affair and the Trust's failures on child protection and other matters would not be raised again.

And the review report, so critical of the board and executive for what was, in my opinion, a virtual dereliction of duty, would be buried forever. Only Sue James and I had a full copy of it. Then there was what I had disclosed as the possibly criminally dishonest report by Mike Brown on the heating failure, written to conceal or at least trivialize a serious clinical incident. I was in no doubt that this was why Sue James wanted me out. The payout and gag would give her closure at taxpayer's expense. And it was a tempting offer.

She then told me in a patronizing way that the settlement would be a very nice birthday present for me. She would find early retirement attractive from her perspective too, she said. I didn't believe a word. Retirement was the last thing on my mind. And hers. So, what to do? Ian asked what would happen if I failed to accept the deal.

"I believe, and Ben Reid believes, that David's position is untenable in the organization and we would seek to remove him by disciplinary procedure if he does not accept."

Ian asked for a break so we could talk things over. We'd worked together for 18 months. Ian knew me well: "I know better than to advise you. What do you think?" When we had met Ben Reid on 5th November Ian told him that I had been "stitched up" by Mike Brown when I was suspended. I believed the same was true now. I was one of the awkward squad who stood up when things were going wrong. There was not a single concern that I had raised that was not valid – but also, more to the point, personally embarrassing to the two who had now decided unilaterally that I had to go. I told Ian that I would need to discuss this with my family as there would be financial consequences for everyone. I was going on holiday for a week in Derbyshire with my children and their children. The sixteen of us were gathering to celebrate Janet's 60th birthday. I asked for two weeks' grace.

Sue James's insincerity was transparent: I felt certain she and Ben Reid wanted me out to contain personal embarrassment. Ian had told me that the lawyers would have been advising them for at least several months. The board had made no decision about me. The SHA had not approved this payment, as a subsequent enquiry to its CEO showed, nor had it required a confidentiality clause. When I made contact, it turned out they had not even heard of me and had no record of my name. When challenged about all this under oath, Sue James said rather lamely that she had not understood the process for severance. She had been taking advice from her Head of HR and the Trust solicitor so her claim to ignorance was scarcely credible.

The irregularities went well beyond that. Such payments and gags cannot be used in the way Sue James was using them. The policy covering settlement and confidentiality clauses is contained in a document known as Maintaining High Professional Standards (MHPS). It specifies that settlement with a gag should not be used, for obvious reasons, in any case that should be dealt with by disciplinary procedure. The Trust had already made allegations that I had refused a lawful and reasonable instruction and ordered me weeks earlier to attend a disciplinary hearing. Sue James stated specifically that failure to accept this deal would be followed by removal by disciplinary procedure. She also made it clear that no obstruction would be put in my way to working elsewhere in the NHS. This is all specifically contrary to policy laid down in MHPS. In some circumstances it would allow a rogue doctor to be rewarded and allowed to find work in some other hospital. As with a number of other senior officers at Walsall, Sue believed herself exempt from local and national policy. Senior managers, under the Chairman's patronage, were effectively a law to themselves. I know, I keep repeating this. It needs to be heard.

The meeting closed with a strange statement from Sue James. "Well, can I just say, I remember being over on Salisbury ward one day and I saw you coming out of a side room with a child in your arms and I thought, "There's a man who loves his job." And it's very clear that you do, David, and that's why we've made this offer for you. Because I do – this is a very sincere offer – I do want you to feel that we value the work you've done." If I did not have the recording and transcript I would doubt that I had heard this.

At the weekend I left for a well-deserved holiday in Derbyshire with my family. When we discussed the offer everyone reacted as I expected, with fierce loyalty. At the family pow-wow Janet said simply, "That's dirty money. If you accept it I'll divorce you." One of my sons added, "Yes, and we'll never speak to you again." I was proud of them and glad that they had made the decision so easy for me.

On my return I responded to Sue James, refusing the offer. "The offer is a bribe at public expense. The disciplinary is a threat. I do not accept bribes and I am not moved by threats," I wrote. During my absence Nadeem Moghal had written to my consultant colleagues indicating that I might not return and asking them to arrange cover for my clinics for the next six months. Done and dusted, Dr Drew! One way or another you will soon not be working at Walsall.

I identified with Socrates at the end of his life. He was given the stark choice, exile or hemlock. On the day he died he reportedly said that he looked forward to going to "a place where they don't murder people for asking questions". I could have chosen a gagged exile with a fat payout and a passport to a new job. I believed that would have been morally wrong, a choice I would have been unable to live with. In any case, I wanted to continue serving Walsall families in the way I had done for many years until retirement suited me. I was certain that I had done all that was required of me by my conscience and my professional code. Sue James was going to have to pour the hemlock down my throat.

34

Foul Play

Holders of public office should be as open as possible about all the decisions and actions they take. They should give reasons for their decisions and restrict information only when the wider public interest demands it.

Nolan Committee on Standards in Public Life on "Openness"

By August I was still waiting for the disciplinary investigation to begin. I exploited one quietish day to write to Ben Reid about three issues that were central to my troubles. If he had taken my letter seriously it would have resulted in the end of the Trust's action against me. Instead he chose to use it to extend the charges against me to include "insubordination".

First, the results of the review should have been disseminated much more widely than they had been. "Neither you nor the executive has accepted the instruction of the review with respect to its dissemination," I wrote. Sue James had been under threat of a vote of no confidence over the last year. She was also known to be looking for a new CEO post. Clearly she was not going to want the board and executive's serious failings, as described in the report, widely known. It would have been in the public interest but it would not have been in her interest. And with Nadeem and Ben Reid on board she was in the driving seat.

Secondly, I could not accept any of the nonsense about imposing my religious views on other staff or refraining from religious reference in the workplace. No complaint had ever been made, rather the opposite. I had not been asked about this matter in either the exclusion investigation or the review. No evidence that I could answer to had ever been presented to me that there was any problem that needed these draconian measures, in fact any measures at all. It was a smokescreen devised and used by management. None of my clinical colleagues who I spent my working life with recognized any truth in it.

Thirdly, there had been repeated suggestions by Trust managers that I was mentally ill. Again, this was a management invention. My outrageous behaviour in speaking up for patients in the way that I did was the main symptom of my madness. I gave Ben an account of these smears and later used it as a submission to the Health Select Committee.

My letter to Ben Reid was headed "Disposing of Dr Drew". It contained necessarily some detail from the review. I also sent it with a covering letter to the most senior consultants in the hospital, to show that Sue James was pulling the wool over their eyes.

I'd followed senior management's dealings with the hospital consultants for many years. The Hospital Consultant Committee was the main arena for discussion of matters directly impinging on them and their work. During 2008 there had been a growing sense of disillusionment with Trust senior management.

The Chair of the Consultants' Committee wrote to Ben Reid in December 2008 expressing the gravest concerns about Walsall Manor Hospital. The background to this letter was that the consultants were preparing to take a vote of no confidence in Sue James's leadership. The letter makes frightening reading:

> I am hoping to apprise you of some of the grave concerns we consultants have regarding the current provision of care, staff morale and management within the Trust.
>
> We perceive a lack of insight and inability to listen when clinicians express concerns over service provision. Changes are railroaded through without consultation, often resulting

in deterioration of the services provided. All disciplines within the Trust are affected.

The overarching view is the lack of insight by middle and senior management as to what is actually required to provide a safe and efficient service.

The review was clear that these were the main problems disabling the paediatric department. The board knew little or nothing of what was happening in the paediatric department. The executive had made inappropriate appointments of managers who had no experience in the discipline, were aggressive and had failed to engage front-line staff. A cost-cutting change programme had been mismanaged and caused havoc in the department. The review had made recommendations to remedy these failings, which included guidance for the board and executive on how to do its job properly, removing some managers and the provision of extra resources. It was clear that all departments had problems with senior and middle management. Sue James at my employment tribunal said under oath that problems were restricted to paediatrics and the Hospital Consultant Committee's concerns had all originated with me. This was specifically untrue. It was also why I believed it was my duty to encourage the hospital consultant body to get insight into the paediatric review.

The Chair of the Consultants' Committee wrote further letters in the same vein to Ben Reid and Sue James later that month. Ben Reid's response, made through the Consultants' Committee Chair, was blunt. We were applying for Foundation Trust status and the PFI build was starting. This was no time to be voting the CEO out. That would put everyone's job at risk. The Consultants' Committee backed down. That did nothing to serve the interests of Walsall patients.

Following the review there were three meetings of the Consultants' Committee, in April, June and September. Every consultant in the hospital knew the paediatric department had had a review and most were anxious to know the outcome.

A minute from the April committee meeting recorded:

> The Independent Review of Paediatric Services is now complete. The Consultant Paediatricians present described the process. They stated that they had not received any feedback, either verbal or written, regarding the outcome of this review. There then followed questions from the floor. The general view was that there was **cause for concern that the report resulting from this review was not available and that neither the paediatricians nor the wider consultant body had yet received any feedback regarding this process.** It was therefore requested that a formal feedback of the report resulting from this review be presented to the Consultants' Committee at the next meeting, either by the paediatricians or more appropriately by the Chief Executive.

The June meeting took this up:

> Dr Drew commented that the minutes of the previous meeting stated that the Chief Executive had been invited to report on the recent review in paediatric services. It was reported from the chair that as the Chief Executive could not attend this current meeting this item had been deferred to the next meeting.

And in September, six months after the review, a minute reported:

> Mr Turner (Associate Medical Director) then commented that he had serious concerns that if the key findings of this report were not circulated widely to all the consultant body

then there was a significant risk that similar managerial issues and failures would be repeated.

The consultants needed the information about mismanagement that this report provided to help address similar issues in their own departments. They repeatedly asked for it. Nick Turner, a senior medical manager, stated openly that failure to share the report with the consultants would result in the problems being replicated in other departments.

I had written to Sue James along the same lines:

> It is important that the consultant committee sees and debates this review. It contains many lessons that all departments could benefit from. Much has been made of the importance of confidentiality but it has been dealt with so far by you in a way that has caused us to slip over the line into secrecy.

Ben Reid and Sue James attended the September Consultants' Committee. This was a swan song for Sue, as she had been appointed as Chief Executive at Derby Royal Hospitals. Ben Reid took the opportunity to eulogize her for seven years of excellent steerage and for delivering the PFI to grateful Walsall residents. The consultants were not impressed but returned to the theme that had originally prompted their desire to call her to account.

> Dr Holland (chair) on behalf of the Consultants' Committee voiced concerns that remained about the delivery of service at middle management level. She highlighted areas of specific concern including medical secretarial support, administration support and outpatient management. It was also the view that there was still significant disengagement of the Consultant body in day-to-day management decisions. Mr Reid confirmed his

own personal commitment to consultant engagement and confirmed that his door was open to all consultants should they have any concerns. Mr Reid commented that he felt that there was a lack of managerial support and that an increase in the number of medical managers may improve this. In response, Dr Balagopal (incoming Chair) commented that he did not feel that increasing the number of medical managers would help solve the problem. He felt that the problem lay in middle management being unable on a regular basis to deal with problems presented to them. This view was supported from the floor.

This was, to my mind, a prime example of a Trust Chairman and CEO who had not got a clue how to engage with the genuine concerns of senior clinicians who knew what they needed to do a decent job and who knew that the standard of middle management was poor. It is management's role to create the right conditions for the clinical front line to do its job. This was not how middle management saw things.

I read out at that meeting the review's instruction that its findings be reported to the wider hospital community. Sue James had, in the summary she sent to the paediatricians, quite deliberately altered this, limiting the instruction to: "paediatric staff and the management team".

She told the meeting that there could be no further discussion of the paediatric review as it was now included in a consultant's disciplinary hearing. Mine. She left for her new post in Derby three months later without having to address the Consultants' Committee on the review. I had predicted from the beginning that she never would speak publicly about it as long as I was around to comment. She should have come clean and shared the review with the consultants as soon as it was published. They might have respected her for that and tried to work with her. But that was not her way.

Even the clinical directors of the various departments, the senior clinicians with management responsibilities, had not been given any details of the review's findings, not even Sue James's abridged account. As we learned at the September meeting, however, the divisional directors, the non-clinical middle managers, had all been briefed on it. Sue James had delegated her Medical Director, Mike Brown, to do this. It was the unprofessional behaviour of Mike Brown that had occasioned the review in the first place. He had been trounced by the review, and many speculated that it precipitated his early retirement soon after. He had, supposedly, not been made party to the full report of the review but he was given the responsibility of briefing the middle managers on it. That gave him a good opportunity to defend himself, which is exactly what he did. Nick Turner was present when Mike Brown gave this talk and, unbeknown to Mike Brown, had an unabridged copy of the report, which I had given him. Nick told the September consultants' meeting that the account given by the Medical Director, Mike Brown, to the managers "was neither accurate nor honest".

It is astonishing that Mike Brown could have been made responsible for disseminating the review findings to the managers. It is astonishing that such criticism of him could be on the written record with no open challenge. He should have been called to account for this. But he had the backing of the Trust Chairman and the CEO, so he was protected from any such inconvenience. And Nadeem Moghal was present at this meeting, silently consenting to this wrongdoing. The following day I met him and challenged him about this. "The review is over. No further discussion. You had your chance."

What is a decent professional person encountering this level of abuse of power to do? I had done my best to challenge Sue James's suppression of the report. I had challenged Nadeem Moghal's complicity in this. I had tried to alert colleagues to this wrongdoing. My thoughts now turned to protecting myself.

35

Dr Drew the Religious Bigot

Preach the Gospel always; only use words if necessary.
attributed to Francis of Assisi

The restrictions imposed on me by Naj Rashid's investigation and
Nadeem Moghal's review would have been understandable if I had
been a tub-thumping, in-your-face, religious zealot. But I was not.
I am not. A clear implication of the instructions was that I force my
religious beliefs on others. I never have: that would be stupid.
Another implication was that I was such a religious loud mouth that
I had to be shut up. The final basis for the instructions was more
explicit and was contained in Nadeem Moghal's later written
clarification to my disciplinary investigation. I was, according to him,
quite simply, a religious bigot.

I am a Christian, a quiet Christian. I prefer to think of myself as
a Christian with questions. I am agnostic on some things, but
committed to the central doctrines of the Christian faith around the
person and life of Christ. I believe the Christian faith is true, not
just for Christians but for everyone. My position is that of St Paul:
when Herod Agrippa asked him if he (Paul) wanted to make him
(Agrippa) a Christian, Paul replied, "Yes, you and everybody else."
If Christianity is true Christians will of course want others to share
it. From the beginning the proclamation of forgiveness in Christ has
been known as Good News.

I am not an evangelist or a preacher or a Bible teacher. I do not
have the gifts or training for that. I am a doctor. I have tried in my
working life to express my faith by doing a good job, by being

diligent, knowledgeable and compassionate. No one in our culture is attracted to Christianity by hearing it shouted from the rooftops. I have always been careful not to abuse my position as a senior doctor to communicate my faith. I have always taken the Franciscan line and tried to model Christ in my behaviour. I have failed of course. But the central theme of Christianity has been my anchor: forgiveness. Every day is a new start.

When I was interviewed for my consultant post in Walsall in 1992 the British Paediatric Association (later to become the Royal College of Paediatrics) sent an adviser. He was Dr Paul Rayner, an endocrine consultant at Birmingham Children's Hospital. After being offered the job I told the committee that I had an interview at another hospital the following week. "What's up, David, don't you think Walsall needs a missionary?" asked Paul. The committee, including the Chief Executive, John Rostill, laughed. They agreed to hold the post open until I made a decision. As it turned out Walsall was the place for me. Twenty years later an employment tribunal in a written judgment decided that it was not acceptable for me to identify myself as a Christian in my workplace. To use the words "as a Christian" was unnecessary and unacceptable. That was quite a culture shift, one that Sue James and Nadeem Moghal would both have approved of.

For many years I was the only white and only Christian consultant in the paediatric department at Walsall. The others were variously Muslim, Hindu or atheist. There was no one who didn't have some view on faith. I always counted discussions about such things as an important part of getting to know my colleagues. The department was a hive of religious tolerance: Dr Muhammad was fond of ending conversations with "The Lord will tell us who is right one day, David. Me." I always appreciated his religion spiced with humour. He quite often at the end of a talk put a slide up that said, "Only God Knows Everything." That to me was an excellent reminder of the Socratic position, which should keep us in our place. Some may find this eccentric but it is preferable to some of the conversation I have heard in medical company.

Difficult ethical decisions, for example, at the end of life, often involved a religious perspective. Dr Muhammad's input with Muslim families was invaluable. Dr Gatrad was an international expert on healthcare delivery to Muslims. Colleagues gave interesting lunchtime talks on visits to Indian Christian mission hospitals or medical aspects of the Hajj or once, even, a meta-analysis of the efficacy of prayer. These all broadened our outlook and, in multicultural Walsall, made us better doctors. I was surprised at how often I was asked by parents about Christianity. Word gets around about a Christian doctor. "I've got a friend who goes to the same church as you," was a common introduction.

We all engaged in some way in the main festivals. Cards were given and received at Christmas. I covered Muslim colleagues' duties in Ramadan and went to break fast with them at dusk. We all enjoyed sumptuous feasts at the Hindu Festival of Lights, Divali. I went to the Guru Nanak Sikh temple, Hindu temples, and mosques, though I never learned as much about other religions as I intended: mostly I was interested in the lives of others.

From 1992 to 2009 we never had a quarrel or a cross word on the subject of religion. Everyone was too grown-up and respectful for that. But in 2009, following my exclusion, the Trust's interest in my faith and how I expressed it in the hospital developed into a war zone. This was driven by two people, Sue James and later on Nadeem Moghal, with help from the head of HR and some hostile middle managers. None of them had a faith as far as I know. Sue James showed an appalling ignorance of religion, and that to some extent explained her inability to accept the possibility that her behaviour was discriminatory.

Nadeem was different. He wanted a secular NHS. "Keep your religion out of the workplace, David" was one of the first instructions he gave me after he arrived. "No crosses at work. The law lords have decided." I do not wear a cross or any religious symbols. That my faith was a major part of my identity and informed much of my professionalism seemed to be lost on him. It was virtually impossible for me to determine where his intolerance came from. He was a closed person. He refused to engage on matters that had been part of normal conversation in the department.

The first hint of trouble came on 25th September 2009 when I met Mike Brown with Ian Mckivett to hear the result of Naj Rashid's investigation. I was told, in the now infamous Recommendation 6.5, "Dr Drew should accept that his own wider personal views and religious beliefs should be kept to himself and should not be imposed on others." This was the first we had heard about religion. Ian called it discriminatory from the start. He told me this was a lever the Trust would use against me. Mike Brown promised but failed to help find out what underlay it.

Over the following weeks I wrote to HR for information. I knew for certain there was nothing I could have done to warrant this instruction. Eventually Sue Wakeman volunteered this:

> I can confirm that there are two witness statements that relate to you sending poems and prayers and using Bible quotes. The comment was that they were inappropriate.

In April I had sent consultant colleagues an email containing the prayer of St Ignatius, the only prayer I ever sent anyone at work. The email read

> Dear Colleagues
>
> Thought I would encourage you with this prayer from St Ignatius Loyola, the founding father of the counter-reformation and the Jesuits. I find this a personal inspiration

in my frail imperfect efforts to serve my patients, their families
and our department. Hope you can find something in it too.

Teach us, good Lord,
to serve you as you deserve,
to give and not to count the cost,
to fight and not to heed the wounds,
to toil and not to seek for rest,
to labour and not to ask for any reward,
save that of knowing that we do your will.

David

We had just been in a difficult job-planning meeting. The prayer is
a classic. It is possibly the most beautiful expression of selfless
service in the English language. Its theme is that the act of service,
the satisfaction gained from service, is in itself our real reward. It
perfectly expresses the spirit of idealism on which the NHS has been
built. But who was I to quarrel with Naj Rashid or Jon Pepper or
Rob Hodgkiss, who all found it "inappropriate". Trust management
had formally accepted that I was imposing my religious views on
colleagues and it must stop.

In fact my consultant colleagues who had received the prayer
expressed gratitude to me for drawing it to their attention. Dr
Gatrad, a Muslim, wrote, "Thanks David, This is lovely and thought
provoking. Rashid" Dr Satish wrote, "Dear David, as an atheist, let
me write to say that I did not find your e-mail objectionable. I
concur with Mike Brown and find it refreshing. I am sorry that it
has been blown out of proportion. Satish" Other consultants told
me that they remembered the prayer from school and were glad to
be reminded of it.

Mike Brown had written to me about the email some days
before suspending me.

Dear David, Very refreshing to be reminded of this prayer, which I remember well (having been educated by the close rivals of the Jesuits the Augustinians, responsible for identifying the genetic basis of life). This is an excellent frame of mind in which to negotiate next year's job plans. I applaud your altruism. Mike.

This clearly was not imposing anything on anyone. I didn't know at that stage which witnesses had made the allegations so I wrote once more to Sue James to ask for details. I still find her response shocking:

We do not usually share witness statements, but you insisted on seeing these and they have had the effect I feared in that you have started to try to work out who said what about you and why.

Of course I wanted to know who said what, and what their evidence was for it. It would also have been useful to know why. Sue James's view was quite clearly that I had no right to this. In a subsequent report to the Royal College review panel the Head of Human Resources described my efforts to get this clarification as an "attempt to find and potentially harass a member of staff ... potentially a very serious disciplinary offence." My legitimate attempt to get transparency was seen as misconduct. The Chief Executive and HR boss had primary responsibility for modelling an open culture. Neither appeared to have any understanding of what this involved.

Finally, after more wrangling, Sue James did a volte-face. After further exchanges about my alleged religious imperialism, in December she wrote, "As I believe the report made clear, and Sue Wakeman and Mike have emphasized to you in your discussion on the outcome of the investigation, this issue was dismissed during the investigation." This was totally untrue but I accepted it as a truce and laid the episode to rest.

Three months later, Nadeem Moghal interviewed me twice for the review. I was asked one brief question about the use of religious language at work. I said it was impossible for a native English person not to use religious references: they are deeply embedded in the language. No more.

I was shocked to read in the report three weeks later that I was instructed (it was a required outcome, a must do) to "Refrain from using religious references in professional communication, verbal or written, regardless of past apparent acceptance of this style".

This was the only instruction I was given by the review that I refused outright to accept, pending evidence of my alleged wrongdoing. It took me a year to obtain documents using the Data Protection Act to understand how the review could have come to such a ludicrous conclusion.

By January 2010 the Trust had produced a 16-page statement of case for the College review, with contributions from Sue James, Sue Wakeman and Mike Brown. At every turn this statement casts me in the worst possible light. Nothing was too trivial to serve that purpose. Even a short email in which I apologized for a moment of bad temper was cited as an example of my communication problems, concentrating on the "temper" but ignoring the apology. The statement is full of inaccuracies and untruths and spin. It ascribes ulterior motives to the most reasonable of actions.

Well before this statement was completed Sue James had written to me to say that the issue of religious misbehaviour had been dropped. But within weeks the allegations of religious misbehaviour were being kept alive in the Trust statement to the review, a statement that I was not allowed to see. The St Ignatius prayer is cited as "a prayer circulated to colleagues for no apparent reason". I had made the reason perfectly clear and it had been applauded by its recipients. Mike Brown's email commending my use of the prayer was said to be "unhelpful, in that it might reasonably be viewed by David Drew as approving his circulation of an unsolicited prayer". The report also refers to two managers objecting in their statements to my "use of prayers". "The case investigator, Mr Rashid, concurred with their views. Mike Brown had accepted recommendation 6.5 that David Drew should stop imposing his religious views on others." This was exactly the opposite of what Sue James had written to me weeks earlier. She had claimed the matter had been dropped. The letter in which she informed me of this was never shown to the review. Senior management was more intent on destroying me than helping the review panel get at the truth.

Nadeem arrived as head of department in June. His position was that all witnesses were given "a cast-iron guarantee of non attribution" and I would not be able to interrogate the evidence. He claimed not to be able to remember what some witnesses had said and there was no extant record of their oral evidence.

It was not until I saw his August statement to Julia Hollywood, the investigator in my disciplinary procedure, that I began to understand the basis of his instruction. Nadeem told Julia that the panel had "examined Naj Rashid's recommendation 6.5 and considered it valid". The prayer had found universal acceptance by its recipients, there had been a mild expression of distaste by two hostile managers who it had *not* been sent to and Sue James had withdrawn recommendation 6.5 months earlier in writing. But these facts were of no importance. And since I was unaware that religion was an issue I had been unable to defend myself. Even Julia Hollywood was not allowed to see Sue James's email withdrawing 6.5. Quite a stitch-up, but so well crafted that it could not have been other than by design.

Nadeem continued in his statement, "People had said to the review panel that David Drew has a habit of saying at meetings, 'I am a Christian therefore...' which in my view was placing himself in a different context. David Drew complained that there had been no earlier complaints about this. This was not altogether surprising as these are difficult matters to raise openly. The confidentiality of the report and the guarantee of non-attribution of comments allowed people to say things that would be too sensitive to voice openly to David Drew." In Nadeem's view, in referring to myself as a Christian, I was claiming a higher value for my opinions. That is the essence of bigotry. He had arrived at this view, and used it in the investigation against me, without even discussing it with me. I knew the alleged evidence this was based on was untrue: I suspected that it came, once again, from hostile middle managers.

In two large files disclosed to an FOI after my dismissal I came across the source of this evil nonsense – and I was correct in my suspicion. Shortly after the Trust Chair had agreed to commission the review and around the time Sue James claimed 6.5 had been dropped, the HR department had started a trawl for material to include in its statement of case against me. In response to a verbal request Jon Pepper wrote the following email to Sandra Berns:

Sandra,

The query about religious views was made in context of inappropriate emails. There have been several meetings where David has put his hand on his heart and said, "I am a Christian" thereby implying that he is speaking the truth. He has sent a prayer to Rob by email.

Thanks
Jon

Apart from its pettiness, its spitefulness, this was specifically untrue. I am not in the habit of going around saying I am a Christian. Everyone I work with knows that. I do not use the gesture described. In my experience it is a gesture more likely to be used by Muslim colleagues. There is, in any case, nothing wrong with it. It was once a cultural norm to speak "as a Christian and a gentleman": Jesus specifically instructs us to let "yes" be "yes" and let "no" be "no"; I do that. In Nadeem's later statement to Julia Hollywood he converts Jon's "There have been several meetings where David has…" to "David Drew has a habit of saying at meetings…". What I knew I never did Jon reported I had done at several meetings and Nadeem amplified into a habit. I had not encountered, in 40 years in medicine, any doctor so given to profane speech as Jon. And he was proud of it, as I had heard him boast. Nadeem was the most zealous advocate of a completely secular NHS I had met. This was an unholy alliance and I was its quarry.

And so I refused to accept the instructions given by Naj Rashid's investigation and Nadeem Moghal's review. I was certain that my behaviour as a Christian in the workplace had been impeccable at all times. My Christian faith had made me a better employee, a more sensitive and caring doctor: it was an asset. I never at any time considered my views superior to those of others because I was a Christian. I had never caused offence and even the allegations made against me under the guarantee of non-attribution were trivial, untrue or vexatious.

I had, according to Martin Brewer, the Trust solicitor who constructed the charge sheet against me, failed to accept a reasonable and lawful instruction. Neither my advisers nor I thought this instruction reasonable or lawful. I stood to be dismissed under employment law for Some Other Substantial Reason (SOSR) solely because I refused to submit to this tyranny.

36

Julia Hollywood – Private Investigator

Now is the dramatic moment of fate, Watson, when you hear a step upon the stair which is walking into your life, and you know not whether for good or ill.

Sherlock Holmes *in The Hound of the Baskervilles*

On 17th August 2010 the newly appointed Medical Director, Amir Khan, wrote to say that my disciplinary procedure was about to start. He would act as case manager and an outside consultant, Julia Hollywood, would lead the investigation. The three allegations made against me were written by Martin Brewer, the Trust solicitor. I had seen them for the first time immediately after the review had published its report in March, when Sue James had unsuccessfully tried to oust me. They were now rehashed with no change.

> First, by refusing to confirm your acceptance of the independent panel's recommendations and therefore failing to agree to normalize, or even to attempt to normalize, working relationships in the best interests of the service, you are in breach of contract, in that, contrary to obligations implied in your employment relationship with the Trust, you have:
>
> failed to co-operate with the Trust in implementing its procedures and failed to obey a lawful and reasonable instruction.

Second, that your refusal to confirm your acceptance of the independent panel's recommendations and to work alongside others in the service in the best interests of the patients and the Trust is a current and continued manifestation of past failings, indicating a lack of willingness to work as part of a cohesive team.

Finally, that your failure to confirm your acceptance of the independent panel's recommendations and work with the Trust in developing and delivering first class paediatric services shows a disregard for the Trust, its staff and the patients, and represents a complete breakdown in trust and confidence between yourself and the Trust as your employer.

When I first read these allegations I knew there was no truth in any of them. The Trust had been forced by the BMA to withdraw them three months earlier. I believed that I could disprove them. I still believed in fair play. I still believed this was England, not some backwater banana republic.

Julia Hollywood, an HR consultant with her own private company in Essex, was hired to investigate the truth or otherwise of the allegations and decide whether I had a case to answer. My first meeting with her was scheduled for 19th August. HR gave me the absolute minimum notice – one working day, in fact. My appointment also coincided with one of my busiest unassisted clinics. At short notice I had to ask a trainee to cover me. This was, in my experience, HR's modus operandi. I never worked out whether it was deliberate or symptomatic of profound incompetence. The review's account of HR supported the latter.

The first meeting lasted two hours, more than twice as long as my meetings with the review panel. A digital recording was made and this was later transcribed. Julia Hollywood was tense. I thought her body language unfriendly from the outset. Her brow was permanently furrowed. She told us several times that she recognized her method of investigation was "unorthodox". The exact method she explained was "to play the devil's advocate". Since my use of supposedly unacceptable religious language was to occupy much of our discussions I found her use of religious metaphor ironic. To me it meant (and felt very much as if) she was taking Sue James's and Nadeem Moghal's view on everything and advocating on behalf of them – not that I am comparing Sue or Nadeem to the Devil of course.

In response to Julia's questions, Ian and I gave a historical account of events from the time of my exclusion eighteen months earlier. To me it was tedious and I struggled to keep it accurate and coherent. Ian pointed out what we had already said until we were blue in the face. The Trust's action against me was to be seen in the context of my whistleblowing. Julia had worked for the BMA as an industrial relations officer earlier in her career: she knew full well that this sort of thing happened. I was clear that I considered I had made a number of disclosures under PIDA. On 31st August I followed this point up in an email:

> We may lose sight of what this is all about. In 2008 I wrote a number of letters to the divisional management and executive raising concerns about patient care and child protection.

But Julia was, as she told us, there to investigate and not to speculate about such things. I felt some sympathy for her. The review was essentially closed off to her. She had a copy of the report but now, in the hands of Sue James and Ben Reid and their legal advice, it had assumed the status of holy writ. Like the Law of the Medes and the Persians, it could not be revoked; it could not be questioned. Ian spoke about our meeting with the panel when we received the report. The panel's view had been, he said, "Our work is done. Any problems with the review, discuss it with the Trust." But the Trust had no access to any of the evidence for any of the review's conclusions. As Nadeem had told me earlier, it was up to Sue James to interpret it as she saw fit. The review panel had concluded that I was not a whistleblower but had given no evidence for its conclusion, which was patently wrong.

Religion came up again. I did not know Julia's background but I suspected she found talking about religion slightly distasteful – in the same way that some at one time may have felt when discussing race or homosexuality. She suggested that irrespective of whether I had ever caused offence with a religious reference, whether or not using such references was a breach of Trust policy, and irrespective of the behaviour of others, I ought to accept my employer's instruction. Since I knew I never had caused any offence and the instruction was discriminatory I could not do so. I was a paediatrician: that was my vocation, my calling. It is quite impossible to keep spirituality out of the life and death affairs of children and their families. It was clear that the whole case against me relating to my faith had been manufactured by certain managers who had taken against me; furthermore, latterly, it had opportunistically been used by Sue James and Nadeem. I asked Julia to get the evidence behind the allegations from Naj Rashid's investigation and Nadeem Moghal's review. She agreed to do this for the next meeting.

That night I had a drink with a friend, a cynical old union man. "You want to know how these things work, David?" he asked. "Well, the HR Director calls the external HR consultant in. There's five or ten thousand pounds on the table. 'Now,' says she, handing him two sheets of paper, '*This* is what we want you to look at, and *this* is what we want you to find. Any questions?'" I took this as a metaphor for the difficulty outside consultants would have in being completely objective, conscious of their need for future commissions. "Why did they bring someone in from Essex, David? We're at the centre of a population hub of six million. Think about it. She's a hired gun." He laughed. I never quite knew whether to take him seriously.

Before the first meeting closed I asked Julia to consult me when arranging the next session so that it could be scheduled at a mutually convenient time. On 2nd September I emailed her, "I would be grateful if future meetings could be arranged with adequate notice so as not to clash with my clinical commitments. I look forward to our next meeting." But I was not at all surprised, after this, that when I received an invitation for the next meeting it was scheduled on my mandatory child-protection training day, nor that it fell at the end of a 24-hour on-call period. Nadeem overruled my decision to attend the "mandatory" child-protection training and I had no choice but to cancel and hope for the best with my night on call.

The second meeting was on 27th September, six weeks after the first. On the 26th I was consultant on call. We were busy: I went home for a late supper, exhausted. That evening there was a torrential rainstorm. The recently opened PFI hospital developed a massive roof leak directly above the paediatric unit. I was called in as management was considering evacuation. On arrival I found water pouring through the ceiling and down the electrical conduits in the corridor. The patients and their parents were fine; so were the nurses. The manager was nowhere to be seen so I went upstairs to investigate. The Trust officer with responsibility for the building was a likable and diligent man, Lincoln Dawkins. I found him on the top floor obviously in charge of the situation. If he'd been my doctor I would have felt confident that I was in safe hands. He assured me there was no need for evacuation.

I went home to bed but didn't sleep. At 4am I was called in to see an ill child with meningitis. She needed transferring for paediatric intensive care but no bed was immediately available in the region. Once I was sure the patient was safe until the paediatric intensive care unit retrieval team arrived, I went home to snatch an hour's sleep. I turned up to Julia's meeting on time. In the corridor I passed a colleague. "David, you look like shit. Go home and get some sleep; I'll cover you today." Little did he know what he was offering.

The meeting lasted an hour. Julia had promised to give me the evidence that underlay the allegation that I had been imposing my religious and wider beliefs on others. I was shown a couple of sentences from the statements Jon Pepper and Rob Hodgkiss made to Naj Rashid. Jon's statement said, "Some of his emails are a little bizarre, quoting the Bible etc." Probably in 18 years of working at the Trust I had used a quoted Bible reference on half a dozen occasions at most, and only to someone who I knew would appreciate it; I had never to the best of my knowledge sent one to Jon, not one. Rob's statement said, "He's also sent me poems and prayers to read, which I find strange." Rob had been copied in on the St Ignatius prayer but it was clearly aimed at the clinicians. That was the only prayer I ever sent anyone in 18 years. I never sent Rob a poem, just one limerick. Julia came to that next. She turned to a short businesslike email I'd written on a departmental administrative matter; it had gone to Rob and the consultants. At the bottom I added the following:

> Be it a business, a club or a nation,
> To complete some immense obligation,
> The job will get done
> If we're working as one,
> It merely takes co-operation."

I thought that witty, brief and relevant. Julia thought it unorthodox and clearly felt that it was "inappropriate". Rob had found it strange. Jon was prepared to whinge about things he had not even received. Curiouser and curiouser! In one other email I had used an Aramaic term to an outside paediatric consultant who I believed was familiar with it. It is the origin of the expression "the writing is on the wall." Because Julia was not familiar with it she thought it "opaque".

So, this was the evidence that in Naj Rashid's hands had amounted to an allegation that I was "imposing my religious opinions on others" and necessitated an instruction that I desist. Months later, when I obtained the full statements courtesy of the Information Commissioner, I found that Rob had finished his statement with, "David has an opinion on everything." In the hands of Naj Rashid this required another instruction: that "Dr Drew must stop imposing his wider opinions on others." There was, in my experience, little if any attempt by the Trust to adequately select or train staff as investigators in disciplinary procedures. And, in the case of my investigation by Naj Rashid, this certainly showed.

Later, using the Data Protection Act, I learned that the Trust had done a trawl of managers (but not clinicians, who, unlike them, were well disposed towards me) to gather information about my "communication style" for its statement of case for the review. Rob had complained that I had sent him a text on Christmas Day. It said, "Rob, have a peaceful Christmas." He had texted a rather grumpy response: "Likewise". In a statement to the Trust he claimed that my action had "grieved him". Nothing was too petty to be included in the Trust's inventory of my strange, bizarre, unorthodox and grievous communications. The story of this unwanted Christmas greeting was told in the media across the world during my employment tribunal. Journalists have an eye for the bizarre.

What Julia wanted to know, as Devil's Advocate, was that if my colleagues found my behaviour strange, unorthodox or even irritating, shouldn't I be willing to accept an instruction from my employer to stop? "Isn't the world grey enough for you already?" was my response. The HR shade of grey, I meant. What kind of employer required its employees to agree to desist from irritating others on pain of dismissal? These matters are settled at a personal level and the employer should only become involved in the event of a serious complaint. The truth was that Rob and Jon had made these comments about me in a statement solicited by the Trust, under a cloak of secrecy; neither had said a single word to me. The meeting came to an end.

Afterwards I wrote to the Trust outlining serious irregularities with Julia's investigation; I concluded as follows:

> I have no doubt that this investigation is unfairly biased against me in the Trust's favour. I do not know whether this is deliberate or raises issues of Julia Hollywood's competence. It must be recognized that Julia Hollywood did this work on a commercially lucrative basis. I wish it to be recorded that I consider the investigation biased against me and should be declared void.

This was ignored. I was so used to that I thought nothing of it.

> *Dear Diary: The Barbarians are at the gates. No inspirational prayer, no limerick, no poem, no antique quotation permitted. No wisdom. No fun. And Christmas is cancelled. The world has grown grey at their touch.*

Julia Hollywood reported to the Trust that I had a case to answer to the allegations. On 12th November Sue Hartley, the Director of Nursing, who would chair my disciplinary hearing, informed me that I would answer the three allegations at a disciplinary hearing. A week later she wrote again to report that a fourth allegation had been added as an afterthought.

> Finally that on 16th August 2010 you disclosed confidential information to a group of colleagues by copying to them a letter and enclosures addressed to the Chairman of the Trust board containing information that he had been asked not to disseminate, and that in so doing you committed an act of

serious insubordination and/or a serious breach of confidentiality and an act or acts of gross misconduct.

Martin Brewer, the Trust's hawkish solicitor, wrote this allegation. It referred to my letter to the Chairman in which I had challenged him about Sue James's failure to disseminate the review. I had in fact volunteered to Julia Hollywood at our first meeting that I had copied this letter to a group of senior consultants in the Trust. She showed no real interest in this at the time and I felt no need to explain myself. She failed to investigate the allegation. She gave me no opportunity to explain why I had taken that step, which I clearly took in the interest of patients. Nevertheless, she concluded, I had a case to answer for it.

The Trust withdrew Amir Khan as case manager shortly before the disciplinary hearing. Sue Hartley, the disciplinary chair, informed us that the Trust solicitor, Martin Brewer, of Mills and Reeves, would replace him. Ian made a written protest to the Trust chairman at this unprecedented action but Ben Reid was having none of it. We then had an extensive correspondence with Sue Hartley on a host of procedural points. But no quarter was given. Six months after Sue James had tried to pay me off and gag me I was out onto open ground, running for the last fence. I had little left in my legs but I was determined to jump it.

37

Faith on Trial

I would challenge any of you to walk through the paediatric department with David and find anything other than a very warm reception from all the staff, patients etc. And the reason for that is because David Drew is a force for good in this Trust.

Ian McKivett, BMA representative: comment addressed to disciplinary panel

Tuesday 14th December 2010 is a day that will live in infamy in my own personal history. With it began my two-day disciplinary hearing. It seemed to me that everything possible was done to disadvantage me at that hearing. I believed then and believe now that the result was predetermined.

Ian and I arrived on time. The room was small, hot and airless. I commented on this and was advised that we could keep the door open if I wished. The panel was seated. Sue Hartley, the recently appointed Director of Nursing (with, ironically, responsibility for safeguarding), was in the chair. Nigel Summer, Trust Vice-Chair, and Colin Holden, a fee-paid, retired NHS HR Director, were on either side. Sue Wakeman, Head of HR, was present for the Trust. Julia Hollywood, investigator to my disciplinary procedure, had been brought up from Essex for the day and helped present the Trust case. Martin Brewer, of Mills and Reeve, Birmingham, the Trust solicitor, was there to present the Trust's case. He was supported by his trainee legal assistant, Kelly Barnet. "I take good notes when I bother but Kelly takes even better notes," he later intoned when cross-examining me. Sue James had told us six months earlier that the board wanted to see the back of me. It looked and felt like seven against two from the outset.

After introductions we got underway. Ian raised a series of objections to the Trust's breach of its disciplinary policy. The most serious of these to my mind was the presence of Martin Brewer at an internal disciplinary hearing. This had been raised in writing with Sue Hartley before the hearing and the BMA had protested to the Trust Chair, Ben Reid. Sue Hartley's definitive response on behalf of the panel was allegedly based on the ruling in *Kulkani v Milton Keynes NHS Trust*. Dr Kulkani went to the High Court seeking to win the right to bring a solicitor to his disciplinary hearing. This was granted primarily on the grounds that, the NHS being a monopoly employer, Dr Kulkani would lose not only his job but also his career if he were dismissed for gross misconduct. Sue Hartley argued that since I had been offered the opportunity for legal representation, it was quite legitimate for the Trust to be represented by its solicitor if it so wished.

This stank. Sue Hartley, both as panel chair and in her subsequent appearance at my employment tribunal, performed poorly. "Out of your depth" were the words used in her cross-examination at ET. It is inconceivable that she would have been able to construct this response herself. It probably came from legal advice, most likely given by Martin Brewer himself. The Trust had never been represented by a solicitor in an internal disciplinary process before. Shortly after my dismissal, the Trust board was approached by the Consultants' Committee with BMA support, and was assured that this would never be repeated. Sue James, in evidence to the employment tribunal, when asked about this, said weakly, "We were advised that we could use a solicitor." But who gave that advice? Once again I can only think that it was the Trust solicitor. The Trust wanted me out and Sue James sent the person most likely to secure that to speak for her.

I had asked about Martin Brewer in the HR department. "We

call him the Rottweiler. We love him because he's on our side," I was told. This man did not look like a Rottweiler: he was rather dumpy and bespectacled in a three-piece pinstripe suit, and in getting himself ready for the day he had not noticed a small food stain on one lapel. To me there was a whiff of the Dickensian grotesque about him; I was underwhelmed. But I was wrong: I underestimated him. At his hands and without any restraint from the panel chair I was about to suffer two of the most unpleasant days in my life.

Ian raised numerous objections. We had asked for a three-day hearing to present our case fully and have time for witnesses. It was a complex case and we had asked for an adjournment until after Christmas so that Ian could give it his full attention. Some of my important witnesses were busy senior doctors now working hundreds of miles away. The panel nevertheless refused to specify a time for them to give evidence. There were similar problems with staff working in the hospital. I had to resort to witness statements to compensate for this. Sue Hartley wrote to witnesses I had asked to attend to tell them they were under no obligation to do so. We had been told that the hearing had to be held before Christmas as Sue James was leaving and would be needed as a witness. When we arrived we were told she would not appear. Nadeem Moghal refused to give evidence. Much of our defence rested on cross-examining these two. The Trust produced no witnesses.

In summing up his criticisms of the process Ian said, "I have made 18 requests to the panel and not one of them has been granted." It was one-sided but we had no choice other than get on with it.

So, Martin Brewer took the floor to present the Trust's case. He was formidable. Even before he started he dominated the room. Ian had to ask him if he was in the chair. "I'm chairing it," Sue Hartley chimed, but we never felt she was. We were disadvantaged from the start. Martin Brewer was an experienced and, as it turned out, aggressive prosecutor. He did all he could to present me in the worst possible light. He admitted he had written the four allegations made against me and that they were legally framed. And here he was on the Trust's behalf using them to indict me.

Martin Brewer turned what should have been an internal hearing effectively into a courtroom, in which we were unfairly disadvantaged. Later, Ian actually told him, "You're cross-examining like it's a tribunal." He told the panel, none of whom had legal training, "I won't give you legal advice but I will tell you what the law says." He behaved in a rude and haughty fashion from the outset – he would never have got away with it in a real court. He treated us with disdain, criticizing Ian's English, correcting his grammar, telling him he was asking "ridiculous" questions; he accused Ian of "spurious and specious self-serving argument"; although I had been the hospital's most senior paediatrician he referred to me as "cheeky"; he described twelve of my senior consultant colleagues in the hospital as "your twelve mates."

He continually cut us off, grimaced and generally demonstrated his irritation. Later, when I presented my case, he would scowl and mime winding a handle, signalling me to speed up. All this was clearly visible to the chair but not once did she restrain him or even seek to do so. The nearest she ever came was, "Please, Martin." When he came to cross-examine me he was thoroughly condescending: "Now it's been interesting to me to watch you guys perform. I know that sounds a bit patronizing." He was the lawyer and as far as he was concerned we were the bumpkins to be ridiculed.

After he had presented the Trust's case we were given an opportunity to cross-examine him. That was rather like playing tennis with Federer: we had no real chance: he sidestepped practically everything we said. When we asked whether others had accepted and then acted on the recommendations (all had nominally accepted but none had acted on them) we were told this was irrelevant. Sue Hartley supported him from the chair. The panel did not want to look at the actions of others, she told us. It was Martin and Sue who looked like the double act. But under the principle of consistency, we said, it is discriminatory not to treat all employees alike. No, said Martin Brewer, the issue was whether the recommendations had been accepted: the others had accepted them; I had not. We were out-gunned but I felt much better for Ian's robust, good-humoured support.

At 10:00am on day two Ian and I began to present my case. I gave an extempore account, largely without notes: I knew my story well. Ian interrupted occasionally and added his own comments when I had finished. We both at some point referred to my whistleblowing history. That was in vain: the review had concluded that I was not a whistleblower. The Trust did not care whether this was true, or whether the evidence for it was good, bad or indifferent, Martin Brewer told us. What mattered was that the Trust had accepted the review. Halfway through his presentation of the Trust case Sue Hartley had announced, "It is not the role of the panel to unpick the recommendations behind the review." I was irreversibly cut off from my own history as a whistleblower by the machinations of the Trust's legal advice. I knew resistance was pointless but even now, reading the transcript, I am proud of the account I gave of my actions.

Julia Hollywood's investigation had relied on two witnesses, Nadeem Moghal and Sue James. I had not been allowed to see the statements they made against me until shortly before the hearing. The statements made scurrilously untrue and unsupportable claims about me. Since Sue Hartley had made it impossible for me to get some of my witnesses into the hearing I asked all four new paediatric consultants, appointed en bloc two years earlier, to provide statements. I gave them examples of Sue James's and Nadeem Moghal's calumnies and asked them to comment.

On Sue James's statement that she "perceived David Drew as

having a negative influence on others, including the newly appointed paediatricians" all four refuted this in graphic detail. I had a very positive influence on all of them, they reported. I was the most helpful consultant when it came to their settling in. (I had worked with these consultants for two years and they knew me well.) Sue James, to the best of my knowledge, had not set foot in the department for the last year. They all spoke of me in such warm and appreciative terms that on several occasions on the audiotape I can be heard crying as I read their statements into the record. The panel sat stony-faced; Martin Brewer smirked.

Similarly, Nadeem Moghal said in his statement, "David Drew's clinical work is good but he can't work effectively with colleagues in the department." But all four consultants in their statements agreed that I worked tirelessly to improve the service, was the most effective consultant, the best team player and an excellent role model for them. They all expressed this in their own way.

The fact that both witnesses to Julia Hollywood's investigation had completely misrepresented me was of no consequence to the panel. Sue Hartley later trivialized these statements: I was a good colleague, she said, that's all. To add insult to injury, Sue Hartley having made it impossible for them to attend in person, Martin Brewer complained that the four consultants had not been willing to come and say this in person: "Not one will stand with him, not one." They would all have stood, given the opportunity. And all did, or offered to do so, at the subsequent employment tribunal. This was open war and the truth was its main casualty.

Finally, Nadeem Moghal complained in his statement that I "habitually, in meetings, referred to [myself] as a Christian and thus claimed a higher status for [my] opinions than others". I knew this was untrue. I had asked Nadeem for evidence for this and he refused to give any. The four consultants in their witness statements confirmed this in the strongest terms: it was complete nonsense. But the panel was not going to unpick the recommendations and did not care whether they were based on true or false testimony. The thing I found most distressing about this whole episode was that I was certain that Nadeem Moghal knew in his heart that there was no truth in his statement. Ian made the point forcefully that in practice, as far as the outcome of the hearing was concerned, it was apparently now irrelevant whether or not I *had* ever transgressed in expressing that I was a Christian. It was now down simply to whether Nadeem Moghal *believed* I had. That is a strange idea of justice.

Three senior consultants to the Trust then appeared as my witnesses. They were hugely supportive of my position: "A doctor has loyalties above and beyond those to his employer. He also serves his patients, his colleagues, his own conscience," the hospital's most senior surgeon told the panel. They all believed the review should have been shared with the hospital consultants. Sue James had promised to do this and had even claimed she had done so. They all believed the report would provide an important opportunity for learning from our mistakes.

I then endured cross-examination from Martin Brewer: I was a lamb led to the slaughter. Ian was a great buffer but, considering Martin Brewer's hostility and his legal erudition, it was hopeless. He always returned to the fact that I had not accepted the recommendations in full, had not, as he said, ticked the box. "It's convenient in corporations to have people who tick boxes and get on with it," I countered, "Paediatricians have to attend to details. That's often a matter of life and death." He scowled. I was surprised that he came down so hard on my religious expression at work. His relentless painful grilling felt like the Inquisition. He spoke of my sending the prayer of St Ignatius in a way that made it seem close to the unforgivable sin. The hearing was not supposed to be unpicking the review but this is what he did, imposing his own view of the witnesses and evidence he referred to. Was I calling Jon Pepper a liar? Or Rob Hodgkiss? I was still not in full possession of what witnesses had actually said because the Trust had kept the documentation from me.

Mercifully, teatime arrived. Afterwards, both sides presented closing submissions and we went home, to reconvene the following Wednesday. "The die is cast," Ian told me before we parted. I felt relief: it was over. My only real anxiety was whether it would be a summary dismissal, which would have pushed us over the financial edge at Christmas.

"You look half dead," Janet greeted me when I arrived home. "Don't worry," I said, "I'll be fine in the morning." That was just as well because the next day we drove to Kent in a blizzard. The journey took eight hours, much of it spent on England's biggest car park, the M25. But Janet's company has always energized me, and a few days with three of our delightful grandchildren and their parents were like a salve applied to an open sore.

By Wednesday, just two days before Christmas, I was sufficiently recovered to return to Walsall to hear Sue Hartley pronounce the death sentence over my career as a children's doctor.

38

Reflections

In the depth of winter, I finally learned that within me there lay an invincible summer.

Albert Camus

I took my dismissal well and so did my family: we had a lovely Christmas. I knew the reality was likely to hit me in the New Year when we got back from Newcastle. On 5th January 2011 I emailed the interim Chief Executive, Michael Scott, to say that I would be appealing the disciplinary panel's decision.

On 6th January – Epiphany, I got up early, intending to be at my desk, dressed for work, by nine: I had a little fight left in me and knew that self-discipline was essential. The appeal statement had to be written but I had become more disorganized than usual. Documents needed filing and I needed a fresh overview of all that had happened. I would adopt a military posture: warrior stance.

As it was I found myself waylaid by a news article on a website I often visited: "Punjab Governor Assassinated in Islamabad," ran the headline. We'd been in Pakistan the previous year, and the parents of one of my patients had insisted we visit his family in Islamabad as well as going to our primary destination, Karachi.

Salman Taseer, the governor, had been shot by one of his bodyguards, an Islamist fanatic. His main crime was that he had stood up for a young Christian woman, Asiya Bibi, who had fallen foul of Pakistan's medieval blasphemy laws. He was a millionaire businessman and a politician; from what I could understand, he was a Muslim but not very religious. Asiya was a village girl going about her household chores when false allegations were made against her.

I was fascinated and found out all I could about the case. My perception of injustice in the way I had been treated all but disappeared. These two, at opposite poles of the social spectrum, had suffered huge injustices: Taseer was dead and Asiya Bibi was (and remains) in prison. I identified with both: one was arrested while going about her legitimate business, the other gunned down for defending a vulnerable child. I remember Nadeem Moghal saying that yes, I might have suffered a degree of injustice but it wasn't exactly human rights abuses in Iraq. He was right. This story put me in my place.

I consciously let go of my case and began to muse on my own past. I looked through old photograph albums, letters and newspaper cuttings, and even emails. I spent hours, whole days, talking with Janet about our adventures. I was filled with a sense of gratitude for the life we had been given. After a few days I found three old boxes filled with scraps of paper.

Somewhere in the late nineties, I forget exactly when, a fashion developed in both undergraduate and postgraduate medical education for encouraging or even requiring formal written reflection on clinical experience. On principle I never did it. Ever. It was a good thing, I'm sure, and some needed to be prodded into doing it. But I was already a reflective person. I used hospital notes, clinic letters, and reports, to reflect on experiences. If that required a bit of traditional wisdom I would include it. Reflection is a Biblical norm. Prayer for me is essentially reflective. It is not principally about asking God for things but about understanding.

In the boxes I found some of my informal scribbled reflections on the wider aspects of my clinical experience: little stories of life and death, loss and grief, success and failure, joy, humour even. Stories I had long forgotten were reanimated by a name on a scrap of paper, a couple of lines of verse, a thumbnail description, a faded photograph. I re-entered a world I had known and been allowed to live in.

Here was a baby who died tragically at a newborn unit I was working in. I had a close relationship with the parents, especially the mother. This verse was written carelessly, hastily, on a postcard.

An Early Death

Words fall like empty prayer
From muted lips
Dumb with despair,
Senses fail to feel,
The heart to care;
I reach out to touch you,
But you are not there.
Can no one sense the strangeness everywhere?
Life's suffocating sadness,
Rage, loss,
The hopelessness
That I must bear.
I do not doubt you share my loss,
You are a stranger,
Yet I feel your care,
For I saw you glance
When I reached to touch my son,
And in your eyes
Reflected grief
Declared you also knew
He was not there.
Words fall still everywhere,
For words are frail
And do not dare to tell
That though I reach the farthest star

That sits within the rim
Of eternity's shell,
My hand shall never rest in his,
He is not,
No, and never will be there.

We knew the crushing loss of our brothers' deaths but not our child's. Even to think about the loss of our own child was too painful to bear.

I was taken back to Nigeria. A young Fulani boy had been brought to hospital by his family; I have no record of his name. He had advanced meningitis and died shortly after arrival. The following week I went to work in the desert around Lake Chad in the far north. We were moving between clinics and dispensaries, staying only a day or two at a time. Thanks to my friend from Jos, Yusuf Ibrahim, who was travelling with us, I was given an opportunity to witness something that missionaries who had worked with the Fulani for a lifetime had not seen, the painful rite of passage of its young men.

Fulani Initiation Ceremony

Two days in the bush
With native beer,
And now they rush upon me.
I do not hear; I do not see,
As raised rods lick the sky,
Hungrily.
Two days with a strange god
I had not known before,
And fragile bonds are fractured.
I do not hear: I do not see,
I am released from fear,

From inconsequential fear,
I am free.
Two days to change a world.
It seems absurd but it is true;
So ends my slavish ignorance,
As the rods scream, "See."
And I reply, "I can",
And, "Hear."
And I reply, "I can".
Now, childhood passes swiftly,
And deep wounds
Unveil, a man.

The boy with no name would never be initiated into manhood. He would be a child forever in his mother's memory. Who is sufficient for such things?

In another scrap I was taken back to a forgotten incident in the refugee camps, 32 years earlier. A hill-tribe man had promised to take me fishing.

Fishing the Mekong

I saved your child,
And in return
You pulled into my yard
At dawn,
In a battered Datsun pick-up truck,
To take us fishing.
The Mekong lies
Beyond the rice fields
From my house.
And getting there
We bounced on rutted roads,

Blood-red
In the morning light,
Halting on the mighty river's edge.
Four dusty men
Who'd been asleep
Then sprang to life
And spread a thirty-metre net
In front of us.
We waded in the river's rapid flow,
You pointing me to the farthest reach.
I was so full of fear I dared not go.
Yet more ashamed to let that show
I plunged into oblivion.
And having played my part,
I swam to shore
Like a drowning rat,
Amazed to see
Nine thrashing fish
Caught in the net.
Your men lit fires,
Then gutted, cleaned and skewered the fish
And grilled it there beside
Sticky rice steaming in green banana leaves.
You poured Mekong whisky
Neat, in plastic cups,
And Coca Cola for the kids.
You fell asleep,
And we, replete
Beneath the sky,
Watched on.
You were at ease because your child
At home lay at his mother's side,
And all was well for you.

But I was left dissatisfied,
My world grown small,
Swallowed whole by your nobility
Your river-wild manliness.

I was taught from early on in my career not to get emotionally involved with patients or parents. Sometimes I was so tired or ill or distracted that there was no more emotion to go round. But I was always more or less involved. It's best to be yourself – or better than yourself if possible. I do not have favourites: all my patients were favourites. Some I have kept photographs of; one is on my desk now with her twin sisters. I remember being telephoned with news of her death on a Saturday morning as I was going out to a meeting at the university. She had been for a minor operation at another hospital and had died at home in the night.

Grieving for Katie

Spring is over for this year,
Summer has been cancelled,
And autumn's promise
Though never near,
Recedes to infinity
With all that we hold dear.
Deep winter is upon us here,
Cold winds, ice-cold winds,
Blast and chill us to the bone
Erasing any hope of summer's cheer.
Ice and Frost chill the night,
Until our world becomes
A single frozen tear.

....
16th October 1994.

And below I'd scribbled, "Unfinished. Unfinishable." I was always slightly ashamed that I could offer little more than doggerel to such tragedies. I went to Katie's funeral in the local parish church. It occurred to me to give the poem to her parents but I got cold feet.

I saw a film about Simon Wiesenthal in Auschwitz. He was later to become the Nazi hunter but here he was a prisoner at the mercy of his captors. It was lovely summer day. The incinerator chimneys were belching smoke into a clear blue sky. "Where is God? Where is he?" asked one prisoner angrily. "He's gone on his holidays."

I never saw the suffering of children or their parents in that way. Why a loving God does not or can not rescue is unanswerable. God is not in the events but in the response to the events. I sympathize with anyone who looks at the world and finds it hard to believe it was created in benevolence. No doubt many of my Christian friends who read this will be disappointed with me for thinking this way and especially for expressing it in public. All I can say is that my doubts have never stopped me living as I believe a Christian should.

As I read more of my scribbling I saw how much I had struggled with Christian faith but always returned to the central truths. I was never afraid to act on those truths. I knew that Jon Pepper's assertion that I would refer to myself as a Christian "thus claiming my opinion was true" and Nadeem's amplification of that claim to the point of him describing me as a bigot who thought his opinions better than others' were groundless. They were both hopelessly ignorant of what a Christian is. Ignorance is the principle enemy of all diversity and the main source of all discrimination.

I have a good memory and a vivid imagination. In a short time I revisited the wonderful life I had been granted as a children's doctor and as a husband and a father. I knew that whatever had happened to me nothing could ever take that away. I had been true to my calling. I had kept faith with my patients and their families. I had kept faith with my own family. And so, in the midst of winter, I basked in a warm glow of, to give it its humblest name, nostalgia.

39

Going through the Motions

Prayers are like those appeals of ours. Either they don't get through or they're returned with "rejected" scrawled across them.
Aleksandr Solzhenitsyn: *One Day in the Life of Ivan Denisovich*

I was still tempted to rummage around in my past but knew this had to end. At the bottom of the last box of memorabilia I found a manila envelope with some tidy shorthand on both sides. It was one of my favourite stories. I had told it several times to illustrate the family distress that a supposedly trivial medical condition can cause.

7pm. Tired. Need food. Desperate to escape. Secretary's phone rang. (I didn't usually answer it after Sue had gone at 5pm.)

"Is Dr Drew there?"

"Speaking."

"Dr Drew, it's George's dad. We haven't seen you for a month. Something's happened. I had to call you."

Many of my patients' parents had open access to me through Sue and were not shy about using it. George had a very severe form of chronic constipation and sometimes wouldn't do a poo for more than a month. He was one of the rare children so resistant to medical treatment that on more than one occasion he'd needed to have his bowels emptied manually under general anaesthetic. I won't describe this. It's not pleasant. For the last year, with the right medication, he'd had his bowels open most days without too much difficulty. But he'd been left with a psychological aversion to using the toilet and still did a poo in his pants. Tonight George's dad sounded excited."

"What's up?"

"I had to call you and tell you, Dr Drew. George is seven next week. Today, for the first time in his life, he's done a poo in the toilet. Proper like!"

"Thanks for letting me know. Tell George he's great. I knew he'd do it in the end."

"I will, Dr Drew."

I was anxious to get off but I could sense something was about to be said.

"I rang to tell you what I did, Dr Drew. I know I shouldn't have done it, but I did."

"What's that?"

"Well," he hesitated, "I put my hand down the toilet. I lifted that turd out and looked it straight in the eyes. And I said, 'You...are...beautiful.'"

His voice cracked and I could hear him crying. I've seen more tears of relief and of joy, than I have of grief in my years as a children's doctor. Severe constipation on the mend was a fertile source of emotional release for parents. Constipation isn't a life-threatening condition but it is a life-spoiler. It can ruin a child's quality of life. Parents of badly constipated children suffer. I have been inundated over the years with gifts from them, more so than from all my other patients put together. Some parents attending for the first visit would walk in and before anything had been said or done burst into tears. After ten minutes in the clinic they might say, 'This is the first time anyone's listened.' And then they would have another cry. In my early years at Walsall a nursing sister told me I was known as the doctor who makes mothers cry. When I protested she said, 'No, it's a good thing. It's like they feel safe with you.' And now I had a father crying down the phone.

"You've done right. Now go and wash your hands and get George to bed. See you in clinic."

George's family story was a microcosm of everything that I'd enjoyed in medicine. In paediatrics there was always the added pleasure and challenge of interacting with parents.

It was late January and this reverie came to its natural end. One cold morning the doorbell rang and five large cardboard boxes were unceremoniously dumped on my doorstep. It was my office contents. I'd been refused permission to clear my desk myself or say goodbye to my colleagues. This felt like ritual humiliation. Or, as a more worldly pal told me, "They're pissing on you, mate." I could think of no reason the Trust would have done it this way other than for its demoralizing effect.

Throughout January practical matters had interrupted my reminiscences. I registered the grounds for my appeal early. Ian Mckivett had done most of the work for this. Then I began to think about my statement of case. The appeal is not simply a re-run of the first hearing. The only grounds for appealing are the employer's failure to adhere to procedure, a penalty being seen as unfair or new evidence. I appealed on all three points, specifying 20 instances. Throughout January I had been asking for a copy of the transcript of the disciplinary hearing and access to my computer to enable me to write my statement. On 11th February I was allowed to use my computer for a few hours under close supervision, specified by Nadeem Moghal "to ensure that patient data does not leave the Trust." That was a barb.

I was now in a position to write my statement of case. I wanted it to be comprehensive, though I believed it was a mere formality. I knew it would help at a later date with preparation for the employment tribunal. I had little doubt that was my next port of call. I believed that my disciplinary hearing had been a kangaroo court. So, for good measure, I included with my statement a short paper titled, "The disciplinary hearing I was subjected to on 14th and 15th December 2010 by my employer, Walsall Hospitals NHS Trust, was in my opinion a kangaroo court."

I had been denied the right to summon witnesses. Their attendance was effectively made impossible. Nadeem's review had actually refused to hear my witnesses. I had been refused the right to cross-examine the only two Trust witnesses in Julia Hollywood's investigation. I had been tried on secret evidence obtained from Trust managers, known to be in conflict with me, who were given an assurance by Nadeem that they would never be held accountable for their evidence. The Trust, by bringing in its lawyer, had turned the disciplinary hearing into a courtroom, where I was on trial. Panel members should have been excluded on grounds of partiality or conflict of interest. The panel was made up of people who, according to Sue James, had already decided I had to go. Colin Holden was paid handsomely for his work and could reasonably be expected to want more of this in future. Human nature being what it is, there was an obvious conflict of interest here, conscious or not. He who pays the piper… Yes, this fitted the definition of a kangaroo court.

My statement of case took a month to compose and was 32 pages long. Writing it was therapeutic. It was an investment. I gave specific accounts of my disclosure under the Public Interest Disclosure Act concerning the repeated heating failures. I referred specifically to Child K and the Trust's catastrophic failures that had sent him home to his death and the Trust's subsequent failure to remedy those failures. I catalogued the concerns I had raised with Sue James about medical and nursing redundancies, poor staffing, patient risk and bullying. I linked this causally with my exclusion by Mike Brown following Karen Palmer's allegations. In fact, I told the whole story. They already knew it but it was my pleasure to dish it up again so that at some future point they would not be able to claim ignorance.

Finally, knowing that for me so much rested on the Trust's attempt to deny my freedom of speech and religious freedom, I attempted in my own untutored way to show that this was unreasonable and unlawful. It flew in the face of natural justice. I read this up in Wikipedia. I argued that the instruction was unlawful on the grounds of the Employment Equality (Religion or Belief) Regulations 2003. I quoted Article 9 of the Universal Convention of Human Rights: the instruction breached Article 9. I read most of this up on the internet but got advice from a couple of lawyer friends. I concluded that, "The Trust's and the review's complaints against me in this matter are in any case vexatious and have been constructed to obscure the real issues behind my suspension and grievance." This was about whistleblowing.

On 18th April Ian and I returned to the Education Centre, where four months earlier Sue Hartley had read out my letter of dismissal. I was on good form, fitter and mentally and physically stronger than I had been for a long time.

Michael Scott chaired the panel. He had been appointed interim Chief Executive until Sue James's replacement was appointed. He had recently left his post as Chief Executive of a London PCT in a scheme that became known as "revolving doors". Redundancies with a large financial settlement were followed by lucrative alternative employment. In Michael Scott's case this was at Walsall on, according to the *Daily Telegraph*, £1,750 a day. Stephen Dorrell, Chair of the Health Select Committee, had described this arrangement as "the sort of thing that gives effective management a really bad name". But Mr Scott seemed to be doing very well on it. It was never Beveridge's intention that the NHS should become a get-rich scheme for a senior managerial elite. But this is the way they had managed to tilt things to their advantage over recent years.

A non-executive director and yet another paid "independent" HR consultant completed the panel. Sue Hartley was there to defend her decision. Colin Holden, on another profitable day out, backed her up. I wondered how much this was costing. Taxpayers' money earmarked for patient care was being used to finish off a good doctor who had spoken up to defend patients. They knew that already and if they read my statement they would be left in no doubt. I had by that time heard many others question the ability of NHS internal hearings to be even-handed. It was unlikely that having come this far any panel the Trust put up would suddenly see the justice of my case.

Ian and I presented the appeal case enthusiastically but with little hope. We knew it would fail. Michael Scott, to me, appeared completely uninterested in the proceedings. His body language and facial expression suggested that he wished he were somewhere else. But, at £1,750 for the day, it can't have been too bad. We finished in the afternoon. The last rites were said and we left.

Outside, Ian anticipated my question. "They didn't listen to a word we said." On our way out of the building we passed a group of medical students. Laughing and chatting away, they appeared entirely carefree. "My course is over now but yours has scarce begun..."

40

The BMA Solicitor

Life is a long preparation for something that never happens.

W B Yeats

It was now more or less certain that I would get the legal help I needed to prove beyond doubt that I had been unfairly dismissed. On the 25th March 2011 the solicitor allocated to my case by the BMA, Avril England of Gateley Wareing, wrote to me for the first time. She sent me a copy of her merit assessment of my case. This was supposed to be a detailed analysis of what chance my case had at the employment tribunal. The three-month deadline for registering my case at the tribunal had already passed and I had neither met nor had a telephone conversation with her about it. I was immersed in preparing my statement for the appeal hearing that was a few weeks away.

Avril was quite open that she had not been provided with all the documentation by the BMA. We had had no direct contact with each other. She was nevertheless able to conclude that she would be representing me for settlement only for claims of unfair dismissal and religious discrimination. No claim for whistleblowing had been registered. Ian at some point had told me she did not think I was a genuine whistleblower. My 40-year career as a paediatrician had crashed because I had done what I considered to be the right thing for my patients and the BMA solicitor could not even be bothered to talk to me or read the documents before writing my case off. I couldn't help feeling things would have been different if I had been a paying client. Gateley Wareing's primary responsibility was to its real client, the BMA. Included in a rather sketchy summary of the background to my case Avril wrote:

> I am further aware that from 2008 onwards, you raised concerns regarding child protection and patient care which you state amounted to whistleblowing. The Trust does not agree that you are a whistleblower. I have not considered the whistleblowing claim in detail. However, from what I have read, I consider you would struggle to prove a link between the concerns you raised and the action taken against you. On this basis, I can not approve BMA funding for a whistleblowing claim. In any event, I am aware that it is not a claim which has been issued before the tribunal.

The truth was, of course, that she had not had all the documentation and had not spoken to me about my case and had no basis for reaching this conclusion. I had laid a clear paper trail on whistleblowing for more than a year before my dismissal. Does any Trust ever agree that an employee it has sacked is a whistleblower? Of course not. That would be an admission that it had broken the law. And as Avril wrote, what did it matter anyway? Registering my claim as a whistleblower was already out of time.

There are six potentially fair reasons for dismissal under Section 98 of the Employment Rights Act 1996 (ERA 1996). These are conduct, capability, redundancy, breach of a statutory restriction, retirement and some other substantial reason ("SOSR").

Avril explained that I had been dismissed under an SOSR. In her view the Trust would be able to establish that there was an SOSR reason that could justify my dismissal. This was naïve and based on no evidence. I had never at any point refused to accept the review that was the whole basis of the SOSR. I had quite simply asked for an opportunity to discuss the grossly unfair instructions about my behaviour as a Christian and the dissemination of the report. Avril had not picked up on this because she had not discussed the matter with me.

She did concede however that many of the Trust's actions could impact on the fairness of my dismissal and she gave a long list of these including the following:

- The allegations made against me by Karen Palmer in April 2009 were unfounded. My exclusion was unwarranted.
- There was no basis for the reference to my behaviour as a Christian in the investigator's report.
- I did not agree to the methods used by the independent review or to be bound by the outcome.
- All the investigation notes of witnesses evidence taken by the independent review panel were destroyed
- The Trust initially tried to go straight to a disciplinary procedure before holding an investigation.
- The Chair of Review, Dr Moghal, was appointed as the Clinical Director of the department soon after the report was published, casting doubt on his independence.
- I was advised by Dr Moghal to accept the findings or I would not be working there much longer, suggesting the disciplinary was pre-determined.
- The Chief Executive encouraged me to take the settlement or I would be dismissed, again suggesting the disciplinary was pre-determined.
- I had difficulty obtaining relevant documentation and had to apply to the Information Commissioner for help. The Information Commissioner forced the Trust to disclose the documentation.
- The Trust advised my witnesses that they did not have to attend if they did not want to, arguably placing undue pressure on them not to attend.
- The Trust case was, unprecedentedly, represented by a solicitor

who was arguably advising both the management team and the panel. There was therefore a possibility that the panel would be biased.

- The disciplinary hearing was held like a court hearing and was intimidating.

"It is for these reasons that I have concluded that there is an argument that the decision to dismiss was predetermined and the disciplinary process was a sham thereby making the dismissal unfair," Avril concluded. In short, it was a kangaroo court.

The truth is that, again, if she had examined the documentation in detail and spoken to me, she would have found the case even stronger than she thought. Any reasonable person would have understood that a good senior doctor who has never had a complaint against him in his long working life could not have been treated so badly by accident.

On the subject of religious discrimination she was unenthusiastic: "On the basis of the limited evidence available to me…". But I would have produced a ream of evidence, fully documented and within a coherent narrative. No, she had included the religious discrimination claim for tactical reasons. That presumably meant to improve the settlement offer. At a later date, in one of the two phone conversations I had with her, I asked about her experience with religious discrimination.

"Have you ever represented anyone for a religious discrimination claim?"

"I'd have to think about that."

"If you had ever been involved in a such a case it's hardly likely you'd forget."

"I've done cases of sex and racial discrimination."

"But that's not what my case is about."

I recognized the evasion tactics I had become so familiar with in my dealings with NHS managers. In that same conversation I asked why, if the religious discrimination claim was entered tactically, the whistleblowing case was not entered on the same ground. No answer to that though she had already admitted funding was the real issue. She must have been aware that if at some point I were to instruct my own lawyers I would not be able to pursue my whistleblowing claim. This is how I came to be lumbered with a religious discrimination case and not the whistleblowing claim that I expected. It resulted in endless misunderstanding and outright hostility from secular groups. The case manufactured by Sue James and Nadeem Moghal about my behaviour as a Christian at work had proved a singularly effective tactic. Even my own lawyer was fooled.

There was in this merit assessment a section entitled "Compensation". I did not even bother to read it. Compensation was never an issue for me. All I wanted was for it to be shown that I had been dismissed by my employer for speaking up for my patients and then allowed to get back to the work I loved.

Avril concluded that the case as she understood it was not strong and compensation would be low. The cost of running the case at ET would be disproportionate, so she would be representing me for settlement only. That was that then.

At the earliest opportunity I responded to this as follows:

> I was under the impression that whistleblowing was the major reason why my dismissal was unfair. Will you please reconsider approving funding for this on the basis of my enclosure which demonstrates unequivocally I believe that I am a whistleblower?

The enclosure was titled, "Why my case against Walsall Hospitals NHS Trust is that of a whistleblower". It gave detailed examples of the concerns I had raised from October 2008 onwards, including specific references to my obligations under "Raising concerns about patient safety" in the GMC's guidance "Maintaining Good Medical Practice" and the Public Interest Disclosure Act. I knew I had done everything to the letter and that there was a clear trail from this to my dismissal in the documents I had obtained from the Trust. I had made repeated evidenced references to whistleblowing in the independent review and in my disciplinary hearing and appeal. There was a wealth of evidence if Avril had only bothered to look and listen.

It took almost a month to get a response to my request that Gateley Wareing reconsider my request for funding my case as whistleblowing. The answer was a resounding "No". Astonishingly, given the account I had provided, the response was that there really was little or no evidence that I had made protected disclosures, and that in any case even if I had this was not why the Trust had dismissed me.

By August the Trust had refused to enter into any negotiation on settlement unless I agreed first to a non-derogatory compromise agreement and a confidentiality clause – a gag. I had already refused this when Sue James offered it in what was to me a very clumsy attempt to sweep a whole load of wrongdoing under the carpet. So, my decision to refuse was not a difficult one. As a consequence, Avril wrote to me on 18th August to announce that she was now off the record.

I had no intention of settling if that involved signing a gag. The story of the concerns I had raised and the treatment I had endured as a consequence was far too important to sell for a few quid. So, Avril was off the record: I was on my own. I read the letter twice. There was nothing in it that I had not expected but nevertheless I experienced a profound mental and physical shock. I am by nature an optimist. I do not get depressed. I'm one of the lucky ones. Quite suddenly though, and without warning, I found myself in an emotional freefall.

I put the letter on my desk, walked out of my study and into our bedroom. I fell on my knees. I do not kneel to pray: that has not been part of my church culture. Nor do I generally share much of my subjective religious experience other than with my family and close friends. I was on my knees in mental and physical agony for several hours. I closed my eyes and looked down into a black hole so deep and so dark that I felt lost and afraid. I knew this was the Whistleblowers' Graveyard that Nadeem had promised me. "Make no mistake, David, that's where you'll end up."

But in that darkness I heard a voice: "Don't be frightened. I'm with you. I'll never fail you nor forsake you." It was not an audible voice; I've never heard such a thing. But it was no less real for being entirely subjective. I said, "Thank you" out loud and got to my feet. I knew I would be given the resources to cope with anything. That wasn't the last time I went down emotionally but I never experienced that level of crisis again. I was uncertain what would come next but felt a profound confidence that I was not alone.

41

The Good Lawyers

It's a strange trade, that of advocacy. Your intellect, your highest heavenly gift, is hung up in the shop window like a loaded pistol for sale.

Thomas Carlyle

On a more human level I was definitely not alone. I had my family and good friends. But I also had the whistleblowers. In January I had made contact with Dr Kim Holt, the paediatrician who had raised concerns over problems at the Haringey clinic. Later, as a result of her concerns being ignored, Baby P was sent home to be murdered. Kim's reward for doing her duty was four years away from work. Although she later received an apology from Great Ormond Street Hospital and returned to her job, she experienced the hell that NHS whistleblowers usually do. Kim's name was forever to be linked to Baby P and my own history was overshadowed by Child K. But that was not what cemented our friendship. We were both passionate about an NHS culture in which it was safe for frontline staff to raise concerns, a culture in which such concerns were valued and put to good use.

Through Kim, I started to meet other whistleblowers. In December 2011 a group of us, with Kim as chair, founded the organization Patients First, dedicated to the protection of patients by supporting whistleblowers and campaigning for the end of all compromise agreements in the NHS. Sharing the stories of others was sobering. So many had worse experiences than mine. They were all first-class professionals, honest to the core and excellent communicators. I felt at home among them.

In September I had written to Professor Hamish Wallace, Registrar at the Royal College of Paediatrics. I gave a detailed account of my experience at Walsall. I listed my disclosures about child-protection services, patient safety, nursing and medical redundancies, understaffing and bullying. I described the review methodology as deeply flawed and unfair and asked the Registrar whether it met the standards that would be expected by the College.

In reply, Professor Wallace expressed sympathy at my sticky end but was unable to help further. The College was only an intermediary and had done no more than recommend two Fellows to conduct the review, he reported. A deed of indemnity had been drawn up, putting all responsibility for the review on the Trust and Nadeem Moghal and Peter Heinz. The College had not seen the review report and showed no interest in doing so. It had effectively washed its hands of it. The College would express no opinion on the review's methods and was unable to share any of its own policy documents on conducting a review. He was not even willing to say if such a policy existed. More openness. This came from the body that describes itself online as "the standard bearer of child health in the medical profession".

Later, in 2013 I registered a formal complaint with the Royal College of Paediatrics about the conduct and outcomes of the review. The College relented its earlier refusal to allow me to see its policy document for the conduct of reviews, the External Clinical Assessment Team protocol. It was clear that the review had breached this at a number of critical points. The College CEO wrote to inform me that the review panel members had all signed gags and were unable to make any comment on the review. The Royal College of Paediatrics joined a list of those who had deliberately withheld information from me that would have served to strengthen my claims as a whistleblower.

I was now faced with the problem of legal representation. I toyed with the possibility of representing myself. I was easily dissuaded from this course, having seen doctors and nurses at the tribunal attempting the same against Trust-funded, experienced barristers. A chance comment in church one Sunday morning led me to Waldrons Solicitors, a West Midlands firm, which had dealt with my brother's estate in 2001. I provided five thousand pages of documentation for the merit assessment. In late October Janet and I met their delightful employment lawyer, Hannah Scott. She had read the documents and I was impressed by her understanding of my case. Three days later she set up a meeting with David McIlroy, a barrister of 3 Paper Buildings.

Meeting David was a revelation. I liked and admired him immediately. He showed an ability to effortlessly assimilate complex facts and define the narrative. He also understood the issues at a human emotional level. He was realistic about employment law and passionate about justice. "You're my man," I thought. The case was a good one for unfair dismissal, victimization and religious discrimination. "Remember, David, there is no such thing as an unlosable case," he told me. Since Avril England had effectively decided that my case was un-winnable I was encouraged by this. On the matter of my specific disclosures the news was good. Three of the four main disclosures were held to be solid and one less so. We discussed the BMA's failure to take my whistleblowing seriously.

We submitted an application to the tribunal to amend my claim to include whistleblowing. It was now seven months out of time. The application specified that disclosures had been made; that they were qualifying disclosures; and that I had suffered detriments as a result of making them. The Trust's legal representatives raised objections on several grounds, including the lateness of the application and the fact that Avril England at the Case Management Discussion in June had stated that there was no whistleblowing or PIDA claim. This was despite the fact that she had written to me to say she had not given detailed consideration to my whistleblowing claim nor seen the documents. I had written to her months earlier that whistleblowing was at the heart of my case and asked her to examine the facts. She had advised that it was unnecessary for me to be involved in the case discussion and I foolishly let that ride.

Meanwhile family issues came to the fore. My mother collapsed in September and was admitted to Derby Royal Hospital. She spent most of the next four months there before discharge to spend her last few days at home with my dad. Ironically, by this time Sue James was CEO and Brigid Stacey Director of Nursing at Derby. Over the next four months I saw Brigid on a number of occasions on the wards. She was open and helpful and visited my mum a couple of times. In my numerous visits I caught no sight of Sue.

My mum had generally good care but I was struck once more by the poor communication and bad attitude of a small minority of staff. When she was admitted I gave my mobile number to her nurse and asked to be contacted in the event of an emergency. I specified that my dad, suffering from profound anxiety and with no means of getting to hospital quickly, should not be contacted: I would speak to him. Such an emergency happened a week later at night, when Mum had a massive bleed due to a problem with blood clotting. The nursing staff rang Dad at night, creating panic. These kinds of thoughtless miscommunication abound in the NHS and cause untold suffering.

On another occasion the ward sister rang me late at night.

"We're going to discharge your mother, hopefully to a cottage hospital."

"At this time of night?"

"I've just had a call from the manager: they're desperate for beds."

"She's not well enough for discharge."

"We have to decide that."

"You know the number of readmissions has doubled in the last year as a result of this kind of early discharge."

"You can't believe everything you read in the papers, Sunshine!"

"I'm not reading it from a newspaper; I've got a report in front of me that has just come out of the Department of Health."

"Oh! And who are you?"

"I'm Phyllis Drew's son and I'm asking you politely not to send my mother out at this time of night."

"Fine."

Imagine Joe Public fighting for his mum in that situation. No hope.

In December, while we were waiting for the application to amend to be heard, I noticed that the Health Select Committee was about to hear evidence from the British Medical Association, the Royal College of Nursing, the Care Quality Commission and the Department of Health on professional responsibility. It included questions on gagging clauses. I sent the House of Commons Health Select Committee details of my own case, including attempts to gag me by the Trust and the BMA. Mark Porter, Chair of the Consultants' Committee, gave evidence for the BMA. My own experience of BMA legal support left me unimpressed with his statements.

I wrote an email to Mark immediately after the hearing, pointing out the contradictions between statements he had made to the committee and my own experience. He appeared to know what the BMA's position was on everything to do with whistleblowing and settlement but little about what happened in practice.

I asked why my case had been entrusted to a relatively inexperienced solicitor. The full merit assessment of my case by my private lawyers included 36 hours of reading and a four-hour face-to-face meeting with a three-strong legal team, including the barrister. Yet the BMA lawyer had refused a face-to-face meeting and had not even bothered to read the documents on my disclosures. Why did Avril England not register my case as a whistleblower? If and when she went off the record my new team could have picked this up without all the work and expense involved in re-labelling. In my case the BMA had made no attempt to support a whistleblower. These were questions which as a paid-up BMA member I deserved answers to.

It took two months for Dr Porter to reply and then it was only after two reminders. He was polite and apologetic. My letter (I had sent an email) had been "mislaid". There is an art to formulating this kind of response. The trick is to say something without really saying anything. In any case I did not get any answers to my questions.

The Health Committee referred to an exposé in *The Times* by Alexei Mostrous. Three London Trusts had gagged doctors, even specifying that they could not speak to professional regulators. These gags were referred to by Stephen Dorrell, the committee chair, as unlawful and unenforceable. As a result I rang Alexei to tell him that I had the next chapter in his account of NHS gags. He sounded doubtful but after I sent him all the correspondence relating to the BMA-mediated gag he wrote an article: "No help for doctor who refused to be gagged". No help from the BMA, that was.

The application to add a whistleblowing claim to my case was heard at Birmingham Employment tribunal in December 2011, a year to the day after my dismissal. It was a long shot and expensive but I found it useful experience. Ms Misra, the Trust's counsel, showed some insight into the BMA's failures when she suggested I apply to them to remedy my losses. I had no interest in remedy, only in getting my disclosures heard. Nevertheless I tucked that suggestion away for later use.

Two months later the Tribunal dismissed the application to have my whistleblowing claims heard.

In January 2012 my mum died peacefully at home, looked after by my dad with the help of some excellent home nursing. I'd wanted to get my name cleared before my mum died but in the event it didn't matter. Late one night we left to drive home. I told her I loved her and she told me the same. She died a few hours later and by the time we returned in the morning her body had been taken away. — *Dear Diary: I will miss Mum but I will not mourn her. She is out of trouble now. But I'm still in it. And Dad, he's still in it.* Only days later Janet had a massive bleed into her eye, tearing her retina off and necessitating major surgery. The NHS rose to the occasion and Janet had the best treatment imaginable. – *Oh Lord, remember David in all his troubles.*

We were now six weeks away from the tribunal hearing. There was still a lot of work to do. The bundles of evidence were agreed, about 2,500 pages in all. My own statement had to be written. Although I was well acquainted with the narrative from start to finish it was important to me personally that it be comprehensive and accurate, besides reading well.

Contrary to Nadeem's warning that I would not get anyone to stand with me I had more offers of support from my colleagues than I could possibly use. I narrowed it down to seven: Ian Mckivett, David Cremonesini, Louise Cremonesini, Iain Darwood, Louise Holland, Bashir Muhammed and Alison Cole.

Ian Mckivett for the BMA was vital. David and Louise Cremonesini, a consultant colleague and his wife, who had been our safeguarding nurse, and Iain Darwood, another consultant colleague, all had first-hand experience of events leading up to my dismissal; none of them worked for the Trust by then. Louise Holland had been chair of the hospital consultants' committee for some years and was in a position to give an authoritative account of what had happened: she had been a great support over my last three years at the Trust; Bashir Muhammad was a paediatric consultant colleague and a Muslim, a real friend: he was able to speak on religious self-expression in the department and Trust; Alison Cole was the Trust's Anglican chaplain: she was able to give a detailed account of religious practices in the Trust. Louise, Bashir and Alison were still employed by the Trust but were not required to attend for cross-examination.

When I received the witness statements I was delighted at the transparently consistent accounts they had given. I did not see how I could possibly lose. It was obvious that any responsibility for the breakdown in the relationship was on the Trust side not mine.

I also asked Dr Cathcart, the Occupational Health Physician, to support me. He refused on the grounds that as he still worked for the Trust there was a conflict of interest. I never understood that. I asked him to attend briefly – to tell the truth, that's all. This would have been embarrassing to the Trust and would have brought out the truth about the psychiatric appointment. It might possibly have damaged his own standing in the Trust. Or he might have feared it would. He was the only person I asked to stand who refused.

The exchange of witness statements was due on the last day of February and we were gripped by excited anticipation. We did not know who would stand for the other side: the Trust's case would not hold up without Sue James so she was a certainty. I was extremely anxious to see Nadeem Moghal cross-examined about his review: he had been reluctant to discuss it in any detail with me; how would he explain his order to destroy all the notes of oral evidence? How would he defend the required outcomes, including the one on religious language with no extant evidence? Both Sue and Nadeem had refused to appear for cross-examination at the disciplinary hearing, though they were the only ones who could cast any real light on why I was being dismissed.

As it was, the Trust applied for an extension to exchange statements and exchange took place two weeks before the hearing – after further delays on their side. The Trust was fielding four witnesses, of whom Sue James was the only one who had been personally involved in the events leading to my dismissal. The chairs of the disciplinary and appeal hearings, Sue Hartley and Michael Scott, and the investigator, Julia Hollywood, were also listed. Their statements put their own spin on events, especially Sue James's. There was nothing in them that could possibly have warranted my dismissal other than the fact that I had got up senior management's noses by speaking for patients. That was my opinion.

The last two weeks before the tribunal were quiet. Janet and I enjoyed each other's company walking in the countryside, refusing to let the injustice I had suffered interfere with our own happiness. We were painfully aware that many others were suffering the same kind of injustice. Vindication seemed to be just around the corner. And after that an opportunity to speak up for and help those others.

42

ET: My Wonderful Witnesses

The purpose of justice is to restore order and for a cleansing.
Jack Whicher in *The Suspicions of Mr Whicher*

I have met many NHS staff who were either facing, or had been to, an employment tribunal with a claim against their Trust. Most found it an ordeal. They had suffered stress and anxiety to varying degrees. Many could not go through with it and had dropped the case or settled with a pay-off and a gag. Our experience was quite different. Apart from the appropriate anxiety caused by wanting to do everything well, we were unmoved. In fact we eagerly anticipated the proceedings: I wanted to give my account; I wanted to defend it; I wanted Janet to see the kind of people who had been prepared to ruin my career. But most of all I wanted to show how a good, loyal doctor can be persecuted – by whatever means available – for expressing concerns about patient care. The BMA lawyers had prevented me from fighting this as a whistleblowing case but in my heart I knew that this was the real reason for my dismissal.

Phoenix House on Newhall Street housed Birmingham's Employment Tribunal. I'd been there a few times to lend support to NHS whistleblowers. It was a shabby set-up but, you might say, satisfactory. On Monday 26th March I was due there on my own account for a two-week hearing. We caught an early train and had time to stop at a coffee shop on the walk from the station. After five minutes, in walked David McIlroy. We chatted briefly but whatever was going on inside his head I did not want to disturb it. We made our excuses and left. There's a lot of waiting around at ET. The claimants' room gives plenty of opportunity for distraction as cases are being discussed with little regard for confidentiality. More of the lives of others.

Eventually we were in court. The panel made its entrance. We all rose and were told to sit. After the preliminaries were over I took the stand. I had decided to swear on the Bible, though doing that was of no importance to me. The panel had read our statements and so I settled down for cross-examination by the Trust's barrister, Ms Misra: I answered her questions for three days, from Tuesday to Thursday. I enjoyed the interaction: she was extremely gentle with me and I do not remember having difficulty with a single question; I knew my answers were straightforward and honest. If possible I referred back to my earlier disclosures and justified my actions on the grounds of my professional responsibility under GMC guidance. The judge, Mr David Kearsley, in one rare interjection, told me that the panel was well aware of these responsibilities, thank you, and needed no further reminder.

On the first day, disaster struck: Janet experienced a sudden total loss of vision in the eye operated on in January. She did not tell me until the hearing adjourned. I called a taxi and we went straight to the Eye Hospital. Tests showed a huge retinal detachment with "macula off". That is the worst kind of detachment and we were told the long-term outlook was poor. Further surgery would be required but with no great urgency. We arrived home late feeling nauseated and desperately unhappy. It had been a good day at the tribunal but all that was forgotten. Our only concern now was for Janet's vision: the problem that predisposed her to the original bleeding and detachment was, we knew, present in the other eye. Even our own synergistic optimism was quenched. I prayed fervently for Janet and we went to bed exhausted. We had a restless night.

I am married to a remarkable woman: in the morning she was much brighter. I made tea while she made the porridge: "We'll not get through today without this," she laughed. She once told me she loved me because I make people laugh. But I love her because she laughs. Proverbs chapter 31 has an insightful description of "the good wife": "She laughs at the days to come." Janet is blessed with that carefree spirit.

Three of my witnesses had professional commitments and their cross-examinations had to be interspersed with my own. I was excluded from these and as a result missed the cross-examinations of Ian Mckivett and David and Louise Cremonesini. I knew Janet would give me a blow-by-blow account, which might even be better than the original, so I was not too worried. I went and picked up a couple of newspapers and read the press reports on our case. Then I found the clerk, Bruce, and chatted to him about the way the tribunal worked. He was Canadian and in former lives had worked as a bounty hunter, an all-in wrestler and in other eccentric professions. He refused to arm wrestle me.

Ian Mckivett's statement was a powerful account of his involvement in my case over two years. He is a gentle, amiable man but his account was robust: it was never agreed that the Independent Review would be a final hearing of my grievance; Dr Moghal had been keen to express his own view as to why there was no place for religion in the workplace but reluctant to share any evidence for my alleged misbehaviour in that respect; religion had not been raised by the panel at our meetings; it was clear to him that the Chief Executive and Trust Chair wanted a speedy disciplinary that was only ever going to end in dismissal; the meetings with Julia Hollywood showed that she had a clear brief to *find* a case to answer: the disciplinary hearing and subsequent appeal were, in his opinion, travesties of justice. He spoke of the aggressive, rude and frankly offensive behaviour of the Trust solicitor, Martin Brewer. He said he had been to a number of meetings with me and that I always bent over backwards to keep things cordial. In 30 years representing doctors he had never come across a case like mine.

David Cremonesini is a gifted paediatrician. He is a big man, half Italian and clever enough to play the wise fool. His statement was equally robust: he described a culture of managerial secrecy and disrespect: his wife, Louise, had resigned as a result of the behaviour of the Divisional Director and Head Nurse. He described a job-planning meeting when the Clinical Director told the consultants to "just fucking accept" what was on offer. He described Nadeem Moghal's behaviour, reporting Nadeem as giving me a hard time, continually putting me down; he described how he used to hear Nadeem shouting at me when we had meetings on our own.

Louise, David's wife, had been appointed Safeguarding Nurse from April 2009 but only lasted eight months: she refused to tolerate the bullying ways of the managers and resigned. She gave an added perspective as a nurse on what was happening in the department. She found the nursing staff development at Walsall was poor, with no progression. There was understaffing on the wards, with sometimes only one qualified nurse and one health care assistant on duty. She was struck by the managers' attitudes and how they spoke to staff: managers shouted and swore at her; a report she had written was praised by the senior safeguarding manager but described as "crap" by the Nurse Manager, Karen Palmer, who herself had no experience in paediatrics or safeguarding. Unlike some who would have loved to quit, she was in a position to do so and did.

Both David and Louise gave evidence that the "Independent" Review of Nursing had turned up high levels of bullying among our nurses. Many of us knew about this. They expressed shock that this was completely expunged from the final written report. Louise had written to the Review Nurse to question this but never received a reply. I had done the same thing and the executive complained that I was harassing the reviewer.

All three robustly defended their stories under cross-examination: that was not too difficult because they were all good, intelligent professionals who were telling the truth. We were doing well.

Three of my witnesses were still employed by the Trust. Their statements were accepted and they were excused cross-examination.

Louise Holland was a radiology consultant at Walsall and was chair of the consultants' committee from 2006 to 2010. Her statement was supportive and factually correct. She spoke of my "single-mindedness in pursuing patients' best interests" and "my exacting attention to detail". The main perspective of her statement was the concerns that I, but also other paediatricians, raised about patient care. She expressed her opinion that my dismissal had resulted largely from my decision to go public over the heating failure and the cold babies.

Dr Bashir John Muhammed is a paediatric consultant of the Muslim faith. His statement typically reflects his own personality. He is a deeply religious man and, I am glad to say, my personal friend.

"I keep my head down. By nature I avoid arguments and confrontations," he wrote.

"I am a practising Muslim and I do practise my faith at work. I have never been made aware that there is a policy preventing me practising my faith at work or using religious language."

"David is a very nice chap. He cares for the patients and the department and fights for them."

Alison Cole is the Anglican Hospital Chaplain at Walsall Healthcare. I asked her to be a witness to give some background to religious life at the Trust. I had also had discussions with her before my dismissal, especially about the Trust reaction to the St Ignatius prayer. In her statement she described her work as a member of a multifaith team that provides pastoral support to patients, staff and visitors. The team also organized celebrations for all the different faiths' major festivals. An unveiling ceremony at the time of the opening of the PFI building had been accompanied by prayers and blessings from all faith groups. The request for the team to do this had come from the Chief Executive herself.

The Chief Executive had also agreed at an earlier date to provide capital funding to construct a dedicated 40-place prayer room for the use of Muslim staff for Friday prayers.

These witnesses made it abundantly clear that the hospital was a place where religious expression was not only tolerated but encouraged. I seemed to be the sole person whose religious expression was not tolerated. And for no evidenced reason. I hoped the judge had noted this discrepancy.

On Thursday I returned to the stand so that Ms Misra could complete her cross-examination. Then, quite suddenly, it was all over, like a tooth being pulled. It had been a therapeutic experience for me not least because of the barrister's extreme courtesy. This was in stark contrast to the behaviour of Martin Brewer at the disciplinary hearing. I do believe Ms Misra gave me a little smile as I finished. "Well done you," she seemed to say. Perhaps I was imagining it.

At noon Iain Darwood was sworn in. Iain is an exceptional doctor. He worked hard at Walsall, always put his patients first and was the epitome of kindness and gentleness. He never hesitated to put me right in areas where my own practice had become a bit outdated. Delivered in his soft South African accent, his corrections were always a pleasure to receive. He left his post at Walsall the year after taking it up – a great loss to us. He had good family reasons for leaving and moved to Hereford. Before he left he told me that he would not in any case have wanted to work in a hospital where five years down the line he could have found himself treated as I had been. Knowing his passion for good patient care, I believed that at a trust like Walsall that would have been more than a theoretical danger.

His statement affirmed what I knew to be true:

David was by far the most supportive consultant. He gave us new consultants our induction. He gave us an understanding of how the department worked, including a history of its problems. He was never negative about anyone. David was the most approachable consultant. His clinical skills and acumen were excellent. He was my role model and mentor. There has always been a suggestion from management that David's mental health was in question. I strongly disagree with that suggestion.

He told the tribunal that soon after his arrival in Walsall he met with the Divisional Director, who told him that I knew everything about the department and everyone in it and would always help. "But you need to remember that David had a bad bike accident some years ago. His mental stability has been in doubt since."

He referred to the potential seriousness of the heating failure and his feelings that I was not listened to. The Nursing Review failed to mention reports by nursing staff of bullying. He used the word "dictatorial" to describe management practices. He confirmed what I had always maintained, my impeccable behaviour as a Christian in the workplace. Finally he gave his overall impression of Nadeem Moghal's role in my dismissal:

"Early on it seemed to me that one of Dr Moghal's considerations was dismissing David. It was difficult to see David being marginalized. There was a sense of 'your time is over.'"

As I had finished my evidence at this point I was allowed to sit in on the cross-examination. Iain is such a mild-mannered man that I was surprised at the passion he showed in his answers, especially when he spoke about the serial bullying of nursing staff by the Head Nurse, Karen Palmer.

I was heartened. What judge could fail to see from the witness statements and the cross-examinations that 99 per cent of the blame for what had happened lay with Trust management?

The day ended. I was happy – as happy as I could be given our other circumstances.

"You've finished giving your evidence now, Dr Drew. There will be no need for you to attend tomorrow," the judge told me.

"I wouldn't miss it for the world, sir," I responded.

"I knew you were going to say that." He laughed at his own joke. I felt good.

Tomorrow was the main event: Sue James, CEO at Walsall at the time of my dismissal and now CEO at Derby Royal Hospital, would go on the stand to face David McIlroy. This would in truth be the first time she had been held accountable for her behaviour.

43

ET: The Corporate Mindset

I promise to tell the truth, the whole truth and nothing but the truth.
Affirmation or Oath required of witnesses

The courtroom had been crowded at times in the first few days partly because of media interest. Michele Paduana from the BBC was there and told me he was running a news item on Friday evening's *Midlands Today*. Cameras would be on the street early on Friday to get footage of Sue James arriving – and of course us. The story was reported widely in the national press and over the next few days across the world. The main focus of interest was the link between my sacking and my sending the prayer. Some but not others saw the significance of this. Our favourite article was "The Toxic Treatment of Dr Drew" by Jenny McCartney in the *Sunday Telegraph*. Without having met me she distilled the essence of my case as told by all eight witnesses. Nina Lakhani at *The Independent* came in person in the second week and wrote an excellent account of my treatment as a whistleblower.

The cameras were outside Phoenix House when we arrived on Thursday and the cameraman recognized us. We did a few walk-ins until he was satisfied. He then asked us to stay, as he didn't know what Sue James looked like. He only had one shot at that and it was a good one. She was smartly dressed and smiling as she passed. I wondered what she felt like inside.

My eight witnesses in their statements and under cross-examination had given a consistent story of what happened from 2008 to 2010. They had been eyewitnesses to the events. Now four witnesses would stand for the Trust. Only one had first-hand experience of the events. The other three had been given responsibility for my disciplinary procedure. The one witness we all wanted to hear from was Nadeem Moghal, the Chair of the Independent Review of Paediatrics, but, as we already knew, the Trust's position was to protect the review and its conduct from all scrutiny. In the circumstances that was an excellent tactical move, and it must have been based on legal advice. It actively prevented my legal team getting at the truth, which I presume was the point.

Sue James had written a nine-page statement. It is quite impossible to summarize her account of events. It would be fair to say, though, that it ran contrary to all eight statements produced on my side. She had become aware of problems in paediatrics in 2008, she said. These were several and were outlined. At the end of this section, unsubtly linking my leadership to the troubles, she wrote, "At this time Dr David Drew was Clinical Director of the department." In fact by this time I was no longer head of department but had been replaced by a doctor inappropriately appointed to that post with Mrs James's approval. The Trust had elsewhere put it on record that I had been regarded for seven years as an effective manager. No mention of this in Mrs James's statement.

As soon as it was recognized there was a problem, "The Trust took steps to *improve the reputation* of the department [my italics]." I find that a curious way of thinking. As a doctor my way is to find out what's wrong and fix it. That's the best way to improve reputation. I have believed for many years that higher management's obsession with reputation is responsible for half the woes of the NHS. The steps taken were outlined: management structures were changed; this was the point at which the executive made inappropriate appointments, bringing in managers with no paediatric experience. Four new consultants were appointed: that would help correct the chronic under-resourcing but, since no one with management experience had been appointed, it left a gaping hole. And David Drew, she stated, was asked to "modernize the department". That was untrue, but it mattered little as by that time I had been removed as Clinical Director.

When referring to my removal she gave her own account, in which I had behaved indiscreetly and had to resign. The Independent Review concluded that because Mike Brown failed to document his actions what actually happened was moot – another part of the review that Sue James preferred to disregard.

My disclosures about problems in the service in 2008/9 became, "I recall that David instigated lengthy correspondence … about various issues within the department." "Lengthy correspondence" always gets a black mark in the tribunal, so this was a safe way of referring to my expressing concerns about babies becoming hypothermic when ward heating failed, about the Trust's failures to remedy factors that led to Kyle Keen's death, about swingeing nursing and medical cuts, etc. In a briefing paper to the board in December 2009, Sue James referred to the "political difficulties" caused by my writing to the PCT about the situation in the department. Reputation was always the determining factor. I would not have written to the PCT if senior management had taken notice of any of my serious concerns about patient care.

She defended my suspension following the Head Nurse's complaint despite the fact that the independent review panel had concluded that this was fundamentally wrong. (There was nothing in any of the allegations against me that would have constituted misconduct even if proven.) The psychiatric appointment was a mistake, she wrote, and the Trust had put its hands up. I was never told this. As with every other thing the Trust got wrong, I never received an acknowledgement or heard a word of apology.

The independent review panel was commissioned because David "did not feel confident that the Trust could investigate the issues he had raised in an unbiased way". Her agreement to this showed, that as a model employer, she was bending over backwards to address my concerns.

"The report contained some strong criticisms of the leadership of the paediatric department and some specific individuals." No mention of how the board and executive, in a virtual dereliction of its governance responsibilities, had allowed this situation to develop, or of the review's critique of this.

She wrote a good statement of her view of events: I was an insatiable complainer, a time-waster, a pedant; but, as a concession, she said I was a strong leader and a respected clinician. Hard to square that other than on the grounds of multiple personality disorder, I thought. The roots of the problems in the department and senior management's singular failure to acknowledge or deal with them were not mentioned. Mrs James came out, in her own account, whiter than white.

I was interested to see how she would stand up under David McIlroy's scrutiny. She took an oath and we were off.

She asked to make a statement before beginning. She would have to limit some of her answers in the interest of staff confidentiality, she said. Mr Kearsley, the judge, told her that she would give full answers to any questions asked: no secrets in this court. She was obviously not used to being put on the spot in this way. She later complained that board minutes disclosed by the Trust were confidential and not intended for public viewing. At one point she claimed one of David McIlroy's questions was "leading" and said she wouldn't answer. "It's his job to ask leading questions, Mrs James. Please answer," the judge advised. Even Ms Misra had to stifle a chortle. The press loved it.

The cross-examination set off at a cracking pace, with barely a pause for an hour. A few facts were established and then the central conundrum of my whole case was exposed.

McIlroy: There would have been no review of the paediatric
    department if Dr Drew had not asked for it?

James: True

McIlroy: His grievance was upheld?

James: True

McIlroy: So the result of Dr Drew raising a grievance, a
    grievance which is largely successful, is that he is
    dismissed?

McIlroy: If there had been no grievance there would have
    been no dismissal would there?

McIlroy: Can you think of any other example of an
    employee being dismissed after they have raised a
    grievance?

The answer Sue James gave to the last three questions was
fundamentally that I refused to accept the independent review panel
recommendations about my behaviour. This was after all the
substance of the original allegations against me.

David McIlroy then turned to procedural fairness, referring to
Trust bullying and harassment, equality and diversity, grievance and
disciplinary policies. Sue James was hazy on some points of detail
but these policies were rather dull and she would usually have had
HR advice available. David was on the trail of fair play and
continually returned to this theme.

On the Rashid investigation:

McIlroy: If Mr Rashid, as claimed, did not discuss the
    recommendations he made, is that unfair?

James: It was not in accordance with policy.

McIlroy You concede it would be unfair.

James: [Could not answer.]

With respect to the review, Sue James agreed she expected it to be carried out with basic fairness. She was responsible for accepting the report and implementing it. She felt she could assume that it was fair because of the seniority and credentials of the panel. David confirmed that she understood my right to basic fairness: to know who made allegations, what the evidence was and to have an opportunity to respond. I recognized some of this ground as I had covered it in my own clumsy fashion in the internal appeal hearing. Sue James understood all this, she said.

> McIlroy: Basic fairness requires that he see the review's evidence.
>
> James: It's for the IRP [independent review panel] to judge that, not me.
>
> McIlroy: Make a judgement.
>
> James: I ceded to the IRP decisions about justice and process.
>
> McIlroy: As part of basic fairness they should have shown Dr Drew the evidence.
>
> James: Ask them.
>
> McIlroy: Your reluctance to answer means there is only one answer.
>
> James: No, we'd ceded the process to the IRP.

No matter how much Sue James was brought back to this point it proved impossible except by her own silence to interrogate her view of the fairness of the IRP. It clearly was not fair. I had made this point repeatedly to Nadeem himself and on through the disciplinary process. David McIlroy would later point out that if you wanted a review doing you could outsource it in this way, accept its conclusions and then no matter how unfair or unjust, the Trust would have no responsibility for it. I had worked all this out long ago and it was hard for me to believe that this had not been done quite deliberately. The review panel and Trust Chair and Chief

Executive were intelligent people with access to excellent legal advice from Mr Martin Brewer.

David McIlroy concentrated on and returned to the religious issues. On the Rashid investigation:

> McIlroy: If religion was never discussed with Dr Drew it would have been unfair to tell him to stop imposing his religion on others?
> James: Yes.

On the review:

> McIlroy: It's not possible to identify from the IRP's conclusions what evidence they were based on?
> James: I agree.

A picture emerged that the instructions relating to not imposing my religious views on others, and stopping all use of religious language at work were, in Sue James's opinion, marginal.

> McIlroy: The instruction on religious references was the least important.
> James: Yes.
> McIlroy: I don't understand why you didn't delete this recommendation.
> James: In hindsight I wish I had.

And later:

> McIlroy: A recommendation [on the use of religious language] was made that shouldn't have been.
> James: Yes.
> McIlroy: There was no evidence. Evidence was never

discussed. This was not a Trust policy. This is not Dr Drew being asked to follow an instruction given to everyone.

James: This sums up why I could not move on this point. It's seen as particularly unfair against Dr Drew but it would have rendered the whole report unsafe.

McIlroy: Removing the instruction is what a reasonable manager would have done, isn't it?

James: A reasonable manager dealing with a reasonable employee may have.

There were repeated frank admissions of unfairness. She was, she claimed, at the end of her tether with me. She treated me unfairly only for the good of the department. She was afraid that the PCT would close the department down. Everyone was treated unfairly she claimed. That was not exactly a vote of confidence in the IRP. David McIlroy pressed the point home, "But it cost Dr Drew his job."

And so little by little David McIlroy whittled the issues down. The only part of the review I had refused to accept in its overtly discriminatory formulation was the instruction relating to religious expression. There was no known evidence to base this on. Sue James accepted it because of the qualifications of the panel members. This was unfair. And she repeatedly admitted it.

I felt she was out of her depth. Her account, in my opinion, was simply not credible. David McIlroy's cross-examination sometimes resulted in frank admission and sometimes silence. Every so often the tribunal panel scribbled notes.

By Monday lunchtime Sue James was released. Julia Hollywood and Sue Hartley were then subjected to the same exacting cross-examination. I have already said as much as I want to about these two. They played vital parts in my disciplinary procedure. In my opinion, Julia showed nothing but implacable hostility on the stand, in her tone of voice, her body language and her resistance to David McIlroy's attempt to get her to soften her opinions on me. She was, of course, the Trust's witness: I imagine she was paid to come and give evidence. Sue Hartley, as far as I could judge, failed to perform: she appeared unable to answer the questions as asked. In her role as chair of my disciplinary hearing David suggested that she was completely out of her depth. She replied that she had chaired many disciplinary hearings. This was not very reassuring. I thought of the poor devils on the receiving end of that. She showed an appalling inability to grasp the issues surrounding equality and diversity.

On the final day Michael Scott, who had been interim CEO for a few months following Sue James's departure, took the stand. He was relaxed and carefree. It seemed to me that he hadn't given any serious attention to my appeal hearing, and even now he seemed only to have a rudimentary understanding of my case and the documentation. He had been brought from Norfolk for the day but contributed next to nothing.

During the morning Janet had a call from the Eye Hospital. A slot was available for her operation that evening. She was disappointed that she would miss David Mcilroy and Ms Misra making their final submissions: she would be travelling by taxi across town and then going through admissions as they spoke.

Final submissions were made in the afternoon. It was the end of eight days of sustained concentration. These submissions are a legal technical presentation, with arguments supported by authorities. Most of it was lost on me but I enjoyed David McIlroy's authoritative style. Ms Misra was softer but soothing. I sat trying to follow the impressively unintelligible things she was saying. I forgot for a while that she was on the other side and enjoyed her slightly musical voice. Ah, in another life we could have been friends.

It was over. I had a quick cup of tea with the lawyers and then went to the hospital. Janet didn't go into theatre until seven o'clock. "We have won, haven't we?" she asked as she was wheeled off. "It looks like it. Fingers crossed." I was grateful to God for his care for Janet, all the more so because he had delegated the hands-on part to the remarkable Mr Ash Sharma at the Midlands Eye Centre. The operation lasted two hours; the surgery had been difficult and when it was completed the retina was splinted in place with an oil bubble, which would need removing a few months down the line.

Back home we settled in to await the tribunals' judgement and the outcome of the surgery. We felt fairly certain of one but very uncertain of the other. We turned out to be wrong about both.

44

Judgment Day

Q. How do you make God laugh?
A. Tell him your plans.

Woody Allen

The tribunal was allowed up to three months to produce a judgment. My main concern now the hearing was over was Janet's convalescence. In the immediate aftermath of her earlier surgery she had been immobilized for ten days, but, with a different technique, this time she was up immediately. Spring was in the air and by mid April we were busy in the garden. I gave little thought to the judgment: a good result seemed certain. I wanted nothing but an end to the struggle so that I could concentrate on my family and give some time to Patients First, helping support other whistleblowers. We drew up lists of things we had most neglected in recent years and planned their repair.

I confess to having had the odd moment of doubt: I had heard a number of people including claimants and lawyers speak of the inconsistency of employment tribunals and the general employer bias. I once attended a tribunal to support an NHS nurse whistleblower who bravely presented her own case. The judge at one point said quite openly that several different panels could result in as many different outcomes for her. These doubts skimmed across the surface and quickly vanished. We practised the neglected art of patient waiting and maintaining normality.

On May Day we slept in and I was in the shower when the phone rang. Janet came into the bathroom with the telephone. "It's

Hannah." Janet looked pale. She had detected bad news in Hannah's tone of voice even though she had said nothing other than "Is David there?"

Hannah [from Waldrons Solicitors] broke the news that the Tribunal had rejected all three of my claims. She was a model of professionalism: concise, factual and unemotional. But she showed her characteristic empathy: she recognized the disappointment I must feel after such a long and difficult journey. She felt it too. I knew she did. She promised to send me the full judgment that morning with her own comments; we briefly discussed the possibility of an appeal. "Thank you so much, Hannah, for everything. I'm afraid I'll have to go. I probably sound like I'm having a panic attack but I've just got out of the shower: I'm shivering." I finished my shower got dressed and went downstairs.

Janet was sitting in the kitchen. She looked ill: I could see she had been crying. I was completely unmoved by the judgment but deeply unhappy at its effect on my wife and the effect it would have on my children when I told them. It was too early to think about this but I knew there was now the prospect of more legal battles, more expense and more disruption to our family life. By early afternoon we had broken the news to our children and our friends. As expected, they expressed total solidarity. Hannah sent the full judgment by email and we agreed the text of a notice to the press:

> This case was never about Dr Drew's capability as a clinician but issues of basic fairness in the employer and employee relationship.
>
> The tribunal heard evidence from both the Trust and Dr Drew's colleagues about the difficulties experienced due to the management style adopted at the hospital. Following Dr Drew raising issues about patient care and safety he was subjected to a recommendation that he not share his religious and wider views. The evidence which formed the

basis for this recommendation and which was not disclosed to Dr Drew, was that one person, in a hospital which employs thousands, had felt that the sending of an inspirational prayer was a bit bizarre and another felt it was a bit inappropriate. Incidentally neither of them was a direct recipient of the email in question. The actual recipients reacted favourably to it…

Dr Drew and his legal team are understandably surprised and disappointed by the tribunal's Judgment and are considering the options for appeal.

Waldrons Solicitors

The *Daily Telegraph* published a piece headed, "Judge tells doctor it is inappropriate to say he is a Christian at work." Unless Christianity were to be singled out it appeared that in the view of this tribunal it was now unacceptable to identify yourself as a belonging to any religion at work. Andrea Williams of the Christian Legal Centre described this judgment as deeply illiberal and wrong: "Being a Christian isn't something you take off when you go to work." Stephen Evans at the National Secular Society said the claims of religious discrimination were unfounded and precisely the kind of nonsense that led to allegations of Christians being marginalized in society.

The National Secular Society had more to say about this on its website: "Latest 'persecuted Christian' case dismissed by employment tribunal." I had, the article said, been dismissed after constantly raising complaints against co-workers. This had produced a "toxic environment" at the hospital. Sue James was quoted: "For two-and-a-half years we had a relationship that was not working." The article's main emphasis was on the authority of Mrs James's evidence. She had, incidentally, described herself at the tribunal as non-religious.

The NSS conclusion delivered a withering blast against Christians:

Yet again we find that when claims of religious discrimination are properly scrutinized they fall flat on their face. The Christian propaganda machine so enthusiastically assisted by certain sections of the British media is attempting to gain special privileges in all areas of life for those who declare themselves to be Christian. It is time their false narrative of Christian persecution in Britain was exposed as the pernicious pack of lies that it is.

I found it hard to recognize any truth in this account of my case. The author was clearly not acquainted with its details but saw in it an opportunity for an anti-Christian rant. I was not interested in special privileges for Christians. I wanted to be allowed to follow a path of quiet service and encourage my colleagues to do the same. That's all.

On a lighter note, in another corner of the secular press, the journal *The Freethinker,* (the voice of atheism since 1881), tweeted a reference to me as "a self-obsessed cretin with his bogus religious discrimination claim". I responded:

"@NHSWhistleblower: Surprised to see @TheFreethinker describe me as self-obsessed cretin so asked Mrs Drew. 'He's only half right.'"

Some of the letters by atheists in the local press in response to my case were openly unpleasant. I was surprised at the venomous reaction I encountered, especially given my own conciliatory stance. On reflection of course it is perhaps not so strange. Religious people, in their behaviour and their engagement with non-believers, have sometimes done little to endear themselves. I did not engage with my critics to defend myself apart from that one tweet. I continued to have interesting and useful exchanges with atheists on Twitter. They were mainly enlightened types with a more liberal education.

They may not have realized it, but they were one with me on St Paul's injunction to the Roman church, "If it is possible, as far as it depends on you, live at peace with all men."

In the afternoon Hannah sent me a copy of the judgment and information about possible responses. Probably I should have been intensely curious about the tribunal's rejection of my claim, and under other circumstances I definitely would have been. But I felt flat and disinterested. I found it hard to grasp the basis in law on which the tribunal had come to its conclusions. The Trust's unfair treatment was now, I thought, compounded by the tribunal's unfair treatment. That's how it felt. I had provided eight witnesses to support my case, as well as sworn statements and opportunity for cross-examination. They had all contradicted Sue James's account of my role in creating a toxic environment in the department by laying the responsibility on management. But the written judgment made not a single reference to any of my witnesses' evidence. They were ignored. My witnesses were as shocked at the result as we were.

Wendy Savage was a famous London obstetrician who had been suspended from clinical practice in 1985. She had been stitched up by her all-male colleagues. They had questioned her competence on the basis of five of her many thousands of cases, which they claimed she had mismanaged. The real issue was that Wendy was empowering women to make their own childbirth decisions, contrary to the established male-dominated culture of the time. She records her lawyer, Brian Raymond, as saying at their first meeting, "Your power in the court, Wendy, is directly proportional to your power outside the court." This summed up my own view of the tribunal's judgment on my case. Mrs James's story had been believed rather than the accounts of a host of more credible and more consistent witnesses.

Janet is better at saying thank you than I am. And she finds more imaginative ways of doing it. So, we went on a shopping trip to the

Birmingham Jewellery Quarter, where she commissioned a silversmith to craft novel pieces of jewellery for each of our team, bracelets for the women and cufflinks for the men. Each item was hand engraved with a phrase adapted from the prayer of St Ignatius. "To give and not to count the cost" went to Hannah. She had given herself unstintingly to us and our case. We joked at the idea of a lawyer who did not count the cost. I was also sure that from the beginning she saw her work as an act of Christian service. To Ian Mckivett of the BMA we gave "To fight for doctors." The BMA is a powerful trade union that fights for contractual rights, pensions etc., for doctors. Ian had fought valiantly for something that is much closer to the care of patients, a doctor who spoke up for them. Two consultant witnesses got "To fight for our patients" on their cufflinks. We tried to personalize the thanks to each one. Each piece had a neat little box containing a minute scroll with the full prayer on it.

As an afterthought Janet had cufflinks made for the surgeon who had saved her eyesight. One was inscribed "Venit", he came. The other "Vidi", I saw. These expressions of gratitude were heartfelt and well deserved. They also provided a delightful distraction from the bad news. Janet benefited from the retail therapy and I enjoyed her pleasure.

I did not know if I had any grounds for appeal in law or, if I had, what chance an appeal would have. I did know that I could not let the matter go. This was no longer simply about the injustice of my own case. I was by now meeting and reading about large numbers of NHS staff in similar difficulties. Regular steering committee meetings at PatientsFirst confirmed that we were dealing with a serious NHS-wide problem. A week later, we met Hannah to discuss the appeal; a month later, David McIlroy had written the grounds and the appeal was registered.

The respondent (that's Walsall Healthcare. I was by now using legal terminology quite casually.) resisted the application, inevitably.

This was overruled and we were granted a full hearing at the Employment Appeal Tribunal in London. The grounds for appeal were quite complicated and uncharacteristically I began to lose interest. I felt like a patient preparing to have his brain tumour removed: I had shown interest in understanding what was involved but only up to a point: of much more importance to me was the surgeon who would be operating. I had immense confidence in David McIlroy. I let go and left it to him. I began to understand that the real fight to secure protection for NHS whistleblowers lay outside the law.

The appeal was largely based on the contention that the original judgment was perverse. I learned that in law perversity essentially means that on the basis of the evidence heard no reasonable person could have come to the conclusions reached. That sounded right to me as a layman. How a tribunal could have produced such a judgment continued to puzzle me. There is no answer other than the way that individual panels interpret employment law. Variation in individual practice is a big issue in clinical medicine and is recognized as undesirable. I have no idea if anyone gives any thought to this in the legal sphere. But they ought to.

In July we were given 5th Feb 2013 as the date for the appeal hearing. By that time I would have been out of clinical practice for more than two years: with GMC revalidation looming, I had with great sadness to admit to myself that I would, as Sue Hartley had predicted, never practise medicine again. What a waste. I promised myself that I would do all I could to ensure that no NHS doctor had to suffer this again.

45

The NeverEnding Story

Every real story is a never ending story.

Michael Ende: *The NeverEnding Story*

By now summer was in full fling and seven long months lay ahead of us before the appeal hearing. Family life had begun to normalize and my professional traumas to recede. We were blessed with two further grandchildren, bringing the total to eight. They were all so beautiful, so full of life, that I found it hard not to cry when I thought of them. And now we were able to spend more time with our family than if I had still been working. This was great physical and psychological therapy. I felt bad that living on a reduced pension and with my legal costs we were unable to help with the expensive task of raising the next generation. I am certain no one else in the family gave that a thought.

I began to strip off my professional identity like excess clothing. I could not afford professional subscriptions to the GMC, Royal College of Paediatrics, Royal College of Physicians, etc. I had a snotty letter from the Royal College of Paediatrics telling me, "You are no longer eligible to use FRCPCH after your name." Hang on, I passed exams for that and worked my backside off as a children's doctor. But I didn't protest: it no longer mattered. I stopped giving medical advice to all and sundry. I enjoyed Janet's company and my children and their children; they saved me. I started serious vegetable gardening. It all came to nothing with the heavy rainfall that summer but I experienced immense pleasure from trying. I cut all the firewood we needed for the following winter. Being indoors was claustrophobic.

The whistleblowers, particularly at PatientsFirst, were a huge encouragement. My favourite was Sharmila Choudhary, who had reported fraud at Ealing Hospital: her shameful treatment by senior management there was reported in the national press. I burned every time I read these accounts. I had much in common with Kim Holt, the Baby P whistleblower, of course. She was the main driving force in PatientsFirst from the outset. In our personalities we were at opposite poles, but we shared a vision of a kinder NHS, where professionals could speak up safely. We both detested the cult of secrecy that was epitomized by gagging staff. David Johnstone, who had been kicked out of CQC by Cynthia Bower for whistleblowing, joined us. Jenni Fecitt had lost her job with NHS Manchester after reporting a colleague working on false qualifications. Edwin Jesudason and Shiban Ahmed, two excellent paediatric surgeons, were ousted by Alder Hey hospital after raising serious concerns. And in the wings, there was Phil Hammond, Medicine Balls of *Private Eye* fame, one of the originals from the Bristol Hearts Scandal. I encountered an endless caravan of excellent professionals who had spoken truth to power and suffered the consequences.

Every so often I would meet a new whistleblower emerging wild-eyed with disbelief from their early encounters on the battlefield. Frequently, this would result in the outpouring of a story that was so emotionally charged, so complex, and assumed so much knowledge, as to be incomprehensible: I knew this person was holding up a mirror to show me what I had looked like only a short time ago. Many whistleblowers' names never reached public attention. Occasionally they resolved their difficulties and limped into an uncertain future. Some accepted a financial settlement, signed a gag and moved on. Hilary Cass, our President at the Royal College of Paediatrics, left Great Ormond Street Hospital under such circumstances. Every individual had to make their own decision on this. For me it would have been wrong to sign a gag. Some brave souls fought it out in the employment tribunal and usually lost.

A growing number of patients, parents and other relatives got in touch with me: I found their stories harrowing and exhausting. I had had very few complaints about the care of my own patients and none that were directly aimed at me. That was certainly not because I made no mistakes. I recognized a familiar pattern: the quest was for truth, an acknowledgment of what had happened, a genuine apology and then corrective steps. Compensation was of course appropriate sometimes but was rarely the main issue. Will Powell rang me after we met on Twitter. He had lost his son Robbie to a medical blunder 23 years earlier. The whole of his life turned into a fight for an acknowledgement of the cover-up of Robbie's death. He had also campaigned tirelessly for a statutory individual duty of candour, Robbie's Law: most patients do not realize that clinicians are under no legal obligation to tell the truth about medical errors.

It was my 65th birthday in October and my eldest son, Simon, suggested writing "the book". I was low and my resistance weak: I caved in. We began a punishing series of digitally recorded interviews that he used to produce draft chapters and an outline for the whole book. I was dubious: I lacked the energy to drag up memories; I dreaded the interviews. But when we came to do the chapters on Thailand and Nigeria and Janet got involved it became an enjoyable stroll down memory lane. Simon drafted "Nigeria" and sent it to me. "I can do better," I thought – and I did, but I would never have started without his first draft. I had to trawl through hundreds of pages of transcripts of the hearings to write some of the chapters. That was a lonely and unbearably painful experience. It brought me to a personal crisis.

I had always paid close attention to the grief of the bereaved parents I worked with. What they most wanted, the only thing they really wanted, could not be given. But that did not mean nothing could be given. I had not lost a child but I had suffered a bereavement. It bore no comparison to the loss and injustice suffered by so many. It was not about war crimes in Iraq. But it was a bereavement. And for almost two years I had refused to acknowledge that. I grew up on the Kubla Ross grief-cycle model. I realized I had more or less been stuck at stage one, denial, since I had been kicked out of Walsall.

I must have been impossible to live with. No one was able to comfort me. I refused to accept the intense humiliation of my sacking. My career had never been about status or ambition but enjoyable acts of service. I had lost what I loved. One of my sons rang me often. He always began, "I know, you're fine, Dad. So I won't ask." I now realize how damaging that was to my relationships and I still have not dealt with it.

I never allowed myself into stage 2, anger. I always dealt with that using humour: perhaps that was my anger. I never became depressed, not to the best of my knowledge. I probably made others depressed. I had always thought of myself as a sensitive and reflective person but I had never allowed myself the space for proper reflection on the more painful experiences in my recent history. A taxi driver took us to the airport and told us he was the reincarnation of an Indian chief. He was deadly serious. He mentioned some personal tragedy and I asked him about it as we pulled in to the drop-off. "We warriors must suffer our pain in silence." He drove off with a noble expression on his face: warrior stance. I had built up my own world in which I had not been hurt and never could be. I messed up on all the grief stages trying to tough it out. I knew for certain, deep down in my pugilistic nature, that stage 5 was a never-event. Acceptance? Never.

The New Year was suddenly upon us. On 18th January it was the first anniversary of my mum's death. We visited my dad: a year of grief lay heavy on him. He had always been a very funny man given to extempore story telling, all drawn from his own experience. Our favourite was about a miner who had sewn his own ear back on with a needle and thread following an accident because he had no time to go to hospital. This always provoked uncontrollable laughter even when we had heard the story many times. But now there were no jokes. The tragic death of two sons had cut him down and Mum's death had left him a shadow of his former self. In the midst of life we are in the midst of death. "Rejoice with those who rejoice: mourn with those who mourn," St Paul counselled the Roman church. How do you laugh and cry at the same time? I don't know but you have to. Do your best.

On 4th February we booked into a noisy hotel next to Euston Station. Janet found a small family-run Sicilian restaurant for supper. She engaged the waitress at first contact: the restaurant wasn't very busy and she came and sat with us for most of our meal. I had little part in their conversation and was happy to listen. It went from Montalbano, "Oh, *Inspector Montalbano*" to *Il Postino*, "Oh Massimo, Massimo, what a tragedy". Pablo Neruda popped up somewhere: I think I introduced him: "Lost in the forest, I broke off a dark twig and lifted its whisper to my thirsty lips." I remembered reading that line with longing one moonless night. "I 'ave not been to the Aeolians myself", Maria confided. They finished talking about the kind of men they would love to eat and moved on to Sicilian food. For a few hours this delightful banter drove employment law from my thoughts. We walked back to Euston, having drunk a little more than we should have, and lay awake listening to the traffic.

Ironically my appeal was to be heard on the day Robert Francis QC published his huge three-volume report on the public inquiry into Mid Staffs. I had attended many evidence sessions in 2011 and as a result had arrived at a much deeper understanding of what had happened to me. We took a long walk from Euston to the Employment Appeal Tribunal on the second floor of Fleetbank House in Salisbury Square. It stands next door to KPMG: "We bring together the right teams at the right time." The Tribunal offices felt impersonal with an over-emphasis on security. No letterbox even.

Before we began, the judge, Jeremy Burke QC, who heard the case alone, told us he realized how important it was to both parties and would accordingly be taking time and effort to ensure fairness. More than six hours of dense legal argument followed. It was an effort but we largely kept up. The proceedings seemed to me a pale imitation of what had actually happened at Walsall Manor Hospital, where once, ages ago, I had been a doctor. There was a small disagreement over whether Sue James had admitted on eight occasions or nine that she had treated me unfairly. What did it matter? Once should be enough. The hearing ended and we left exhausted. David McIlroy had performed splendidly but, realistically, told us it was all in the balance. "I've given it my best shot."

We were given 4th May as the deadline for Mr Burke to produce his judgment: the day came and went. We were only interested in win or lose. Understanding what we now did of the system, a win seemed unlikely. Win or lose, the two outcomes promised entirely different futures, but we knew they were both imposters with their false promises: our happiness lay elsewhere. I knew, or believed I knew, that a win would give me a platform for campaigning for the protection of NHS whistleblowers and the end of bullying. David would conquer Goliath and the Philistines would flee: one of my favourite stories.

In May I was invited to join the *Nursing Times* Speak Out Safely campaign by the editor Jenni Middleton: I was booked to speak on a whistleblowing forum at the National Patient Safety Congress at Symphony Hall in Birmingham. In the morning session Niall Dickson, Chief Executive of the GMC, held a conversation with Kim Holt from the platform. The GMC expected, he told us, that doctors would speak up to protect patients.

To me this was the height of hypocrisy: the GMC had been given full details of my efforts to speak up for patients and had been quoted in *The Times* as promising to look into my treatment, but nothing had come of this promise. Kim and I had gone to meet Niall Dickson in his splendid office, but still the answer was the same:

nothing could be done to help a doctor who had been true to his code and suffered the consequences.

As I listened to Niall Dickson speaking I sensed outrage welling up inside me, one of my few experiences of anger, and then crushing chest pain almost took me to the ground. It passed in a few minutes; I gave my talk in the afternoon and then took myself off to hospital for emergency angiograms and stents.

I was out of hospital in a couple of days but feeling old and defeated. The next day I started walking. My cardiac rehab nurse, Nam, did a home visit: "Whatever's going on inside your head, it's got to stop, David." Janet embraced her as a kindred soul and reinforced the message: "Hey, we're right. Listen to us." I tried to but did not know how. After two weeks I was readmitted in the night with severe anaphylactic shock, probably a reaction to one of the drugs: my hands and feet swelled to thrice their usual size; the angina once again held me in a grip of steel. I saw the tunnel; there was a light; then, intravenous steroids, antihistamines and heroin. The next day I tweeted about the tunnel and the light: "No one there, just a notice 'Unfinished business, get back.'" My cardiac rehab nurse texted asking why she had to find out from Twitter that I was back in hospital. That's the shape of the future, Nam.

The 16th August was a landmark. It was three years to the day since I had written to 14 senior consultant colleagues telling them the review was being kept from them: that had earned me my insubordination badge. I had a cardiology appointment at noon. We were leaving the house when the telephone rang: it was Steve Green at Waldrons. Bad news: the appeal was lost. He was bitterly disappointed and wanted to talk but we were late. "Speak to you later, Steve. Look after yourself. And don't worry about us, we'll be fine."

And we were. More than fine. The train journey to Birmingham gave us time to explore each other's feelings: neither of us had experienced a single pang; we didn't even feel relief. It was so matter of fact. Shell shock? Denial? Time would test that. It did and nothing changed. No anguish, no regret, no nothing. Kubla-Ross gave me the nod as if to say, "This, for you, is what acceptance looks like."

We walked through the urban sunshine from the station to the hospital. Our hearts were light: laughter came tumbling out of us like it does out of young lovers. We were met by an automatic check-in. No friendly, or even frosty, receptionist to welcome us. My number, 247, came up on the screen. I checked my pulse before we went into the consulting room: 54 beats per minute: I was on the road to recovery. The cardiologist was pleasant and efficient. All was well. Fit for discharge. I had a one per cent chance of dying of a "cardiac event" each year for the rest of my life. What do patients make of such numbers?

We went home to begin the rest of our life.

"It's over," I said to Janet as I filled the kettle.

"This will never be over."

It may take the rest of our life together to resolve that dispute.

Dramatis personae

The main action in my story took place at Walsall Manor Hospital between 2005 and 2010. These are the important characters in the drama. Not in order of appearance.

Walsall Healthcare NHS Trust board members:
Ben Reid OBE: Walsall Healthcare NHS Trust Chairman
Stuart Gray: Non-executive director

Executive:
Sue James: CEO
Mike Brown: Medical Director
Brigid Stacey: Director of Nursing until 2010
Sue Wakeman: Head of Human Resources

Women and Children's Service Managers:
Rob Hodgkiss: Divisional Director
Jon Pepper (Gynaecology consultant): Clinical Director
Karen Palmer: Head Nurse

Consultant paediatricians:
Rashid Gatrad, Bashir Muhammed. Anil Bagchi, Gyan Sinha, Rajneesh Walia, Satish Bangalore, David Cremenosini, Iain Darwood
Alyson Skinner

Other clinical staff:
Simon Langford: Paediatric Matron
Dr Malcolm Cathcart: Occupational Health consultant

Investigating panel following exclusion:
Naj Rashid (A&E consultant)
Sandra Berns (HR officer)

Independent Review Panel recommended by the Royal College of Paediatrics:
Nadeem Moghal FRCPCH (Chair)
Peter Heinz FRCPCH
Sarah Faulkner (Independent HR consultant)

Disciplinary hearing panel:
Sue Hartley (Director of Nursing Services and Chair)
Nigel Summer (Trust Vice-chairman)
Colin Holden (Independent external member)

Appeal hearing panel:
Michael Scott (Interim CEO and Chair)
Phil Ashmore (Non-executive director)
David Holmes (Independent external member)

Others
Ian McKivett: BMA representative
Julia Hollywood: Independent Disciplinary investigator
Martin Brewer (Mills and Reeve): Walsall Healthcare NHS Trust solicitor
Pauline Pilkington: Director of Children's Services at Walsall Council
Elaine Hurry: Designated Safeguarding Nurse at Walsall Primary Care Trust
Helen Goodyear: Paediatric Sub-dean at West Midlands deanery
Nick Turner: ENT surgeon and Associate Medical Director
Tim Muscroft: Senior surgeon
Andrew Hartland: Consultant in chemical pathology
Louise Holland: Chair, Hospital consultants' committee

Timeline

Whistleblower stories are usually complex. This rudimentary timeline is offered as an aid to any reader who might find it helpful.

January 1992: I start as a consultant paediatrician at Walsall Manor Hospital.

April 2001: Appointed Clinical Director (head of department) in paediatrics

January 2005: Death of Dr Anil 'Nil' Bagchi

January 2006: Appointment of Dr Rajneesh Walia

June 2006: Death of Kyle Keen

April 2008: Removal of Dr Walia as neonatal clinical lead

April 2008: My removal as Clinical Director

April to June 2008: Off work with illness

June 2008: Return to work

September 2008: Appointment of foundation safeguarding nurse

October 2008 to April 2009: I report my concerns about patient care, child protection, understaffing etc.

April 2009: I am excluded from the hospital.

April to September 2009: Exclusion and my subsequent illnesses

26th October 2009: My principal disclosure letter to CEO

5th November 2009: A meeting with the Trust Chair and CEO with my BMA representative

November/December 2009: Meetings with CEO to address managerial bullying

18th December 2009: Heating failure on children's ward

20th January 2010: Appearance on BBC *Midlands Today* to report repeated heating failure

4th/5th March: Independent Review Panel interviews

26th March: Review report issued to Trust

June 2010: Dr Moghal, Review chair, starts as Paediatric Clinical Director.

26th June 2008: CEO offers me a large extraordinary payment coupled with a gag to leave.

August 2010: Disciplinary procedure starts.

August/September 2010: Meetings with disciplinary investigator

14th/15th December 2010: Disciplinary hearing

22nd December 2010: Disciplinary judgment

18th April 2011: Appeal hearing

26th March 2012: Birmingham Employment Tribunal

1st May 2012: Tribunal judgment

5th February 2013: Employment Appeal Tribunal

16th August 2013: Employment Appeal Tribunal judgment